PRAISE FOR *SLOW TRAINS TO VENICE*

'Like the trains he travels on, Tom Chesshyre meanders through Europe and the result is entertaining and enjoyable.'

Christian Wolmar, author of *Blood, Iron and Gold:*
How the Railways Transformed the World

'At a time when European unity is fraying at an alarming rate, here comes Tom Chesshyre's travelogue to remind us of the virtues of connectedness. Better still, his explorations are made by train, and use the Continent's historic, unpredictable routes from the era before high-speed rail. A diverting and thought-provoking read.'

Simon Bradley, author of *The Railways*

'Meander through Europe in the excellent company of Tom Chesshyre, who relishes the joys of slow travel and seizes every opportunity that a journey presents: drifting as a flâneur in Lille, following in the tracks of James Joyce in a literary exploration of Ljubljana, cosseted in luxury on a trans-Ukrainian express, all decorated with a wealth of detail and intrigue.

As Tom discovers, it's not just Brexit Britain – the whole Continent is in disarray. But at least Europe's railways still bind us together.'

Simon Calder, *The Independent*

'One of the most engaging and enterprising of today's travel writers, Chesshyre has an eye ever-alert for telling detail and balances the romance of train travel with its sometimes-challenging realities… but for all its good humour, the book impresses as a poignant elegy for the Europe which Britain once embraced.'

Stephen McClarence, travel writer, *The Daily Telegraph* and *The Times*

'An engaging picaresque series of encounters and reflections on Europe as many of its countries struggle to find common ground amid the populist reaction to its dilemmas.'

Anthony Lambert, author of *Lost Railway Journeys*
from Around the World

'Beethoven with attitude, masochism in Lviv, the smell of cigarettes in the corridor, adventurous great aunts who travelled on the roofs of crowded trains, Carniolan pork-garlic sausage, Jimi Hendrix in the Slovene Ethnographic Museum and, of course, the 13:49 from Wrocław. Tom Chesshyre pays homage to a Europe that we are leaving behind and perhaps never understood. Che bella corsa! He is the master of slow locomotion.'

Roger Boyes, *The Times*

SLOW TRAINS
TO VENICE

We are grateful for permission to reproduce the following material in this volume:
Notes on Nationalism by George Orwell (copyright © George Orwell, 1945)
Reprinted by permission of Bill Hamilton as the Literary Executor of the Estate of the Late Sonia Brownell Orwell.
Locomotive by Julian Tuwim © Fundacja im. Juliana Tuwima i Ireny Tuwim, Warszawa 2006, Poland.

Disclaimer
Every effort has been made to obtain the necessary permissions with reference to copyrighted material; should there be any omissions in this respect we apologise and shall be pleased to make the appropriate acknowledgements in any future edition.

An Hachette UK Company
www.hachette.co.uk

Summersdale Publishers Ltd
Part of Octopus Publishing Group Limited
Carmelite House
50 Victoria Embankment
LONDON
EC4Y 0DZ
UK

www.summersdale.com

Printed and bound by CPI Group (UK) Ltd, Croydon, CR0 4YY

ISBN: 978-1-78783-299-2

Substantial discounts on bulk quantities of Summersdale books are available to corporations, professional associations and other organisations. For details contact general enquiries: telephone: +44 (0) 1243 771107 or email: enquiries@summersdale.com.

TOM CHESSHYRE
SLOW TRAINS TO VENICE

A 4,000-Mile
Adventure Across Europe

summersdale

For Kasia

ABOUT THE AUTHOR

Tom Chesshyre worked as a travel writer on *The Times* for 21 years. He has contributed to *The Guardian*, *The Daily Telegraph*, *The Sunday Telegraph*, *The Independent*, *Daily Express*, *Daily Mail* and *The Mail on Sunday*. He has also written for *Condé Nast Traveller*, where he was contributing editor, *National Geographic*, and *Geographical*, the magazine of the Royal Geographical Society. He is the author of *How Low Can You Go? Round Europe for 1p Each Way (Plus Tax)*; *To Hull and Back: On Holiday in Unsung Britain*; *Tales from the Fast Trains: Europe at 186 MPH*; *A Tourist in the Arab Spring*; *Gatecrashing Paradise: Misadventures in the Real Maldives*; *Ticket to Ride: Around the World on 49 Unusual Train Journeys*; and *From Source to Sea: Notes from a 215-mile Walk Along the River Thames*. He contributed pieces to *The Irresponsible Traveller: Tales of Scrapes and Narrow Escapes* and to *The Times Companion 2017*. He helped research *WG Grace: An Intimate Biography* by Robert Low and *Carlos: Portrait of a Terrorist* by Colin Smith. He lives in Mortlake in London.

In some instances, names of those encountered during the train journeys for this book have been altered.

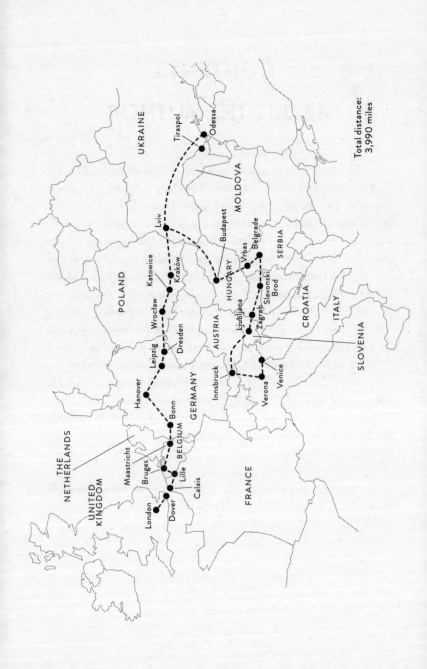

Total distance: 3,990 miles

CONTENTS

The steam hissed. Someone cleared his throat.
No one left and no one came
On the bare platform. What I saw
Was Adlestrop – only the name.
Edward Thomas, 'Adlestrop'

The general uncertainty as to what is really happening makes it easier to
cling to lunatic beliefs. Since nothing is ever quite proved or disproved,
the most unmistakable fact can be impudently denied.
George Orwell, *Notes on Nationalism*

The only way to be sure of catching a train is to miss the one before it.
G. K. Chesterton

PREFACE

On 19 September 1946, Winston Churchill delivered a speech at the University of Zurich in which he stated 'we must build a kind of United States of Europe'. Britain's leader during the war against fascism continued: 'In this way only will hundreds of millions of toilers be able to regain the simple joys and hopes which make life worth living.' He attacked 'frightful nationalistic quarrels' and exclaimed in his finale: 'Let Europe arise!'

I love Europe. I love trains. With Brexit negotiations tortuously unwinding I decided to combine these twin passions. I would let everything go for a while. I would set forth on trains from my home in London in mid-spring and slowly descend whichever way the rails took me to Venice. I would be a free spirit heading south towards the famous stop-off of the world's best-known service, the *Orient Express*.

My purpose was threefold. I wanted, with fresh eyes from my carriage, to see the continent that Churchill and our ancestors liberated. I wanted to get away from deliberations over 'tariff-free zones' and seemingly endless political rows about Britain's 'departure' from my destination.

I wanted also, quite simply, to enjoy the ride. To take as many slow trains as I could and allow lazy days to slip by while gazing at the scenery, meeting new people and listening to the clatter of wheels on the tracks.

CHAPTER ONE

MORTLAKE IN LONDON TO CALAIS IN FRANCE

CONTINENT CALLING

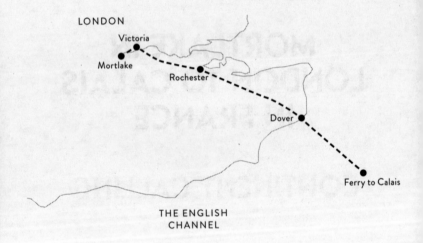

LONDON

Victoria

Mortlake

Rochester

Dover

Ferry to Calais

THE ENGLISH
CHANNEL

The 07:37 from Mortlake to Clapham Junction is two minutes late. Which is lucky, as that is exactly how late I happen to be.

On board commuters peck at mobile phones. Nobody reads a newspaper (not even a *Metro*). It is a grey, grisly morning and the carriage smells of wet dog. Suburbs slip by as do familiar stations: Barnes, Putney, Wandsworth Town. We arrive at Clapham Junction. I disembark Train Number One, with its cherry-red South Western Railway carriages, blue-and-yellow doors and tangerine stripes.

At platform 12, I board the 07:58 to Victoria, an apple-green Southern train with more twitchy-fingered passengers. Battersea Power Station's towers loom beside the Thames. An officious announcement requests we report anything that 'doesn't look right' to the British Transport Police – 'See it. Say it. Sorted.' – making me wonder how many terrorist attacks have ever been nipped in the bud by one of these Big Brother-style messages.

I cross Victoria Station's busy concourse, dodging yet more zombies-with-phones and a man in a hoodie who asks for spare change. At platform six, I board the 08:34 to Dover Priory, a lilac Southeastern train that re-crosses the river. I am on my way to France. All being well, in three weeks I shall arrive in Venice. In between I'm not quite sure what will happen... just as I've always planned.

Leaving Britain by slow trains is liberating. The Dover Priory carriages are almost empty. These days most train-goers to France opt for the high-speed Eurostar service: two hours and 15 minutes to Paris, or just 80 minutes to Lille (186 miles per hour). From Victoria to Dover is two hours and three minutes, with 17 stops along the way. This is the way I intend to get to La Serenissima. No rushing about. No hurry. No stressing. No need for it. Early on a weekday, going in the opposite direction to London commuters, the 08:34 feels like a ghost train.

For a while, at least. A man with gelled hair plonks himself in the set of four seats ahead of mine. Without seeming to notice me or care that he has chosen such close proximity when the rest of the carriage is free, he begins a long, loud scattergun phone conversation.

'She lay down starkers naked so she could get some last sun. She literally took off her trousers, the lot. I'll send you the link from the *Daily Mail*,' he begins, pausing for a split second before telling whoever is on the other end of the line (and me) that 'things are good' with him at the moment, that he has a date with a woman from Bromley this evening, that he will buy an iPad later today and has placed an advert to sell his car in *Auto Trader* magazine.

I move seats as we trundle past council estates in Peckham and pull into St Mary Cray Station, where the train's guard says: 'We're arriving five minutes early. We'll wait a while. There's nothing to worry about, we're just five minutes early.' My slow train has, evidently, been going too fast.

There is already a tantalising sense of escape – of slipping beneath the radar of modern life. Emails: I won't read them. Phone calls: let them leave messages. As the countryside opens up into mesmerising fields of lemon-yellow rape seed, I settle back and allow south-east England to pass gently by. The great train writer Paul Theroux once said that tourists 'don't know where they've been', whereas travellers 'don't know where they're going'. Well, I have my target, but there are plenty of *don't knows* ahead. It is a marvellous feeling.

The guard checks my ticket. I have an Interrail Pass covering a month. This golden ticket allows me to go wherever I want in 30 European countries on most services (a few private rail operators have not signed up). I have an Interrail Pass Guide explaining the ins-and-outs, as well as a map showing the network of lines and which train companies require reservations, for which you must pay extra. Before boarding each train you are required to fill out a space in a logbook that comes with the Interrail Pass with the date of travel and time of your train as well as its departure point and destination. My first entry shows Mortlake and Dover; you do not have to worry about detailing each connection.

This ticket has an almost hallowed reputation among train guards, as I am soon to discover. The grey-haired Southeastern conductor barely glances at the floppy green document, such is his trust in its authenticity. The ticket covers one journey out of the UK and one journey back home. The rest must be taken abroad, with no limit on the number of trips with my type of pass.

'Where are you going?' he asks.

When I tell him Dover, he simply replies: 'Yes, you're on the right one,' and ambles off.

I close my eyes. The train judders and hums. We stop at Sole Street Station, then pass banks of cow parsley and ivy, undulating countryside and the Royal Mail depot at Rochester. The surface of the River Medway has a smoky-white glare as the turrets of Rochester Castle arise. We have been going about an hour. It seems almost impossible that Charles Dickens used to walk from London, sometimes through the night, to his house at Gad's Hill in Higham, not so far away here in Kent; a good 30 miles.

At Chatham, the eel-nosed locomotive of a high-speed train gleams on an adjacent platform. Terraced houses that remind me of *Coronation Street* mark the outskirts of Gillingham, where we pass close to the stands and floodlights of Gillingham Football Club's Priestfield Stadium. At Rainham there's a *BRITAIN RUNS ON RAIL* sign and a shuttered pub named The Railway. Electricity pylons, long glasshouses with fruit crops, and vineyards emerge on the run-up to Canterbury East, where flags bearing St George's crosses and Union Jacks flutter on poles in back gardens (Kent voted overwhelmingly to leave the European Union in the Brexit referendum in June 2016 with 59 per cent of its 970,000 voters wanting out).

And so we arrive at Dover Priory, bang on time at 10:39.

* * *

During this description of an adventure by rail, I will from time to time, when I can, provide details of the exact trains on which I have travelled. I am well aware of the *rail enthusiast* contingency (never *trainspotter* – I know better than that). So, making an effort on my first trip, I go to the station supervisor's office to ask what kind of train the 08:43 from Victoria was. I cannot tell from looking at it, as some train lovers would in an instant (no doubt).

A tall employee eating a sausage roll looks at me, shrugs and turns to a shorter man sitting behind a counter at a desk. This is Simon, the Dover Priory Station supervisor. He seems pleased to have been asked and replies that it was an Electrostar 375 from the 1990s with eight carriages. So there you have it. I tell them about my journey ahead. Simon and Warren, the sausage-roll-eating customer services officer, appear delighted. Warren asks if I know the way to the ferry port. I say I don't and he accompanies me to the front of the plain, white art deco station, giving me extensive directions.

'Good luck,' he beams, patting my hand twice during our handshake.

Nice people at Dover Priory Station.

Before going to the port, however, I take a look at the centre of town. It's not all about the trains on this foray by rail. I want to provide a series of snapshots of the places along the way (or else it could simply become a Groundhog Day of locomotives and carriages). Destinations matter.

The town centre is down a hill and has a pedestrianised high street with a PRICEL£SS FURNITURE shop, a Poundland and a PoundStore. A group of drunks clutch cider cans and put the world to rights on a corner by an HSBC bank. Poppies hang from lamp posts and a mural by the town hall war memorial shows soldiers gazing seawards. Lines written by the poet Laurence Binyon in the 1914 poem 'For the Fallen' are inscribed across the mural's skyline.

> They mingle not with their laughing comrades again;
> They sit no more with familiar tables of home;
> They have no lot in our labour of the day-time;
> They sleep beyond England's foam.

Dover has, of course, always been in a crucial defensive position. With Binyon's words reverberating I go up to the medieval castle. It was in tunnels here that the evacuation of soldiers from Dunkirk was overseen during Operation Dynamo in May 1940. William the Conqueror passed by in October 1066 on his way to Westminster. Fortifications were reinforced during the Napoleonic Wars; garrison numbers at the time were increased, with underground lodgings added by the clifftop. It is for good reason that Dover is nicknamed the Key to England. It feels as though this is a place where many important decisions have been made over the centuries (which indeed they have). A tantalising sense of history hangs in the air.

After inspecting the ancient battlements, I look across the silvery sea and the sprawl of the ferry port. Then I scamper down the hill and walk along the main road as lorries roar by (their drivers without a worry in the world about tariffs and traffic jams, for the time being). The port has become a 'secure area' due to illegal immigration and 'other concerns' says the P&O Ferries ticket man, so I cannot just walk to the ferry. Instead I wait for the Port Service Bus in a room with a work of art made of tiles saying 'Port of Dover: Gateway to Britain'. Beneath the words, Stonehenge, St Paul's Cathedral and a village cricket game are depicted (all white faces among the players).

The bus whisks the eight foot passengers across the secure area. We board the *Spirit of Britain*, where I sit on the afterdeck with a beer (why not?) and regard the not-so-white cliffs of Dover (they're quite grey, really). Massive seagulls with cold yellow eyes rest on the handrails. The engine growls softly. We pull away in a trail of English foam, heading for Calais. 'Goodbye, England,' says a child with his mother.

To maintain my train mood I begin reading *Murder on the Orient Express* by Agatha Christie. The opening scene has Hercule Poirot wrapped in scarves and wearing a hat on a freezing platform at the station in Aleppo in Syria. He is heading to Istanbul on the *Taurus Express* and of him 'nothing was visible but a pink-tipped nose and the two points of an upward curled moustache'.

It does not take the world famous detective long to start poking about, quickly noticing the close relationship between a colonel and a 'young English lady', two of his fellow passengers. 'The train, it is as dangerous as a sea voyage!' he muses. 'Rather an odd little comedy that I watch here.'

The *Spirit of Britain* was not built in Britain. It was made in Rauma in Finland and completed in 2011. The length is 213 metres. The gross tonnage is 48,000. The top speed is 22 knots. There are a dozen decks. It can hold 180 lorries, 195 cars and 2,000 passengers. I learn all of this from a model of the vessel near the Shop Ahoy! duty-free shop. Good transport buff stuff.

Televisions built into walls and hanging from the ceiling advertise breathalyser tests, cheap wine with a 'carry to car' service and deals on Johnny Depp cologne. I stare ahead at the dark-grey sea through the salt-stained windows of one of the bow lounges. Little black wavelets ripple across the otherwise placid water and, before long, cliffs and long oatmeal-coloured beaches appear. A church steeple shoots upwards. Vodafone sends me a text message telling me 'WELCOME TO FRANCE' and an announcement is made that the Vegas Slots fruit machines are being switched off: 'Do not insert further coins!' We enter the harbour at Calais. Foot passengers are assembled and I am soon walking through drizzle past high walls with rolls of barbed wire and graffiti scrawled on the road that (rather optimistically) demands: 'OPEN THE BORDER'.

I am on European Union soil, with its funny rules written by funny bureaucrats with funny accents.

I am off around the Continent – trains all the way.

CHAPTER TWO

CALAIS IN FRANCE TO BRUGES IN BELGIUM

'ZER IS NO TRAIN TODAY'

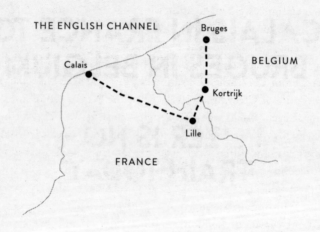

THE ENGLISH CHANNEL

Bruges

BELGIUM

Calais

Kortrijk

Lille

FRANCE

Calais is 21 miles from Britain and it's a strange place with an intriguing history. Recent notoriety, of course, came in the form of the Jungle camp of asylum seekers hoping to enter Britain (not far from the ferry port). This was closed in October 2016 after complaints from the UK that France was not doing enough to prevent people hiding on vehicles on trains through the Channel Tunnel; President Macron has since informed any would-be refugees and migrants that northern France is a 'dead end' and that attempting to cross the Channel is pointless. Nevertheless, more than 115,000 such attempts were made in the year before my journey (this is just the figure covering those caught).

For more than 200 years Calais was part of Britain, so in the past asylum seekers would have achieved their aim simply by being here. From 1347, when Edward III of England annexed Calais after the Battle of Crécy, until 1558, when the French led by Henry II won it back, Calais was a key English port. At its peak, a third of the English government's revenue is said to have come from the port's customs duties, with wool trade being the most important source of income. At the time it was known as 'the brightest jewel in the English crown'. It was also an official parliamentary borough. Dick Whittington was mayor for a while (in 1407, while also acting as Lord Mayor of London). Upon losing the port, Mary Tudor famously said: 'When I am dead and opened, you shall find Calais lying in my heart.'

The port played an important role in World War Two. During the Siege of Calais in May 1940, more than 3,000 British troops alongside 800 French soldiers faced a German barrage for six days. This brave resistance diverted Nazi divisions from Dunkirk, giving the evacuation there a greater chance of success.

Julius Caesar set sail to Britain from Calais. Napoleon considered invading Britain from Calais. A lot has gone on in Calais.

Première Classe in a downpour
Arrival in Calais

It is a three-mile walk from the ferry port to the centre of Calais along a long nondescript road lined with warehouses with more high fences with barbed wire. I am the only passenger who has chosen this route into the city. The other foot passengers appear to have taken taxis or buses. Perhaps that is because it is pouring. I have put on my pac-a-mac – looking like a true rail enthusiast – and I am splashing through puddles following a road that leads to what I take to be the main church tower, the one I had seen from the sea.

In this bedraggled fashion I head towards the Hôtel Première Classe Calais Centre-Gare, right opposite Gare de Calais Ville. During these journeys I am going to put up for the night as close to stations as possible to make onward trips easier the next day. I have also chosen to go cheaply, if not dirt cheap. My budget is around 40–50 euros a night. The Première Classe Calais Centre-Gare ticks all the boxes.

The long road eventually curves round towards the 'church'. Beyond a sex shop offering 'gadgets and films', I come to this structure and find it is not, in fact, a place of worship. It is the ornate Hôtel de Ville, built in an OTT Flemish Renaissance style with a rocket-shaped bell tower rising to 75 metres. So says a little information panel. The building dates from 1925 and was damaged during World War Two but remarkably survived the worst of the bombing. Most of the city centre was razed.

Hôtel Première Classe Calais Centre-Gare is just around the corner next to Le Klub and Les Pirates Bar.

First impressions are not the best. It looks like a small prison with a grey concrete facade and a front door that has been permanently, one would presume, concreted up. To enter you must go to a side entrance by a car park. I am soon in a tiny red and white room complete with a bed with a beige blanket and a cereal-box-sized television on a high shelf. Not so bad after all – comfortable enough. I look outside through a grimy window. A group of furtive individuals walks past; surely asylum seekers considering how to cross the Channel, although perhaps I'm jumping to conclusions. My room, rather pleasingly, directly faces the station and the Buffet de la Gare.

It has stopped raining. I go for a wander and soon find myself in Parc Richelieu, inspecting a statue of General de Gaulle and Winston Churchill, erected in 2017. Churchill has been captured smoking a cigar and leaning on a cane. De Gaulle, who is about a foot taller, wears a long buttoned-up mackintosh and a determined expression. Further on in this little park, I come to a plaque remembering Emma, Lady Hamilton, Lord Nelson's lover who died in Calais after falling into debt and hard times aged just 49.

Calais has plenty of watering holes, catering no doubt to those on booze cruises, although I cannot see many Brits about. L'Hovercraft Bar, Le Buzz and Le London Bridge pub by the main square seem the most popular. There's another statue of de Gaulle here, this time with his wife, who was from Calais.

I cross to the other side of the square and walk along the harbour to Fort Risban, originally built by the English to help take Calais in the fourteenth century. Rain begins to pelt down and I take shelter in Brasserie de la Mer, where I eat a delicious bubbling bouillabaisse listening to Stevie Wonder hits on a stereo before returning to my room to read *Murder on the Orient Express*. Poirot is about to take 'sleeping-car accommodation in the Stamboul–Calais coach'. I am at the destination of the detective with the 'upward curled moustache'.

Back at my hotel, feeling content after the excellent bouillabaisse, I find it is not, however, easy to sleep.

Through the thin walls of my room I hear a rather worrying domestic drama unfold.

'Why were you talking that ****?' says the man, in Cockney-English.

Female response, also in Cockney-English: 'No, no, no.'

Man: 'Let's just get all this **** out and throw it all away.'

Woman: 'No, no, no.'

Man: 'What have I done wrong?'

Inaudible response.

Man: 'Your attitude makes me feel that it's all gone to pot.'

Woman: 'No, no, no.'

Never mind *Murder on the Orient Express*, for a while I'm concerned about *Murder in the Hôtel Première Classe Calais Centre-Gare*. Eventually I drop off, wondering: *Why do people go on holiday to argue with one another? Why now?* And, I must heartlessly admit: *Why can't they do it somewhere else?*

'This polis cracked my tooth'
A morning in Calais

In the morning I meet the Eritreans, but before I do so I go to the station. My intention today is to travel to Dunkirk, as I have never been and I would like to see the famous beaches where Britain – and Europe, for that matter – was saved from the Nazis. However, there is a problem.

'Zer is no train today,' says the almost bald station guard. He has fluffy clumps of hair, hazel eyes, glasses and an inscrutable manner.

'What do you mean?' I ask.

'Zer is a strike,' he replies. 'You may take a bus to Dunkirk at twelve thirty.'

'But I don't want to take a bus.'

'Zer is no train today,' he says.

Damn it. I should have checked this out before setting off. The French railway people seem to be on strike. Of course they are! What a great start. I go outside and contemplate my next step. The station guard has informed me that the strike will also be on tomorrow. I am stuck in Calais, train-less, for the foreseeable future.

Or so it would appear.

I go back into the station and look at the bus options on the departure screen. Then I notice that the 15:39 to Lille has a little train symbol, rather than a bus symbol. I ask the station guard about this.

'*Oui*, zer is a train to Lille,' he concedes.

It is the only train of the day. One of the French train drivers, it would appear, is not on strike. *Très bien!* Or even, *magnifique!*

So, I'm going to Lille.

First, however, I head for the neighbourhood of Calais that was once the Jungle. My target is L'Auberge des Migrants. Even though the Jungle has officially shut down, many Channel-crossing hopefuls are still to be found on the streets of Calais.

The route takes me through a suburb with a football ground and the local communist party headquarters. Outside the latter posters belonging to the General Confederation of Labour, the second largest trade union in France, declare: '*La régression sociale ne se négocie pas, elle se combat!*' (Social regression does not negotiate, it fights). This is the biggest union within the Société Nationale des Chemins de Fer Français (SNCF), the state-owned French rail company, and its members are behind the current rail disruption. President Macron intends to cut pay and reduce retirement and benefit terms for rail employees in return for helping to bail out SNCF's debt, currently running at a staggering fifty billion euros. The union, naturally, is unhappy and there are fears that the move could be a first step towards privatisation.

It's an intriguing scenario that some are referring to as Macron's 'Thatcher Moment'. Will he really see off the unions? French rail workers, known as *cheminots* and who number about 150,000, do have it rather good. The retirement age for conductors and train drivers is 52 and for those in administrative positions, 57 years old. This compares to an average retirement age in France in the private sector of 62. On top of this, pension payment is based on the previous six months' salary, not an average of the employee's salary over the previous 25 years (the norm elsewhere in France).

Then add a condition of employment known as *licenciement économique*, a redundancy rule that some regard as a 'job for life', so long as employees do not retire, resign or get sacked for poor behaviour, a 35-hour week, 28 days of annual holiday (three more days than other French workers) and the possibility of 22 days of RTT, *réduction de temps de travail*, for drivers, which is effectively extra holiday for those working over 35 hours a week. Then bear in mind that spouses and children under the age of 16 can receive 16 rail fares a year for ten per cent of the full ticket price (an allowance that costs SNCF around 25 million euros a year).

Yes, the *cheminots* do have it extremely good, which is why they are on strike: they want to keep it *extremely good*. Yet to understand the stand-off, the outsider must also appreciate that the French railway, nationalised since the 1930s, is a much-loved part of the nation's welfare state. The French take pride in their railway, especially its *grands projets* such as the Ligne à Grande Vitesse Sud-Est between Paris and Lyons that opened in 1983, Europe's first fully-fledged high-speed railway. Do not underestimate the power of your driver or conductor in France. This is a country where strikes still work – if that is not a contradiction in terms – although SNCF is considering a radical option to get round the stalemate: driverless trains. With no drivers, there can be no driver strikes. That's the idea, anyway. *Téléconducteurs* at control centres may soon oversee 'drone trains'. Welcome to the future! Let's hope the computers don't crash, causing the trains to do the same.

Pondering this I plod on past a retail estate and a Japanese Wok restaurant in the direction of the former Jungle.

I'm drawn here as I want to lay eyes on this key neighbourhood in Britain's recent history. The threat of a 'flood' of migrants and refugees to the UK was, after all, one of the main reasons Britain voted out of Europe in June 2016. Leavers wanted to 'take back control' and the Jungle was, if you like, the symbolic epicentre of their worst fears.

Down Boulevard de l'Égalité I go, eventually turning left at a Lidl supermarket into Rue Clément Ader.

This is where I meet the Eritreans. Fikru and Girma are idling along Rue Clément Ader and I ask if they have a moment to talk. They do. They probably have a lot of moments while waiting around homeless and stateless in Calais.

Fikru wears a leather jacket, ripped jeans and a green headscarf. He has a wide smile with a prominent broken front tooth. Girma is clothed in jeans, a green jacket and a hooded top. They say they are 18 years old, brothers and that they left Eritrea three years ago via Sudan, Libya and a ship to Italy that took four days across the Mediterranean Sea.

I am with people who have risked all to reach Calais.

Fikru is despondent. 'We have no life,' he says. 'Problem with *polis*.' He pauses.

'We have no working. Three years, no working. Three years we are not calling Eritrea.'

Girma cuts in. 'It is problem. We have no one.'

Fikru tells me: 'This *polis* cracked my tooth.'

He grins to reveal the full damage to his ruined smile.

Then he clutches his leg.

'Seven days ago, stick on leg.'

The police, he says, attacked him.

We talk a little longer. I can sense they are nervous about drawing attention to themselves (too much publicity could be painful). So I wish them luck, offer Fikru ten euros – which he gladly accepts – and ask if I can take their picture.

Both quickly shake their heads.

Then they shuffle and limp along Rue Clément Ader. Not far from the Lidl they sit on old plastic crates beneath a litter-strewn hedge.

For now, at least, this seems to be home.

* * *

L'Auberge des Migrants is across the way. It is not, as the name suggests, an inn. It is a depot offering support to the 400 or so asylum seekers still in Calais despite the dismantling of the Jungle (probably many more, 400 is an official figure). The outfit is run by 30 volunteers. Food, clothing, free mobile phone charging and legal information on asylum rules are offered from vans that circulate in the city.

At first I talk to Luke, a bushy-bearded British man, who cagily tells me: 'All across Europe there is hostility towards refugees. France is not exempt from that. We are trying to show humanity to refugees.'

Luke is sitting in a hut by a chalkboard upon which figures are scrawled referring to the number of sleeping bags, duvets and emergency foil blankets that have been distributed in the previous month. Another board reports that 1,200 meals have been delivered in the past day. A sign says: *'À coeurs vaillants, rien d'impossible'* (With valiant hearts, nothing is impossible).

Across from this hut is a van with a small table at the back.

Inside I find another Brit: Rowan Farrell, co-founder of the Refugee Info Bus. This UK-registered charity helps immigrants seeking asylum understand the intricacies of asylum laws. The van has a generator and Wi-Fi antennae that allows up to 80 people to use the internet for free. Leaflets are in seven languages including Pashto (spoken in Afghanistan). The majority of those in Calais are from Afghanistan, Eritrea, Ethiopia, Iran, Iraq and Syria.

'If someone's in Calais, they're trying to get to the UK, obviously,' says Rowan. 'They must prove that they are in fear of recrimination in their country. It's individual. Food and shelter are important but so is the bigger view. Often refugees just don't know anything regarding their rights.'

The whole point of the Refugee Info Bus is to fill this void. Rowan founded the charity after coming to work on behalf of refugees in the Jungle and realising that a lack of legal know-how was a major problem. Previously he had worked as a photographer.

He asks about my trip, and I explain what I'm up to.

It turns out Rowan loves trains, too, and he is soon telling me that he once went on the overnight sleeper train between Lviv and Odessa in Ukraine. Lviv, he says, is a beautiful city that feels strongly part of Europe without being within the European Union (which gives me ideas about the route ahead). He had gone there for a photography project soon after Russia, breaking international law, invaded Ukraine to 'take back' Crimea in 2014.

There seems to be a lot of 'taking back' going on at the moment.

My eye is caught by a pile of cricket bats in a corner of the yard.

'Afghanis love cricket,' Rowan explains matter-of-factly.

After an appeal, a team in the UK has kindly donated their spares so Afghani asylum seekers in Calais can practise their favourite game while waiting for their paperwork (should it be forthcoming).

We say goodbye and I return along Boulevard de L'Égalité.

I have two pit stops to make before the train to Lille.

The first is just along the boulevard at Ville de Calais Cimetière Sud, where I pay homage to the Britons who defended the city against the Germans in May 1940. Row upon row of Commonwealth War Graves are surrounded by neat box hedges. Each inscription on the gravestones is a reminder of the great debt owed to the soldiers of World War Two.

'P. W Amos. The King's Royal Rifle Corps. 26/5/40. Aged 24,' reads one stone, 'H. J. Dungay. The Rifle Brigade. 24/5/40. Aged 29,' says another. 'A soldier of the 1939–1945 war. The King's Royal Rifle Corps. Known Unto God,' says yet another. Not all bodies were identified. About 300 British troops were killed in the heroic, bloody siege.

Afterwards I go to the Musée Mémoir 39–45 Calais in Parc Saint-Pierre, right by the station. The museum is in an eerie former Nazi bunker that stretches almost 200 metres. Inside, displays cover the terrifying events of May 1940 as well as the outcome of the war, when Canadian units freed the port in 1944. An original poster dated 13 July 1940 catches my eye: 'Every English People [*sic*] who lives in Calais as well as every English person who is staying here for some time and who is more than eighteen years old, is obliged to come immediately to the *ORTSKOMMANDANTUR* in the Town Hall of Calais. Every English people, who will not come immediately, will be considered as a spy and judged accordingly.'

Spine-chilling words, just 21 miles from Dover.

Churchill's 'frightful nationalistic quarrels' came very close to our shores.

'Not all those who wander are lost'
Calais to Lille

Before boarding the 15:39 to Lille, I check out the cosy little Buffet de la Gare. How could any train lover not poke their nose in the cosy little Buffet de la Gare in Calais?

Inside are faux leather booths, a copper-topped bar, a flashing pinball machine and a drinker who has slumped his head on the table while clutching his mobile phone (perhaps he's been here all day waiting for the only train out of Calais). A lovely old railway poster bears a picture of the Calais town hall and the words: *CHEMIN DE FER DU NORD. CALAIS: SON PORT, SA PLAGE, SES DENTELLES* (NORTHERN RAILWAY. CALAIS: ITS PORT, ITS BEACH, ITS LACE).

Calais has long been famous for its lace. In the nineteenth century many English manufacturers moved from Nottingham to Calais to take advantage of cheaper working conditions. Apparently, the Duchess of Cambridge and Amal Clooney, no less, wore *dentelles de Calais* dresses at their weddings.

So it must be pretty good.

I pick up a copy of *Nord Littoral*, a local paper that runs a story headlined: '*4 MOIS DE PRISON POUR AVOIR FRAPPÉ UN POLICIER*' (FOUR MONTHS JAIL FOR HITTING A POLICE

OFFICER). A man named Jamal Khurchach from Morocco, who has been in the country since 2007, has been found guilty of an attack on La Police Aux Frontières after crying 'Allahu akbar'. The court decision is: *'Il a l'obligation de quitter le territoire français.'*

Goodbye and good riddance, more or less.

* * *

The only train out of Calais is a sleek double-decker due to call at Audruicq, Watten-Éperlecques, Saint-Omer, Hazebrouck, Strazeele, Bailleul and Armentières. It is to arrive in Lille at 16:59. This is, as it happens, exactly the same journey time (80 minutes) for the Eurostar service from London's St Pancras Station to Lille.

A group of refugees huddles by the platform. They must have imagined that this would be a quiet place to rest for a while in the city centre. When they see the passengers of the day's only train heading for them en masse they nervously leap up and scurry to the exit.

Calais is such an unusual, transitory place. Amid the booze cruisers and transport lorries refugees float like ghosts. Sit still for a while on a public bench just about anywhere in the port and the apparitions will come and go, each with a story of a long journey behind them and an uncertain future ahead. The city feels like a frontier where lives hang in the balance and business is done; as it has for centuries past. Ghosts of the past mingle with the ghosts of today. It is the perfect place to begin a continental train ride. From one famous frontier the tracks stretch ahead, with many more to come.

On board the 15:39 I settle into a blue-grey seat on the top deck. The train departs on time and we pass a terrace of redbrick houses and sidings occupied by locomotives and carriages; out of action due to the strike, no doubt. Street art and graffiti of the sort found in ghettoes in American cities covers the walls along the track before the train rattles across a canal and countryside opens up. The horn blows. A startled pheasant flaps across a field. Tan-coloured cows raise their heads at this unusual interruption to their afternoon: a train in France that is actually moving.

The toilets, I discover, are locked; part of the *cheminots'* strike. Small towns and villages come and go. At Audruicq we cross a muddy brown river. At Watten-Éperlecques a conductor with a flat cap enters the carriage but does not check tickets (yet another act of protest?). At Hazebrouck we pull in by a Skoda dealership and a church with a tall steeple. At Saint-Omer a caravan park and a series of enormous glasshouses materialise. Bailleul is home to a Lidl and a musical instrument shop. Armentières is notable for its large number of rusty disused train tracks with broken electricity cables hanging above. Maybe Armentières was once a much bigger deal than today. Something seems to have gone wrong in Armentières.

We continue beneath a mushroom-coloured sky. The countryside between stations is moss-green with wispy poplar trees lining lanes leading to remote villages in folds of undulating land. The dreamy feeling of escape that I enjoyed in Kent returns. Trains soon deliver you from the reality of everyday life... if you let them. Just sit back and follow the tracks.

In the dim light of this overcast day the carriage lights flicker as though considering going on strike themselves. We depart the countryside and enter a suburb of terraced houses. Shiny apartments rise next to cranes on building sites with the skeletons of more shiny apartments to come. The train pulls into platform 15 of Gare de Lille Flandres. We are bang on time.

I gather my backpack. This bag is small but heavy. Inside are several books: *Murder on the Orient Express* (of course), *The Lady Vanishes* (a thriller by Ethel Lina White published in 1936 and later turned into a film by Alfred Hitchcock), *A Legacy of Spies* by John le Carré, *From Russia, With Love* by Ian Fleming (which includes train scenes), the *European Rail Timetable*, produced by the former compilers of the *Thomas Cook European Rail Timetable*, and a copy of *Europe By Rail: The Definitive Guide* by Nicky Gardner and Susanne Kries.

The latter makes essential reading. The authors clearly understand the freedom of train travel without much of a plan. 'Serendipity' is key and rail travellers such as myself should be 'led by a whim', they say. J. R. R. Tolkien is their hero. 'Not all those who wander are lost,' as he writes in *The Lord of the Rings*.

With this in mind – having had no idea this morning that I would go to Lille – I step onto platform 15.

Gare de Lille Flandres is a flamboyant building from the late nineteenth century with windows shaped like giant croquet hoops and a grand facade with a clock tower. It has a peculiar atmosphere on this strike day. Hardly anyone is about and the station feels like a place of peaceful contemplation. There are palm trees planted in boxes. There are long rows of passenger-less benches. The tracks are empty: no trains around, other than our one. A woman with a baby in a pram pedals on an exercise bicycle that is creating energy to power her mobile phone. A faint whirring emanates from this unusual public phone-charger. Messages about the *grève* (strike) flash up on screens. Gare de Lille Flandres really is quiet, as though we have arrived in a church.

From here it is a short walk, about a minute, to the Hôtel Première Classe Lille Centre. With serendipity, I hope, and on a whim, I realise, I have booked a room here despite the *no, no, nos* of last night.

My new Première Classe is, I am unsurprised to discover, a far cry from The Ritz. The hotel is on a little street with a run of kebab shops, deep-fried chicken outlets and a Night Shop selling cheap booze, outside which is a group of men who are gesticulating in an animated fashion as I arrive. My room is on the fourth floor, reached via a hall with a threadbare carpet. It has three narrow single beds; quite why I have been given so many, I am unsure. A strong smell of lemon fills the air, probably from a cleaning product. When guests on the floor above flush the toilet or have a shower, a deluge of water rushes down a pipe in a corner. The colour scheme is glaring orange and red. The bathroom is the size of a telephone box and is pink and apricot. Hôtel Première Classe Lille Centre is not for the queasy.

It will do (it will have to).

I go out and pass the facade of Gare de Lille Flandres to visit Gare de Lille Europe, the station where the Eurostar service arrives, as it has done since the trains from London through the Channel Tunnel began in 1994. Lille is the first major stop in France on the route from Britain on the way to both Paris and Brussels; quicker to reach than Birmingham is from London.

Britain does seem to be closer to Europe than ever, whether the 'bad boys' of Brexit like it or not.

Gare de Lille Europe is hellish. The station is buried deep within a large shopping mall crammed with international brands – H&M, Primark, Uniqlo, Zara, Starbucks and much else. Inanely grinning greeters in garish red waistcoats lurk near the entrance. Irritating muzak plays. Shoppers jostle and shuffle by, many with eyes locked on mobile phones.

You could be in a mall just about anywhere: Abu Dhabi, Texas, Milton Keynes, Hong Kong. I do not hang round. I follow a group of twenty-somethings through the exit. When we are outside one of the women in this group spits her chewing gum at a friend and laughs loudly after doing so.

Mon Dieu! As Hercule Poirot might say.

Then I go to a charming little restaurant with a view of Gare de Lille Flandres where I eat a delicious local dish named *l'assiette de potjevleesch*, a pot of chicken served cold in a jelly alongside cold potatoes, beans, gherkins and olives. Then I return to my orange and red room with its pink and apricot bathroom. Then someone has a shower on the floor above. Then I fall fast asleep on one of my three Première Classe beds.

'How can anyone govern a nation that has 246 different kinds of cheese?'

Lille to Bruges, via Kortrijk

The French train strike seems to be ongoing but there appears to be one practical solution: get out of France. Quickly.

Being so close to Belgium, this turns out to be quite easy. There is a train to Cortrai in Belgium at 15:08 on Belgian Rail. From Kortrijk (the spelling used in Belgium, Cortrai is the French version) I can catch a connection to Bruges at 15:58, arriving at 16:55.

Seeing as I have a month-long Interrail Pass I really do have the freedom of the tracks. Why not roll into the 'Venice of the North', as some refer to Bruges, before reaching the real Venice in a few weeks' time? All I have to do is write the date, time and destination in the 'travel diary' section of the ticket, as I have done for the previous journeys.

This settled, I go online and book a room at the Charlie Rockets Jeugdherberg, a hostel in the centre of Bruges with cheap private rooms, not too far from the station. Bathrooms are down a hall but the place looks jolly enough with pictures of a bar with an American theme including a model of the Statue of Liberty wrapped in a Stars and Stripes, various old US number plates and posters of Elvis Presley, Marilyn Monroe and John Travolta. Much jollier than Première Classe, despite my growing fondness for the quirks of this chain.

* * *

In the spirit of Gardner, Kries and Tolkien, I let serendipity lead me round the streets of Lille.

Hearing music emanating from within, my first stop is at Église Saint-Maurice, just around the corner from Première Classe. This is a magnificent Gothic church with parts dating from the fourteenth century. Morning mass is on and I sit on one of the pews by a giant stone column listening to hymns reverberate across the chamber. It is all quite pleasant, even though I can understand little of what is going on. At the end of the mass, an elderly woman next to me turns to shake my hand. The rest of the congregation shakes their neighbours' hands, too.

Before I know it, I find myself in conversation with Père Xavier Behaegel, the priest who oversaw the service.

Very sociable at Église Saint-Maurice.

He is tall and willowy, in his early forties, with kind eyes and a yellow tunic.

Somewhat foolishly I ask if he is the head priest.

'Oh no, that would be the Pope,' he replies, straight-faced.

Even more foolishly, I ask instead whether he is in charge at Église Saint-Maurice.

His eyes shoot upwards.

'That would be the good Lord above,' he says.

Père Behaegel has a dry sense of humour.

After this start we talk for a while about Europe. The subject comes up after he asks where I am from.

'It is a shame that you want to leave us,' he says, referring to Brexit. 'It is very important to live together in Europe. Since World War Two this has been important. These are dangerous times for peace.'

He pauses and then says softly: 'Peace is fragile. We need to believe in peace.'

Lille was occupied by the Germans during both world wars, so perhaps *Lillois*, the name for locals, have a greater appreciation of this than others. The city name comes from *l'île* (the island), due to the existence of a prominent island on the River Duele. It has always been an important city, from the cloth fairs of the twelfth century through to the days of its control by the Duchy of Burgundy, to its period under the United Provinces of the Netherlands, before being taken back by Louis XIV of France in 1668, and its fierce resistance to the Austrians in 1792. The city's first train line, a connection with Paris, opened in 1846. Lille is famous for being where the anti-tuberculosis vaccine BCG (Bacillus Calmette-Guérin) was developed by Albert Calmette and Camille Guérin in the early 1920s. Before the Germans returned in World War Two, many *Lillois* left the city. Memories of bad behaviour during German occupation in the earlier war were still fresh in the locals' minds.

After Père Behaegel learns I have just come from Calais, we turn to the subject of migration. Refugees, he says, are not just a problem in the port. He has put up two 17-year-old refugees from Mali in his own home, providing them with food and shelter for the past ten months.

'We have to do something to welcome refugees. We can't just turn our backs,' he says gently.

An elderly woman begins to speak to Père Behaegel and I leave the church to perform my second religious act of the day. Well, sort of.

I enter L'Abbaye, a bar on the edge of the Grand Place.

Why not? I am, I suppose, on *holiday*. My 'reasoning' from the ferry is as true now as it was then. Other people are here in this 'abbey', drinking beer. It is noon on Sunday and this is what *Lillois* seem to do. A tall glass (half a litre) is delivered. The beer is delicious and it feels decadent as a buzz sets in. I am safe in the knowledge that my train awaits. I can sit here and simply *do nothing* for a while. Afterwards, I can float around Lille for an hour or two; a *flâneur* in the land that created the word.

What could be better? I sip my beer. Lille seems a wonderful place. Tourists led by a guide shuffle by exclaiming in awe as they lay eyes on the Grand Place for the first time. Church bells peal. A solitary man to my left orders another beer after polishing off a plate of sausages. A couple huddling in a corner whisper sweet nothings to one another.

I'm in no hurry. That's the whole point of this trip. Turn up in a new place, take a look around, and move on. Why worry about anything? There is nothing to worry about. Enjoy Europe. It's out there waiting at the end of the railway lines.

I finish my drink and cross the Grand Place, passing the memorial of the siege of 1792. This column celebrates the city's defence against the Austrians, who numbered about 20,000 and who destroyed Lille's main church in their attack. The column is topped by a bronze statue of a goddess, who points the finger of her left hand to the ground as if to say 'We saved this soil'. It is known locally as the Column of the Goddess and is a famous meeting point, rather like Eros in London's Piccadilly Circus.

All around are tall, ornate buildings, some with distinctive roofs with step shapes that remind me of Aztec temples. Lille is part of French Flanders and the architecture is noticeably different to places further south in the country. On the far side of the square is the most flamboyant structure of all: La Vieille Bourse de Lille (the old stock exchange). Gilded spikes adorn the rooftop and stone figurines decorate the burgundy-striped facade. In its centre, reached through archways, is a courtyard with second-hand book stalls that are very tempting but not a good idea for those about to travel with a backpack across Europe who already have quite a few books. The stock exchange was completed in 1652 and this historic yard feels like the symbolic centre of the city.

I drift on, my *flâneur*-feet taking me beyond the opera house to Maison Natale de Charles de Gaulle. The man who led the Resistance against the Nazis during World War Two was born here on 22 November 1890 and the house has been maintained as it was during his childhood years. Apart from being the leader of the government in exile during World War Two, de Gaulle was prime minister from 1958 to 1959 and president of France from 1959 for a decade. During his time as president he oversaw the country's nuclear programme (so that France became the world's fourth nuclear power) and sought an alliance with Germany to counteract growing American influence across the globe. De Gaulle was a big critic of the Vietnam War. He twice vetoed British entry into the European Economic Community, the precursor of the European Union, as he regarded Britain as too closely tied to America. Britain eventually joined the European Union in 1973 under Prime Minister Edward Heath. De Gaulle is regarded as the most important politician in post-war France and it is intriguing to think of Churchill's sparring partner-to-be playing in the garden of this quiet neighbourhood not far from the Grand Place.

De Gaulle was renowned for his turn of phrase. 'Patriotism is when love of your own people comes first; nationalism, when hate for people other than your own comes first,' he once said. Later, he commented: 'I have come to the conclusion that politics are too serious a matter to be left to the politicians.' Which rings rather true today. He also once muttered: 'The more I get to know men, the more I find myself loving dogs.' As well as: 'How can anyone govern a nation that has two hundred and forty-six different kinds of cheese?' This is perhaps my favourite.

* * *

As I have mentioned, the French have a soft spot for trains and they are rightly proud of their excellent high-speed TGVs (*Trains à Grande Vitesse*). The French pioneered 'express' services that did not stop at every station as early as the 1840s. Indeed, the term 'express' comes from them. They also pioneered carriage designs in those early days and a Frenchman, Marc Seguin, even advised George Stephenson to use a tubular boiler in his famous *Rocket* locomotive. This was to become a crucial component of the loco during its trip along the world's first proper railway line, the Liverpool and Manchester Railway, on 15 September 1830 (reaching a heady 35 miles per hour). After this, the highly successful Chemins de Fer du Nord rail company was created in 1845, helped by cash backing from the Rothschild family (*chemin du fer* means 'path of iron'). Its great profitability came from key routes between Paris and French ports such as Calais, Boulogne and Dunkirk.

The country rapidly succumbed to railway mania – just as Britain had – and many lines were added across the nation. As the years went by politicians gave financial backing to little countryside connections run by private companies to gain favour among voters; trains really were popular. However, these were expensive to maintain and they became untenable. Eventually, in 1938, all lines and services were nationalised under the SNCF. This organisation has run them ever since and is, as I have said, a matter of national pride. Trains mean a lot in France.

So I am sad not to spend longer in this railway-infatuated country (even though I was never going to jump on a speedy TGV).

But things happen, I decide, for a reason. I return to Gare de Lille Flandres, where I board the 15:08 to Belgium.

With a honk of the horn and a hissing sound we depart. Through skylights in the high metal hoops of the station roof, shafts of dappled light descend on the platforms. A seemingly homeless man shadow boxes standing next to one of the palm trees. Another, slumped on a bench, stares blankly into the distance. A patrol of four soldiers dressed in camouflage struts by. They clutch sub-machine guns and wear jackboots and bulletproof vests. Soldiers and northern France seem to go hand in hand.

The names of the stations before Kortrijk flash on a screen: Roubaix, Tourcoing, Mouscron. The conductor enters the carriage. He has a comical look. His orange-banded peaked cap is at a jaunty angle, his orange tie is half-undone, his long grey sideburns almost meet his chin, his Buddy Holly glasses are askew, and his grey jacket hangs loosely from his shoulders (at least two sizes too large). He tells me that we are in an MR96 electric train; not that this means anything to me. Then he asks where I am eventually going and I tell him Venice but that I may go via Ukraine as I've heard it is interesting there, perhaps weaving back to Italy through the Balkans.

'That is a long way,' he says.

This is undoubtedly true.

With that, he departs.

We arrive shortly at our first station, Roubaix, where a sign says *il est interdit de traverser les voies* (it is forbidden to cross the tracks). We pull into Tourcoing Station, where a station manager wearing a bright red jacket regards the train as though he owns it. Then we stop at Mouscron, where a message appears on a digital screen in the corner of my carriage saying: *We komen aan in Moeskroen* (we welcome you in Moeskroen).

The conductor walks by and I ask him when we arrived in Belgium.

'Right now,' he says.

The name, I now notice, is given on signs in the station as 'Mouscron-Moeskroen'.

I have escaped strike-ridden France! One less tourist to bolster the coffers of Élysée Palace, sent packing because the trains aren't running! One more tourist heading for a tourist honeypot in West Flanders. Once again, I'm feeling the thrill of the vagabond spirit of rail travel. Anywhere is possible. Anywhere is where I'm going to go. Anywhere the tracks lead.

The train moves on crossing damp farmland where oxen with long horns look as though they belong in the American West. The sky is leaden. Bulbous clouds hang low as rain sweeps across patchwork fields. Belgium has turned into a magical, mysterious blur, a tapestry of shades of grey.

It's good to be tucked away in the warmth of the 15:08 from Lille. At Kortrijk, however, I disembark and await the 15:58 to 'Brugge' and 'Oostende'. This duly arrives: a sleek double-decker locomotive (Siemens-made). We are soon clattering onwards stopping at Izegem, Roeselare, Lichtervelde and Torhout – places I've never heard of, all lurking in the gloom.

Beyond Torhout more enormous cattle munch grass in a field and solemn grey horses stand by a white picket fence as though regarding our own 'iron horse' thoughtfully. At Zedelgem, true to Edward Thomas's classic train poem 'Adlestrop', no one leaves and no one joins our train. We rattle on across flat, hazy landscape, shortly arriving in Bruges.

True to the timetable, it is 16:55. Not quite knowing the way, I follow crowds over a wide road assuming rightly or wrongly that most people will be going to the centre of the capital of West Flanders. A woman ahead of me strikes an unusual figure. She wears a black leather miniskirt and knee-high suede boots. In one hand she clasps a cigarette. In the other is a half-drunk bottle of wine. She totters along a narrow cobbled street leading to a tall church. Perhaps she is going to confession and needs to steady her nerves.

* * *

Bruges is very busy indeed. The woman in the leather miniskirt slips out of sight down an alley. A large group of tourists from the Far East takes selfies by a glimmering waterway. The lane narrows and bends. It becomes even busier; impossible to walk at a normal pace with so many people. A wide, sloping market square emerges with a towering belfry on its southern side. Tall redbrick buildings with A-shaped roofs and pairs of arched windows line the northern side of the square, their silhouettes forming a series of neat triangles. I go east down a passageway where I come to the Charlie Rockets Jeugdherberg, another redbrick building with an A-shaped roof. I check in by the Statue of Liberty, where the receptionist tells me 'the owners just like America' when I ask about the hostel's obsession with the US. I drop my bag in my shoebox room, which has a bunk bed, and return downstairs for a drink by a poster of Woody Allen.

Blues music plays. Spaniards twist the handles of a table football game and yell: 'Oi, oi, oi! Eh, eh, eh!', and from time to time 'Goooooooal!'

I read a copy of *Le Monde* I bought earlier. A front-page story is all about *Génération Identitaire*, a *groupuscule de l'extrême droit* (a far-right group), that erected barriers as a symbolic anti-immigration protest at the French border with Italy at Col de l'Échelle, a snowy pass at 1,762 metres in the Alps where many African migrants have entered France in recent months. The group also unfurled a poster that read in English: *Closed border. You will not make Europe your home. No way. Back to your homeland.*

Charming. The background to the story is the reinsertion of French border controls with Italy in the aftermath of the 2015 terrorist attacks. As slipping into France in the south has become difficult many migrants and refugees have attempted to enter via the mountains, risking hypothermia as they are usually poorly dressed for the freezing conditions. Crossings have been made at Col de l'Échelle as well as at the nearby ski resort of Montgenèvre, another pass.

On the day of the *Génération Identitaire* protest, an opposing group in favour of protecting asylum seekers in the dangerous mountains had helped 30 people enter the country at Montgenèvre. Border police intercepted the pro-migrant group, making two arrests.

Before reaching Calais just getting into France is difficult enough, it seems.

Nevertheless, applications for asylum in France stood at more than 100,000 in 2017, a record high – and in response to the scuffles in the mountains, Gérard Collomb, the French interior minister, announced the deployment of extra police to 'ensure absolute respect for the control of the border'. Marine Le Pen, leader of France's far-right National Rally party, applauded the move and called for even more border protection.

Meanwhile, *Le Monde* has an update on the train strikes. They are continuing and it does not seem certain when they will end.

Too tired to explore Bruges until the morning, I dine on 'fries and Flemish stew' at the Pitta Snack restaurant across the street from the hostel (highly recommended, though possibly not so good for your cholesterol levels). Then I return to my shoebox and fall asleep to the sweet sound of soul music rising through the floorboards.

Three cities in three days.

The journey has just begun.

CHAPTER THREE

BRUGES IN BELGIUM TO BONN IN GERMANY, VIA MAASTRICHT IN THE NETHERLANDS

'WE MUST SEND YOU A TIE!'

The word 'overtourism' was recently submitted for inclusion in the *Collins English Dictionary*. It is defined thus: 'The phenomenon of a popular destination or sight becoming overrun with tourists in an unsustainable way.'

Well, my eventual destination is certainly up there in the ranks of places affected by this modern curse. The serenity of La Serenissima can take a bit of a knock when vast cruise ships pull in. That's if the evidence of regular anti-tourism protests in Venice is anything to go by. More than 2,000 people took to the streets in the latest march demanding action and since then the city's mayor has announced a series of measures to reduce the strain, including restricting access on roads leading to Rialto Bridge and St Mark's Square.

Similar protests have been held in Barcelona, which attracted 32 million visitors in 2017, far outnumbering its 1.6 million residents. On one occasion an anti-tourist group even slashed the tyres of rental bikes and a tourist bus.

There have also been rumblings of discontent over the sheer scale of tourism in cities to which flights are now so dirt cheap such as Prague, which suffers particularly badly from visiting stag groups, as well as Dubrovnik, where the mayor is considering capping tourist numbers to 4,000 a day, and Amsterdam, where tourist chiefs are scratching their heads over how to reduce the flow of tourists at key sights at certain times of day.

Bruges is yet another victim of its own success.

More than six million tourists visit the city each year and a recent study by Vincent Nijs, a senior researcher at Visit Flanders, the local tourist board, revealed that there are on average 126 visitors per day per 100 residents; the population of the city centre of Bruges is just 19,500. On peak days local residents can be outnumbered three to one.

The beautiful city, with its picturesque buildings dating back centuries and lovely canals (hence the 'Venice of the North' tag), has long been aware of the problem. Since 1995 hotel construction has been limited and a strategy has been adopted to concentrate tourism in the south of the city. Both policies have worked, with the limitation on hotels meaning that of its six million visitors, only two million stay overnight. The rest are day trippers.

But Bruges is still very busy, as I discovered simply walking from the station. The irony of this is that when the first tourists arrived in the city they were seeking quiet and contemplation. Bruges had fallen into decline after the Zwin channel linking the city to the North Sea began to silt up in the early sixteenth century, preventing access for ships. Trade in Flemish cloth, grain and spices dropped off, with the port of Antwerp picking up the business. The city, with what is considered the world's oldest stock exchange (1309), was in a terrible state; its medieval heyday a distant memory. Like Lille, it had once been an important centre of the Duchy of Burgundy and was also famous for being where William Caxton printed the first book in English, the *Recuyell of the Historyes of Troye* (1473).

By the end of the 1800s the population had plummeted from 200,000 in medieval times to fewer than 50,000. Bruges was a place to escape the crowds, and the nineteenth-century tourists loved its faded grandeur. Of his visit in 1820, William Wordsworth commented that the city enjoyed 'a deeper peace than that in deserts found'.

Now, however, there are so many tourists that some local *frieten* (chip) shops offer locals discounts as the deluge of visitors has pushed up prices. Meanwhile, no fewer than 2,000 guides operate in the city, and great animosity reigns between official guides with *Gidsenbond* (guide association) qualifications and untrained rivals who provide 'free' tours in return for tips at the end.

Some are even said to have got into fisticuffs, although Renaat Landuyt, the mayor, refutes this: 'I know there is tension between the guides. But the police tell me no significant incidents have been identified. Except for angrily looking at each other.'

Which is not a crime... and might actually be quite entertaining to witness.

I decide to keep an eye out for the angry tour guides of Bruges. Things have certainly changed since Wordsworth's day.

To the belfry, to the station
A morning in Bruges

I wake early to avoid the crowds. In the breakfast room of the Charlie Rockets Jeugdherberg a bald waiter challenges me over whether I have paid for breakfast and seems suspicious even though I am on his list. I sit next to the picture of Woody Allen once again and eat an overcooked hard-boiled egg accompanied by two slices of white-bread toast and a cup of feeble coffee. 'Heartbreak Hotel' plays on the stereo, which feels about right.

To check the weather, I go to the door. It is chilly and raining heavily. In the doorway a twenty-something man with a beard lurks. He is holding a bottle and smoking. He appears to have been up all night.

'Good morning,' he says.

'Beer?' I ask, looking at the bottle.

'Yes, beer,' he replies and holds out the bottle, inviting me to take a sip.

I decline and he looks slightly hurt. Then he shrugs, blows a plume of smoke and continues his morning vigil of Hoogstraat.

I walk back through the breakfast room, where the bald waiter eyes me cagily once again (he clearly runs a tight ship), and go upstairs to collect my backpack, pausing at a sign I had not previously noticed in the hall: 'PLEASE RESPECT THE REST BETWEEN 12 AND [blank space] O'CLOCK AT NIGHT.' Someone appears to have peeled away the final time. 'NO PARTY'S [*SIC*] IN THE ROOMS AT NIGHT.' And: 'CURFEW 4AM.' Perhaps the bald waiter is responsible for this sign. Perhaps the man with the beard missed the curfew.

So I hit the streets of Bruges – an overtourist about to indulge in overtourism, just one of the city's six million each year.

Hoogstraat is almost empty. The beer drinker has vanished. I make my way in the rain towards the Markt square beneath an umbrella. An accordion player crouches in a passage playing a melancholy tune. A horse and carriage for tourists rattles past. A beggar shivers by the doorway of the Pitta Snack restaurant.

On Markt square a woman from the Far East in pink trousers is taking selfies in front of the striking medieval belfry. She has placed her phone on a tripod and is carefully arranging her hair ready for a timer. I watch for a while as she repeats this routine, considering whether to ask if she would like me to take her picture. But she seems so preoccupied I leave her in peace.

The belfry is closed. It opens at 9.30 a.m. I want to climb to the top to see the city from above. The tower dates from 1240, built on the proceeds of the original Bruges boom-time. If I am going to weave my way across Europe by train, I want to visit a few of the iconic sights, and this is certainly one of them. The American poet Henry Wadsworth Longfellow (1807–1882) visited Bruges at the height of its cult period when tourists first came to wallow in its curious otherworldliness. He describes watching the sun rise from the tower in his poem 'The Belfry of Bruges':

> In the market-place of Bruges stands
> the belfry old and brown;
> Thrice consumed and thrice rebuilded,
> still it watches o'er the town.
> As the summer morn was breaking,
> on that lofty tower I stood,
> And the world threw off the darkness,
> like the weeds of widowhood.
> Thick with towns and hamlets studded,
> and with streams and vapors gray,

> Like a shield embossed with silver,
>> round and vast the landscape lay.
> At my feet the city slumbered.
>> From its chimneys, here and there,
> Wreaths of snow-white smoke, ascending,
>> vanished, ghost-like into the air.

Longfellow goes on to imagine the 'shadowy phantoms' of the past when pageants were held and Flemish merchants bustled in the square. His mention of 'thrice consumed' refers to fires that destroyed the belfry. The poem ends with Longfellow saying that 'hours had passed away like minutes' during his reverie as he gazes across the now 'sun-illumined square'.

I love it. Glimpses of history glitter through the verses, one of which mentions 'proud Maximilian, kneeling humbly on the ground'. This is a reference to Archduke Maximilian, the Habsburg heir, who was imprisoned in 1488 on the site of the current Cafe Craenenburg, on the west of the square. To kill time before the belfry opens I go for a coffee at the cafe, watching the horse-and-carriages gathering for the day as rain streams off the awning onto the cobbles.

Maximilian was held here for three months by guildsmen of Bruges who were annoyed that he wanted to limit the city's privileges. This was an error of judgement. Maximilian made many promises to the guildsmen and was eventually released, only for his father Frederick III to take revenge on those concerned. Then, when Maximilian became emperor in 1493, he did his level best to favour Antwerp over Bruges in matters of trade. It was from around this time that the city's fortunes took a dramatic turn for the worse.

This is just one tale connected to Cafe Craenenburg. A short 'history' written on the placemat also explains that in 1468 Margaret of York watched the games of knights that took place in the square to celebrate her marriage to Charles the Bold. Probably from almost exactly where I am sitting now.

So many shadowy phantoms. Yet more lurk by the damp-looking monument in the centre of the square dedicated to Pieter de Coninck, of the guild of weavers, and Jan Breydel, the dean of the guild of butchers. These men led a force of Flemish rebels that snuck into Bruges on 18 May 1302 and massacred a French garrison, killing anyone unable to pronounce correctly the Flemish shibboleth *schild en vriend* (shield and friend). The day is known as the Bruges Matin. Later that year, on 11 July, the rebels went on to defeat the French at the Battle of the Golden Spurs near Kortrijk, my stop on the way to Bruges. This date is now a holiday for the Flemish community in Belgium. Longfellow mentions the victors 'marching homeward from the bloody battle' into Markt square.

I go to the tower, ascending its 366 steps on a corkscrew staircase amid many tourists to reach the top, 83 metres up. Quite a workout with a backpack. A queue had already formed at 9.30 a.m. and it's a tight squeeze on the stairs.

From above, the labyrinthine lanes and twisting waterways of Bruges suddenly seem to make sense; from the streets, the city is a maze. Rain sweeps across the medieval buildings of Markt square, where tourists with pink umbrellas have gathered, looking like human confetti. Haze lingers above the countryside beyond the city limit (Longfellow's 'vapors gray' still rising). Church spires poke through the gloom, as old and brown as the belfry. Channels between the townhouses emit a magnesium gleam. It is a misty, mellow view.

I soak up the atmosphere of Bruges from above for a while, before getting a rude awakening as the bells toll. Wow, do they toll. The sound seems to seep through your bones. A notice says there are 47 bells weighing 27.5 tonnes. And I can believe it.

I make my way down.

Then – already breaking my book-buying rule – I pick up a copy of *Bruges-La-Morte* by Georges Rodenbach at a bookshop on the way to the station. This peculiar novel was first published in 1892 during the Victorian tourist days. It's an intriguing tale about a man coming to terms with the death of his wife as he wanders through the city 'in the muted atmosphere of the waterways and the deserted streets'. The book, as I soon find, uniquely captures the 'melancholy joy' of those strange ghostly days.

That was then, when Bruges was being rediscovered.

Now, even on a rainy morning, it's choc-a-bloc with pac-a-macs, umbrellas and guides (though I never lay eyes on any of the grumpy ones).

I enter Station Brugge to catch the 10:58 to Liège-Guillemins.

Meeting the conductors
Bruges to Maastricht via Liège

Station Brugge is plain and ugly from the outside. Its current structure dates from 1938 and is in an art deco style with a *B* for Belgian Rail above the main door. Inside, however, is a beautiful tiled artwork in gold, purple and grey depicting the country's cities with a background of Flemish characters including weavers, merchants, knights and country maidens. Tall ships flutter above the cities, as though setting sail for faraway lands. The floor has a striking zigzag pattern and the original ticket booths have little wooden triangular tables for sorting out your paperwork. All rather pleasant.

The 10:58 is marked for Brussels and Eupen on the sign on the platform, which confuses me at first. However, extra information flickers on a digital display to indicate that Liège-Guillemins is one of the stops. It is due to arrive there at 13:02. Then I must catch the 13:40 from Liège-Guillemins to Maastricht, arriving at 14:13. I have long been fascinated by Maastricht due to its now infamous European Union treaty, signed in 1992. Why not head to the place where all the fuss that led to Brexit began? It's only a couple of rides away.

A red and white train pulls in. I board the red and white train. Belgian Rail is what I am calling the train service of Belgium, and its website is indeed belgianrail.be. However, things are not quite as simple as this. The service has two names, one Dutch (Nationale Maatschappij der Belgische Spoorwegen), and the other French (La Société Nationale des Chemins de Fer Belges). In order to satisfy the Dutch-speaking Flemish population, 59 per cent of the population, and the French-speaking Walloon community, 40 per cent, the Belgian national railway company likes to be officially known as NMBS/SNCB. However, most foreigners refer to it as SNCB.

Got that? I'm not sure I have.

Railways are important in Belgium and this nitpicking over names hints at why. Belgium was formed in 1830 when the Flemish and Walloons, mainly Roman Catholic, broke away from the Netherlands in the north, where the Dutch Reformed Church held sway. This revolution was followed by the appointment of Leopold I as the new country's first king in 1831.

Having witnessed the success of railways in Britain, Leopold called in George Stephenson to design the locomotives for Belgian's inaugural railway, which opened in May 1835. Both Leopold and Stephenson were on board this first train on a railway on the Continent, which ran between Brussels and Mechelen. This was the start of an acceleration of construction overseen by the state that soon witnessed lines linking Antwerp, Ostend, Liège and Namur.

For Leopold, railways were key to establishing a sense of national unity after the revolution. The lines literally connected the Flemish with the Walloons. They also provided transport for trade with Germany; crucial given that rivers of the north in the Netherlands could no longer be accessed.

His plans worked and to this day there is great national pride regarding railways in Belgium (whatever you want to call the company that runs them).

* * *

We are soon moving along towards Gent-Sint-Pieters across flat countryside populated by piebald cows. The carriage is comfortable with plush blue seats and just a handful of passengers. A tall conductor wearing a grey uniform with orange lapels and a peaked cap with an orange band enters. His tie, slightly askew, is covered in orange and grey 'B' symbols. There is something inherently comical – a bit Benny Hill – about Belgian train conductors.

With a flamboyant flourish he takes my ticket and regards the document carefully for a few moments.

'Do not forget to check the train box,' he says.

There is a column, which seems rather pointless to me, in which you must tick to indicate whether you are travelling by train, bus or boat. Of course I'm travelling by train! You could, I concede, be on a rail replacement bus and there are some ferry services that are covered, including Stena Line from Britain, Irish Ferries, Viking Line in Scandinavia and Blue Star Ferries in Greece.

The tall conductor looks at me severely, though I can tell he isn't really that fussed. He's just messing about. He departs and we glide into Gent-Sint-Pieters, crossing a dark green river. There seem to be a very large number of railway tracks at Gent-Sint-Pieters, as though it's a particularly important station in Belgium. Indeed it is: the third busiest in the country, handling 17 million passengers a year. Belgians, perhaps because of the standing that railways had in the time of the fledgling nation, love trains just as much as the French. Were there time to hop off and look about, I could explore this slightly eccentric station, with its colourful murals, ornate arches and splendid tower from 1912, completed before the city's hosting of the World Fair in 1913 (I have been to Ghent before).

As we wait by the platform a small, doleful woman in a shawl enters the carriage and shuffles along the aisle dropping little notes by every passenger: *'SONT PAUVRES AVEC TROIS ENFANTES QUE JE TRAVAILLE. AIDEZ MOI VOUS PLAIT ACHETER DE LA NOURITTOURE AUX ENFANTS ET A PAYER LES GAZ,*

L'ELECTRITIE, D'EAU. DIEU BENISSE ENCORE, ADIEU.' (WE ARE POOR WITH THREE CHILDREN THAT I WORK FOR. HELP ME PLEASE BUY FOOD FOR THE CHILDREN AND PAY THE GAS, THE ELECTRICITY AND THE WATER. GOD BLESS YOU AGAIN. FAREWELL.) She does not return to collect the notes. Perhaps the tall conductor intercepted her.

I catch a glimpse of the station's tower as we draw away and then I witness a little scene. First class is just beyond a partition and I overhear the tall conductor in action once again. He has a problem on his hands.

'What does this say?' he asks the passenger, pointing at a sign.

'One,' replies the passenger.

'What does this say?' he asks, pointing at the ticket.

'Two,' replies the passenger.

'You are Two but you are in One,' says the conductor.

'Ah, we did not know!' says the passenger.

The tall conductor then tells the passenger that he and his partner have not filled out their ticket properly.

'Ah, we did not know!'

The tall conductor looks very exasperated.

The passengers, who are tourists, come and join me in Two.

We continue beneath a smoky-grey sky as I read *Bruges-La-Morte*. The protagonist is exploring the 'tangle' of the city's streets ('tangle' is the perfect word for Bruges), feeling depressed and recognising that his emotions are somehow echoed in the city's rundown architecture. He is shortly to make a discovery: a woman living in Bruges who looks identical to his former wife. He quickly becomes infatuated. This is where the plot really takes off. The book is not one long downbeat ramble, although a great deal of it is. *Bruges-La-Morte* is a dark novel with a cult following for that very reason. I'm already hooked.

Another big city looms ahead: suburbs, spires and cavernous stations arising in the haze. Names are provided in Dutch and French in Brussels, where we stop by a sign for Brussel-Zuid Station (Dutch for Brussels South). I'm deeply tempted to get off and explore the Belgian capital, but I've already booked a room in Maastricht – and anyway, I've set myself a mission this afternoon and want to arrive with a few hours clear.

A Eurostar locomotive purrs on the opposite platform, ready to fire off in the direction of Amsterdam. Our train creaks onwards – this is a particularly creaky one. I ask the conductors, who have sat down near me, what kind of train we are in. The tall conductor has been joined by another conductor, shorter with grey hair, a potbelly and a ridiculous row of pens poking out of his jacket.

'An intercity electric with cars from 1998 and a locomotive from 2005,' says the tall conductor.

Our current speed is 200 kilometres an hour (125 miles per hour), which is – I must concede – not very slow. However, the pace will soon reduce to 140 kilometres an hour near Liège (87 miles per hour). Not really *slow*, but *slower*.

The tall conductor is named Lucas and the shorter conductor is named Louis. Louis gives me his personally-printed card, with his email, Facebook details and Flickr account; his hobby is photography. Both speak good English.

'Is it common for people to fare dodge?' I ask.

'Oh yes, always,' says Louis. 'They try to avoid us. It's a game you play on every journey. You win some, you lose some.'

The fine for those without tickets is 75 euros (£67).

'We will call the police to arrive at the next station if someone does not have their ID card,' says Lucas, who seems to be completely on top of rules and regulations. All Belgians over the age of 12 are issued with national identification cards, they explain, and all those over the age of 15 must carry them if more than 200 metres from their homes. Foreigners must be in possession of either passports or ID cards from their own countries.

Lucas has worked on the Belgian railways for 20 years and Louis has worked nine. They talk about the historical importance of railways in Belgium. 'Since the beginning of the state!' exclaims Lucas.

They ask about my journey and I describe my ideas about where to go next.

'If we had known before, we could have taken you to the driver,' says Louis.

These really are very nice Belgian train conductors.

'We must send you a tie!' says Lucas.

'We must send you a belt as well!' says Louis. The belts have the distinctive 'B' on the buckle.

'Do not worry, we have plenty of them!' says Louis.

They take my address.

We arrive at Liège-Guillemins. I shake their hands and disembark. What great service on the 10:58 from Bruges.

* * *

Liège-Guillemins Station looks like a UFO. This is by far the most modern station yet, designed by the star Spanish architect Santiago Calatrava and opened in 2009. A white curving roof soars above creating a bright, airy space with glass-brick platforms allowing light to filter into a clever shopping hall below. At one end of this hall is Grand Café de la Gare, a fancy restaurant offering veal steaks and cocktails served amid potted cacti and designer lamps. A courtyard with a large sign saying 'LIÈGE TOGETHER' is at the front of the station. I walk across the road from here and consider going for a drink in Le Tube bar, but it seems a bit *Bruges-La-Morte* with a solitary drinker on a barstool and no other customers. Anyway, I had better not get into bad habits. Too easy to pop into bars at midday on a grand train tour of Europe (though now and then won't hurt).

Back in the station I await the 13:40 to Maastricht.

The train soon arrives.

The 13:40 is an eye-opener, with two battered old carriages filthy with graffiti and grime. Mould grows on window frames and along panels by the roof. It seems almost an insult to the beautiful shiny station that this wreck has had the temerity to show up. But on board I find myself in an orange compartment with drawings of lions and antelopes on the walls, and seats in shades of caramel and acorn-brown. Despite the ruined exterior, there is something delightfully retro, almost hipster-ish, about the 13:40 to Maastricht.

To maintain my dialogue with the train conductors of Belgium, I ask the bushy-bearded conductor – another Belgian Rail comedy character – about the train. His peaked cap is at an angle and the elastic strap of his slip-on tie is visible beneath the curled collars of his Belgian Rail shirt (such a tie, if Lucas and Louis keep their word, is soon to be in my very own possession). What looks like a sandwich packet pokes out of a pocket of his jacket.

'Electric locomotive. 1980s,' he says glumly but pleasantly enough, before smiling weakly and scurrying away.

Three policemen wearing bulletproof vests join the carriage. They are chewing gum and have an aura of 'Do not **** with us'. I decide not to ask *them* any questions. Instead I watch as the train crosses a wide brown river and pulls into Visé, where the policemen wordlessly depart, probably as this is the last station before the Netherlands. Beyond Eijsden, now in the Netherlands, we enter an emerald forest that appears to glow green in the golden early afternoon sun. For a while as we pass though this emerald tunnel I simply enjoy the serenity of the setting.

Shortly afterwards, our clapped-out carriages arrive in Maastricht.

Another city, another interesting station. This one dates from 1913 and is terrific. Light falls in dusty shafts across the ticket hall through tall stained-glass windows depicting medieval knights and maidens. Purple-brick walls rise to a high beamed roof. Squint your eyes and you can imagine magnificent feasts: medieval banquets with roast wild boar and geese, flagons of wine. This is some kind of Gothic dream.

A florist occupies one corner. A neon sign advertising Bavaria beer flickers above an arched passage in another. Being so close to Belgium, the station used to have a border control (where the florist now is).

The Schengen Agreement, signed in Schengen in Luxembourg in 1985 to allow travel without border control within the European Union, put an end to that. As things stand, 22 of the 28 members of the EU participate, with Romania, Bulgaria, Croatia, Cyprus waiting to join and the United Kingdom and Ireland having opted out. How long this set-up lasts is another matter. Things in Europe do seem to be slowly falling apart.

The station is quite a long way from the old town centre, where I have booked a night at Botel.

This is a hotel in a boat that floats on the River Maas in Dutch, or the River Meuse in French, or the River Mouze in Walloon. I walk towards *the river*, take a left, cross a bridge, take another left, cross a little park and a road and there it is, bobbing ever so slightly on the river beyond a gangway with artificial grass. Inside, three elderly women are playing cards at one of the wooden tables in the lilac and blue bar. This room also acts as the reception. Every now and then, I am soon to notice, the three elderly women break from their game and go outside for a smoke. Cackles rise from the pontoon deck. Then, after their break, silence resumes as cards are played. This sequence is repeated regularly. They appear to be having a wonderful time.

Mirrors are angled by the low ceiling so passengers of old could see the best view (perhaps useful for a card cheat). The receptionist at the check-in desk has cropped hair and wears a ribbed grey jumper. By his side are a pair of binoculars and a flashlight. He reminds me of the actor Kenneth Williams, although perhaps not in full *Carry On* mode.

'My favourite is the one to Darjeeling,' he says when he learns of my trip so far. 'Darjeeling! Darjeeling! The hill trains. Oh, I love rail travel!'

He tells me the bar closes at midnight. He says Botel has been a hotel for 20 years. Prior to that it took passengers on the Rhine. Visitors to Botel come from 'China, Spain, the Netherlands, Germany and everywhere'.

I ask the receptionist where the Maastricht Treaty was signed in the city. It would be interesting to visit the spot (to do so was my 'mission', mentioned earlier). He turns and points through the window.

'Where was it signed? Over there,' he says. He is pointing towards a large jagged building on the other side of the river.

'It is the regional government headquarters, about two miles away. Maybe they will let you in.'

'This is where it was signed'
Maastricht

Maybe. I drop my bag in a tiny cabin with a sliding door. It is directly above the bar and has a little shower and a sink with taps emitting scorching water. The bed is hard and can only be accessed from one side as it is flush against a wall. From the cabin window on one side I can see the jagged government building across the choppy surface of the River Maas/Meuse/Mouze. On the other are the occasionally smoking and cackling card players on the pontoon deck.

Over a bridge I come to my first evidence of Maastricht's infamy. This is Plein 1992 (Square 1992), named after the year of the signing of the treaty that led to the European Union and the euro. It is a wide-open concrete square with bronze tiles embedded in the paving. These tiles are marked with '1992' and the symbol for the euro. To one side is a cafe, an off-licence, a home-living shop, a boarded-up shop and a long row of bike racks. On the other is a library and a theatre. Botel is directly across the river from Plein 1992.

From here, it takes about 20 minutes to reach the headquarters of the government of the Dutch province of Limburg. It is windy and sunny as I arrive at the jagged buildings and ask a man wearing a flowery shirt and a gold chain if this is indeed where the Maastricht Treaty was signed.

'Yes, just walk in and sign in,' he says.

He is an official of the province of Limburg, which seems to have a casual dress code. He is in jeans and looks as though he has just attended a barbecue.

I ask him what the people of Maastricht think of the Maastricht Treaty.

'We are very proud,' he says.

I ask him what the people of Maastricht think of Britain leaving the European Union.

'We think it is a shame,' he says.

Then he tells me I should hurry up as the office is about to close and I may not get in. So I go to the reception and a security guard says I cannot see the room and the table where the Maastricht Treaty was signed as I have not made an appointment. I ask if he can ask someone if I can. He considers this and makes a phone call. After a few moments, he puts the phone down.

'You must go through the car park and cross the bridge,' he says.

I do so, coming to an island with a long row of empty flag posts and one flag post with a flag depicting the red lion of Limburg. Cords rattle on the empty flag posts. I enter a marble reception and am soon meeting Peter Schrijen, the *clustermanager* of the province of Limburg.

I have never met a *clustermanager* before (the title appears to mean press officer). He is more formally dressed than his colleague, wearing a suit. He is balding and has a grey moustache and a wide smile. Peter – Mr Schrijen seems too serious; he is far too laid-back for that – tells me he, too, is proud of the Maastricht Treaty and that the city has just gained a European Heritage Label. This status puts Maastricht alongside 37 other important places in the history of Europe including the Acropolis in Athens, the city of Strasbourg and the Solidarity docks in Gdańsk.

Even though I have no appointment Peter is pleased to show me around. The Dutch are, of course, famously relaxed and Peter is no exception.

We are soon in a circular room with a white marble floor, whitewashed walls and an intricate ceiling with a spider's web of white beams.

'This is where the negotiations happened. It was very important that it was a round room as it was important that nobody was at the head of the table,' Peter says.

We go upstairs to a corresponding circular room with a mustard yellow carpet, a large crystal chandelier and a view of the river through tall windows.

'This is where it was signed,' Peter says.

He takes me to the exact spot where the table with the document once stood. Through a doorway and along a passage we come to this pistachio-coloured table. A copy of the treaty is in a glass cabinet beside the table along with a photomontage of the signatories. The original, Peter says, is now in Rome.

Douglas Hurd, Britain's then foreign secretary, is shown pen in hand, raising an eyebrow slightly beneath his shock of frizzy white hair. The date is 7 February 1992. Hurd was later to say: 'If Margaret Thatcher had been prime minister at the time, there would have been no Treaty of Maastricht.' Thatcher had stepped down less than two years before in November 1990. Hurd himself was staunchly pro-European.

John Major, the then prime minister, was pro-European, too, naturally. Major had negotiated the details of the treaty here in Maastricht in December 1991, securing one big concession for the UK: an opt-out from the single currency. Even so, the bitter rebellion among his backbench members of parliament soon had him dubbing them 'bastards' and the issue of Europe was to dog his time in office.

Maastricht was the start of a lot – and Brexit is the latest twist.

I ask Peter about Brexit.

'Unbelievable,' he says. 'Simply unbelievable. I do not understand why Britain wants Brexit.'

He pauses. 'It's all emotion. You should not let emotion determine what you do in politics.'

For a while Peter is quite emotional himself.

Then he snaps back into his chilled-out style, telling me how the Limburg government intends to open its Maastricht Treaty archive to visitors, providing touchscreen computers with information. 'It is very important that people understand what Maastricht means,' he says.

We drink coffee in his office and Peter gives me a set of 25th anniversary Maastricht Treaty stamps. We talk for quite a while about this and that: Peter's sponsorship of a grave at the Netherlands American Cemetery for World War Two soldiers, and his recent visit to Versailles, where he was driven mad by pushy tourists taking selfies. I find it hard to believe Peter could be too annoyed about anything at all.

It is beyond the usual office closing time when I leave the little government island with its weeping willows and empty flag poles. On these, the flags of the dozen signatory countries once flew. The cords are still rattling in the afternoon wind and one seems to be especially noisy, whipping against its pole almost in a frenzy.

Perhaps that was where the Union Jack hung.

* * *

For dinner I eat horse stew in the old town. *Zoervleis*, a local speciality, is perhaps an acquired taste. The thick stew has a sweet and sour vinegary flavour, served with chunky chips, mayonnaise and a pot of apple sauce. I try the dish at Cafe Sjiek in the pretty old town close to the ancient Basilica of Our Lady. The place is packed with many others eating zoervleis, too. You enter via heavy red curtains into a tight candlelit space and may have to wait for a table, or a place at the bar as I do. There is a hushed atmosphere, almost a secret society feel, as though the consumption of *zoervleis* is somehow taboo. Eventually, if you are dining alone as I am, a spot at the bar becomes free and you are given a placemat and a very friendly barman takes your order, nodding with appreciation when you utter the word *zoervleis*. The stew comes quickly, served piping hot in an orange cooking pot, straight from the oven. The barman offers ground pepper from a huge pepper grinder. The sweetness of the apple balances the vinegary, odd stew – and it is best not to think too much about horses if you are fond of the creatures.

During several spells, the last being from 1794 to 1814, Maastricht was part of France, so maybe the French penchant for eating horse stuck. After French rule Maastricht almost became part of newly formed Belgium in 1830, but the city's garrison sided with William I, the Dutch king, despite locals favouring the Belgian revolutionaries. It was formally deemed part of the Netherlands during the 1839 Treaty of London.

Politics and this little city of about 120,000 have a long history.

Feeling full, I return to Botel via various cobbled squares where students have gathered; Maastricht has a major Dutch university. The cacklers are still playing cards in the Botel bar. Long cargo ships slip across the ink-black water, some at least a hundred metres long. I read *Bruges-La-Morte,* which is frankly not getting any cheerier, and contemplate where to go next on my rail map of Europe.

A very large country lies not far to the east.

In the morning my fifth nation looms on the horizon, close by down the tracks.

'No trains are going to those places you want to go to'
Maastricht to Bonn

This is my plan: to catch the 10:20 from Maastricht to Heerlen, arriving at 10:42, followed by the 10:56 from Heerlen to Herzogenrath, arriving at 11:10, then the 11:29 from Herzogenrath to Aachen, arriving at 11:45, then the 11:51 from Aachen to Cologne, arriving at 12:44, and the 12:56 from Cologne to Bonn arriving at 13:25. What could possibly go wrong?

I want to go to Bonn. A friend once told me that Bonn, Germany's de facto capital from 1949 until the reunification of east and west in 1990, is quite beautiful.

So I strike off towards the station, passing the battlements of the old city fort and a neighbourhood with a place called Headshop selling bongs and 'vision seeds'. This is just down the road from the Easy Going Coffeeshop. I wonder if the likes of Douglas Hurd, John Major and Jacques Delors ever popped by in 1992. Somehow I doubt it, though anything, I suppose, is possible.

At the station I learn that the employees of the Arriva train company, the one covering the first part of my complicated route, are on strike.

I discover this at the information desk, where a Nederlandse Spoorwegen (Dutch Railways) assistant wearing a red scarf, a smart blue blazer and a brooch shaped like a butterfly says: 'No trains are going to those places you want to go to.'

She says this very pleasantly.

I mention Bonn.

'Oh, there is a way to get there,' she says. Then she explains that I need to go back to Liège-Guillemins on Belgian Rail, catch another train to Cologne and another to Bonn.

I compliment her on her English.

'Oh, I used to live in England,' she says.

No one else is around and it is a while till my next train. I ask her whereabouts in England.

'Cambridge and then London, where I worked and met an Irishman and moved with him to Ballycastle in Northern Ireland,' she says, very precisely.

'What was your work in London?' I ask.

'Oh, I was a sales assistant at D. H. Evans on Oxford Street,' she replies. 'In the Christmas department to start with, then stationery,' she explains – just to make sure I know what her exact positions at D. H. Evans had been.

'What was your work in Northern Ireland?' I ask.

'Oh, I didn't work there,' she says, almost as though I ought to have known that. 'I just went with my boyfriend. He was a student,' she adds, as though that ought to have been evident, too (as if I already knew her).

'Of course! Of course!' I reply, or something like that.

She smiles and adjusts her butterfly brooch.

I had not expected this conversation. Were it not for a couple who have just arrived to inquire about tickets we could have ordered coffees from the station cafe and had a good long chinwag. Even Dutch rail workers, when they are not on strike, are almost horizontal.

I go to platform 5A to await the 10:19 to Liège-Guillemins.

Unlike in Belgium, railways in the Netherlands took a while to get going: firstly, because the state, with William I at the helm, was less enamoured by trains than Belgium's Leopold I, and secondly because of its many marshes, canals and rivers, which required expensive bridges. The first line opened in 1839 between Amsterdam and Haarlem, four years after the original track in Belgium. The railway expanded to cover the journey from Amsterdam to The Hague later, with no fewer than 58 swinging bridges. Without these, important waterways for shipping would have been blocked.

The state-owned Nederlandse Spoorwegen was formed in 1938, an amalgamation of two private railways that had begun to struggle financially in the wake of World War One. It is the main train operator in the Netherlands and also the busiest railway in the European Union, with 38,000 employees and an incredible 4,800 domestic services a day with 1.1 million passengers. The population of the Netherlands is 17.2 million. A lot of Dutch people travel by train.

On platform 5A, I see my first rail enthusiast in the Netherlands.

He is on an opposite platform and he is wearing an anorak, of course. It is, however, a stylish anorak. He casually smokes a cigarette, or perhaps something stronger. We are, after all, in the Netherlands. He takes various pictures of my train as it arrives. Then he saunters off, apparently extremely satisfied. Rail enthusiasts seem to be particularly cool in the Netherlands.

Like yesterday's train along this line, the 10:19 to Liège-Guillemins is another wreck. Almost all the carriage paint has peeled off. The exterior is scratched and ruined. Mould grows on the windows. Yet again, however, the interior is snazzy and smart with a 1980s retro look. Maybe that's why they have been saved from the scrapheap.

Yet another comedy conductor with a hipster beard checks my ticket and nods. The train creaks away.

This is an enjoyable ride. The movement along the track feels relaxing as familiar landscape opens up. Yachts tack in a flutter of sails on a river. Street art flashes by, one piece depicting Angelina Jolie looking sultry next to a colourful scrawl of indecipherable squiggles. A train putters slowly past hauling wagons heaped with gravel as though struggling to manage the load. A hawk hovers above a field as the horn blasts and the conductor returns to the front of the 10:19 to Liège-Guillemins. There is not much else to report on the journey between Maastricht and Liège – not that this bothers me.

Maybe I am already becoming addicted to the motion of the line. Moving onwards is a joy: somehow settling and calming.

I have a declaration to make here. I said in chapter one that Dover Castle felt like a place of decisions over the centuries. Well, yes, many important ones on a national level, but I made a personal decision, too.

On the clifftop at Dover I placed a phone call that will bring about a big change of direction in my working life. Not that I had quite expected such drastic action when I set off from Mortlake, but as the train rolled onwards from Victoria through Kent with Europe lying ahead, my thoughts, which had been percolating for some time, seemed to rattle rapidly into order: the liberation of the rails, if you like, set them free. Without intending to sound too deep and meaningful, I realised I wanted to take stock, to move on literally along the railway lines and in other ways, too. *Au revoir* yesterday! *Bonjour* who knows what?

The clickety-clack of the track already had me under its spell.

Maybe that's why the railway feels so comforting right now. A new uncertain future lies ahead, but for now I am on an adventure on Europe's train lines, sliding forth, ready for whatever may be, into the unknown.

* * *

The train arrives in Liège at 10:51 and I board my first Deutsche Bahn train, a sleek affair painted with long red streaks. The letters 'ICE' are inscribed on the locomotive.

OK, so this is not a slow one. It looks damn fast. These German Intercity-Expresses travel at up to 300 kilometres an hour (188 miles per hour), the speed of a Formula One car on the straight. Slow train? No way. However, let me just point out that the distance between Maastricht and Bonn is 69 miles and my total journey time is 2 hours 36 minutes. This works out at about 28 miles an hour, almost the exact same speed as Usain Bolt's top running pace during a 100-metre sprint. Were the Jamaican able to keep going for 2 hours 36 minutes, we would reach Bonn at the same time. My journey is as fast as a (very fast) human being.

After the battered old jalopy from Maastricht, ICE is a revelation. Fields flash by. Farms. Lakes. Woodland. ICE seems to swallow the landscape. Oaks with crows fluttering in treetops: gone. Gulp! Small towns: gone! Gulp! Factories producing goodness knows what, church steeples, gently winding rivers. Gulp! Gulp! Gulp!

The Deutsche Bahn conductor is a congenial chap. Conductors are now my friends. Like almost all the male conductors I have encountered so far, this one has a beard. He cheerfully tells me we are on an ICE dating from 2001 and are travelling at 200 kilometres an hour (125 miles per hour). The train has eight carriages, he informs me, of which two are first class and six are second class.

'For this information: fifty euros,' he says, grinning.

I check out the dining carriage but am not tempted by the picture of pallid-looking waffles – and as I consider the sandwiches, which don't look so great either, we stop at Aachen at 11:42, where a text message flashes up saying: 'WELCOME TO GERMANY'.

These text announcements, if you discount the passport check at Dover, have constituted 'border control' on this journey so far.

The train paces onwards beneath billowing oyster-coloured clouds. This is an industrial landscape with flashes of 'rustic' in between (mainly allotments; Germans in these parts seem to love allotments). Cargo trains chunter by. The cooling towers of a power station steamily arise. We tear through a place called Horrem in the blink of an eye. It is difficult to say much about Horrem as we're so soon through it. This is the problem with fast trains.

On the edge of Cologne an enormous piece of graffiti close to a fetish shop says 'I LOVE YOU'. The tracks are elevated here with busy city streets below. It's as though we've taken a secret path into the heart of Cologne, coming to a halt right by its famous cathedral.

At Cologne Station we wait a long time for the doors to open – this is a safety precaution to do with our train coupling with another train, an announcement informs us. We might fall between the platform and the carriages during a jolt when the coupling happens, so the doors are locked. When they finally open, I check out the soaring twin towers of the hulking Gothic cathedral. This is one of the most magnificent sights in Europe. The towers rise to 157 metres and for a while Cologne Cathedral was the tallest structure on the globe. No time to hang around, though! I've set my sights on Bonn and the train awaits.

This is a double-decker: a big red beast.

It departs at 12:32, gliding past a long wall of multi-coloured street art and yet more cargo trains. The settling motion of the carriages along the rails hits me yet again, as it did on the stretch after Maastricht. This time I take a catnap, opening my eyes when we stop at Brühl Station, where the first thing I see is a rail enthusiast snapping our train with a mobile phone.

There must, I reflect, be an awful lot of pictures of trains in the world – albums upon albums, gigabytes upon gigabytes. All of trains. Trains sitting at stations. Trains passing by in a blur. Trains with numbers on them. Trains, trains, trains!

Having been on many trains I still cannot work out this fascination. For me, they take you places you may never otherwise have been, they may be quite comfortable and they are, as I have said, a way of escape. That's why I like trains: the escapism, the romance of the tracks winding onwards. I watch the rail enthusiast move along the carriages taking yet more photographs. Each to his own, I suppose. I close my eyes once more as we slide down the line towards a very interesting city.

* * *

We arrive in Bonn Hauptbahnhof at 12:55.

Hauptbahnhof means 'central station' in German, and this one dates from the 1880s, with a rose-red stone facade decorated with stone urns, carvings of flowers and a stone lion.

It is a distinguished building, but outside it's noisy and confusing. A big construction project of some sort is underway. I cross a road and try to work out which way to go. On the far side of the site, a drunken woman clutching a bottle staggers in a doorway. A nasty piece of graffiti says: 'ONLY HATE'.

I seem to find the correct street. I walk past the Galactic Head- und Growshop, with a Rastafarian figure displayed in the window next to a series of 'bongs'. Marijuana leaves are printed on the front window. People in this part of Europe seem to have a slightly different attitude towards the drug than we do back home. Marijuana is not actually legal for recreational use in Germany but police usually turn a blind eye to minor possession and shops like this show that it is, despite the letter of the law, basically accepted.

I keep on walking up a hill to the Max Hostel. A sign on the door says 'sorry we're closed'. The hostel opens at 4 p.m. I am not having the best of luck so far in the de facto capital of Germany between 1949 and 1990.

Then I join the communists.

There are a lot of them, on a corner near Max Hostel. They seem to be having a party.

CHAPTER FOUR

BONN IN GERMANY TO WROCŁAW IN POLAND, VIA LEIPZIG IN GERMANY

'EARL GREY OR ENGLISH BREAKFAST?'

On a journey by train around Europe there are many opportunities to be nosy. You have bought your ticket and the Continent awaits. You can poke around and do what you want. Let the train tracks take you where they will and then *let things happen*.

Today, for a while, I take part in a communist rally.

It is 1 May and the neighbourhood around Max Hostel is full of communists. Most have settled at a little park on a corner of Heerstrasse and Vorgebirgsstrasse next to a school. Folk music plays and the smell of a barbecue wafts in the air. A lot of people are milling about wearing red.

Julia is at a trestle table near a ruby awning adorned by the words: '*TAG DER BEFREIUNG DEUTSCHEN FASCHISMUS – NIE WIEDER FASCHISMUS*' (DAY OF LIBERATION OF GERMAN FASCISM – NEVER AGAIN FASCISM). The date beside this message is 9 May 1945. This was the day, using Moscow time, that the Nazis surrendered at the end of World War Two. The more formal Victory in Europe Day is, of course, 8 May 1945.

A lot of days appear to be being celebrated today. It is, according to another banner, International Workers' Day as well as Anti-Capitalist Action Day.

Bucking the general trend of red, Julia wears a black T-shirt. She has a milky complexion and a sharp eye. At first, she is quite fierce towards me. Maybe I look like a terrible capitalist – a selfish seeker of personal profit who shuns equality in pursuit of dirty euros to spend on things for myself and no one else. This is a possibility, I grant.

'People here are from communist groups,' she begins.

I had gathered as much.

'We are raising money for refugees,' she continues. 'I believe refugees should be made welcome. We should stop blocking the border and give them jobs and flats. The German government is guilty in Syria. It supports Erdoğan to bomb Syria.'

Germany's government, led by Chancellor Angela Merkel, recently invited President Recep Tayyip Erdoğan of Turkey for a state visit. Meanwhile, Turkish military jets have just bombed Afrin, a city in northern Syria where Kurdish groups are believed to be based. Turkey has defended its actions on the grounds that it says these groups commit terrorism within its borders.

There are more than three million Germans of Turkish descent due to a policy of inviting *Gastarbeiter* (guest workers) to Germany in the 1960s. Although the workers were initially only invited to stay to work for two years, the rules were relaxed in 1964 to allow permanent stays. Ties between Germany and Turkey are strong.

Julia, a trainee nurse in her twenties, believes refugees should be accepted on humanitarian grounds. She goes on to say that today's rally aims to highlight Erdoğan's actions as well as the need for lower prices for flats and for higher wages for all.

Julia has become quite chatty. Her activism landed her in trouble last summer, she says, when she was arrested during a protest against Donald Trump at a G20 summit held in Hamburg: 'The police just grabbed people or kicked or punched them. They held me for three days.'

Julia tells me all about getting a lawyer and the difficulties of organising her release. Then she introduces me to her friend Fabian, who smiles and shakes my hand. The communists and I are getting along just fine. Fabian has fluffy hair and wears a T-shirt with a logo that says *'GEGEN NAZIS'* (AGAINST NAZIS).

Julia and Fabian ask about my journey. I explain my trip by trains, the slow roundabout way, to Venice. They are interested in the visit to Maastricht and we talk about the European Union for a while. Julia and Fabian have strong views.

'We condemn the European Union,' says Fabian, explaining that he regards the EU as a profit-driven organisation.

Lucas, another communist, has joined us. He agrees. 'We don't really care about Britain leaving the EU. We are against a union of nations if it is only a capitalist group.'

Julia and Fabian murmur approvingly. Julia tells Lucas about my train adventure. It turns out he works for Deutsche Bahn, and his job is to conduct passenger surveys at stations.

He points to the barbecue in the corner.

'Come and eat some food,' he says.

I seem to have been well and truly accepted by the communists of Bonn.

I go over and discover that in order to eat I must buy a food voucher. Smoothies are also available, named after Che Guevara (blueberry) and Rosa Luxemburg, the Polish Marxist activist (strawberry).

I eat a very good salad and a spicy chicken dish.

Afterwards, I meet Miran, aged 21, an economics student. His father is from the Kurdish part of Iraq and his mother is German.

'The government here wants to be close to Erdoğan because of economic interests,' he says. He explains that he has joined street demonstrations to raise complaints about Turkish strikes in northern Syria. However, some of these have been broken up by the police and on one occasion he was attacked with pepper spray.

Miran recently went on hunger strike. He says he went without food for five days while protesting about what is happening in northern Syria outside the United Nations Office in Geneva.

I ask how he felt not eating for so long.

'It was like a fight against myself,' he says. 'But I was with other people on hunger strike so I was strong.'

Miran is also involved with a radical youth organisation formed to break up far-right rallies. 'There are many far-right groups,' he says. 'When there is a rally we try to know where they are and block the street.'

Miran has to go. A friend is seeking his advice. Perhaps more action is planned soon.

I sit on a wall for a while near a Karl Marx banner, listening to reggae and drinking a Rosa Luxemburg smoothie.

A little bit of politics.

It has been an unusual start in Bonn.

Beethoven and banter
An afternoon in Bonn

After the communist rally, I head into the city centre, temporarily joining another rally, this one marching on behalf of worker rights.

Bonn seems to be a hive of political activity.

Due to International Workers' Day all the shops are shut, but there is a large marketplace where arts and crafts, fruit, vegetables, sausages and beer are to be had. The tourist information office is, I discover, closed, too. I have no city map and my phone has run out of battery.

I am, quite happily, lost. I wander around the old city watching many marchers on yet more rallies striding through Bonn campaigning for justice of various sorts. By the bronze statue of Ludwig van Beethoven, Bonn's best-known son, in the market square, a group wearing badges and lemon-yellow scarves, who I take to be trade unionists, are contentedly eating foot-long sausages dripping with mustard during a pause from beating the streets. The great composer looms over them clasping a pen and looking severe, his chin jutting out in a manner that suggests 'Dare you challenge me? That would not be a good idea' – and his right foot thrust forwards as though he doesn't approve of the trade unionists, or anyone else roundabouts, for that matter. His whole aspect seems to say: 'Come and have a go, if you think you're hard enough.' I never knew Beethoven was such a tough guy.

Nearby in a side street a brass band plays an uplifting rendition of 'Amazing Grace'. The music draws me to watch as mellow notes reverberate down little lanes with buildings from centuries past. The lyrics rise like ghosts as the tubas, trombones and trumpets combine in honey-smooth harmony.

> Amazing grace! (how sweet the sound)
> That sav'd a wretch like me!
> I once was lost, but now am found,
> Was blind, but now I see.

As though answering my predicament, a series of tiny red signs on corners point in the direction of Bonn's mainly closed tourist sights. One of these is Beethoven-Haus. I set forth in this direction following the tiny red signs and coming to what turns out to be, as far as I can tell, the only 'attraction' open today.

This is Beethoven's birthplace, at 20 Bonngasse, where the composer lived until he moved to Vienna aged 21. The distinguished building has a pale pink facade and green-and-red door. It is set over three floors, with a small garden at the back. Beethoven was born here in December 1770 and the museum has been open since 1889, run by the Beethoven-Haus Society.

The many interesting exhibits include Beethoven's old travel desk, a viola he played when a boy, his final grand piano, and a bust from 1812. As with the statue in the square, the composer looks terrifyingly fierce here, too.

On the second floor I learn that Beethoven suffered hearing loss early in his life. Aged 30 he was already using ear trumpets and 'conversation books' so he could communicate with others. The conservation books, I learn, have proved incredibly helpful to Beethoven scholars. Maybe struggling to hear what people had to say made Beethoven so apparently grumpy.

The room in which he was believed to have been born is also on this floor, as is the most gruesome exhibit at the museum: Beethoven's death mask. This was made about a dozen years after his death and has a grim, haunting quality. A display explains that Beethoven's skull was opened soon after his death during an autopsy into the cause of his deafness. The composer died aged 56 in 1827.

What a brilliant little museum.

I rejoin Bonngasse and drift onwards in the afternoon sunshine, getting pleasurably lost once again before coming to the striking white, colonnaded exterior of the Altes Rathaus (old town hall). A plaque explains that Theodor Heuss, the first president of the Federal Republic of Germany (FRG), gave an address here in September 1949.

Bonn was chosen as the country's capital by the FRG's first chancellor, Konrad Adenauer, who wanted a temporary capital in preparation for the country's reunification. Being from nearby Cologne – he was a former mayor of that city – and knowing Bonn well, Adenauer believed Bonn was a good pick. He felt that a larger city such as Cologne or Frankfurt acting as a temporary capital might make reunification of east and west less likely. These cities could take on a permanent quality, and politicians might consequently lose sight of reunification. Berlin as capital under a reunified country was always Adenauer's target.

The Altes Rathaus steps, overlooking Bischofsplatz, are the perfect location for a speech. The plaque explains that John F. Kennedy gave a rousing address here in 1963, followed by Mikhail Gorbachev in 1989 and Nelson Mandela in 1996 (among many others).

Kennedy's words seem to transcend the years that have followed, especially recently. 'I have crossed the Atlantic at a crucial time in the life of the Grand Alliance,' he said on the steps of the Altes Rathaus. 'Our unity was forged in an hour of danger; it must be vigorously advanced in this period of relative calm. Our Alliance was founded to deter a new war – but we must also work together on behalf of world peace. Our strategy was born in a divided Europe – but it must look to the goal of European unity and an end to the divisions of people and country.'

Europe and its key post-war role in supplying peace on the Continent cropping up yet again. Like Churchill before him, Kennedy recognised the importance of European togetherness. Europe was no longer the 'seedbed of worldwide war', he declared. Rather, it should be regarded as 'a source of strength to all the forces of freedom'.

* * *

On this uplifting note I return up the hill past the communist barbecue to the Max Hostel, where I check in to a cranberry-coloured room and have a long nap.

It is early evening when I awake. Two twenty-somethings with dreadlocks who I overheard earlier talking about the Arab-Israeli situation in the kitchen are still talking about the Arab-Israeli situation two hours on. I sit on a comfortable green leather armchair listening to their chatter while reading *Bruges-La-Morte*. After a while, a man with a stubbly face and a faraway expression sits on the blue sofa near me and begins to talk. He wears a grey vest, cargo shorts and black Adidas trainers with white socks.

He has a lot to say.

My new friend is, I rapidly discover, a student of 'global change management' at Eberswalde University of Sustainable Development in north-east Germany. He and a group of others, who are busy making dinner in the kitchen, are here for a seminar. They are from all over the world including Germany, Pakistan, Mexico and Brazil. He is Spanish – I never do get his name – and describes himself as a 'typical immigrant' to Germany.

After studying forestry in Spain, he left for Germany six years ago due to the country's financial troubles, finding himself unemployed for a while. Then he worked at different 'black jobs'.

'Black jobs?' I ask.

He wags his finger at me (he has a habit of doing this).

'Black market jobs,' he says.

Some of these involved working in kitchens or as a waiter. He also had 'stadium jobs... you know, Rhianna, basketball games'.

He wags his finger and leans forward as though about to communicate an extremely important point.

'The German people,' he says. 'They are very polite but it is difficult to gain their confidence.'

He stayed in Liverpool once, he says. 'Very friendly people. In England, people say they're chav. They say: Leeev-er-pool, Leeev-er-pool, I hate Leeev-er-pool. But I loved them. I lived on Anfield Road.'

He had a month-long grant to study in the city. Afterwards he had taken part in a forestry project in Guatemala before returning to Spain and working in construction and as a waiter in Menorca. This was when he realised the Spanish economy was in a 'very big crisis'.

He wags his finger and leans even further forwards.

'Berlin is very multicultural,' he says, switching tack. 'But this is a lot of small individual groups, it is not homogenous.'

Wag.

'To get a good position you must speak German. They demand it!' he says.

Wag.

'I do speak a little, but it is very, very difficult to speak good German. It is a hand-cap.'

'A handicap?' I ask.

'Yes, yes!' he replies.

Wag.

'For Germans, Germany is the most important thing,' he says with a final flourish.

Wag, wag, wag.

* * *

I return to my cranberry-coloured room and glance at a copy of *General-Anzeiger*, a local paper. The impending *royale Hochzeit* (royal wedding) of Harry and Meghan is front-page news, turning to a full page of analysis on page three. I also have an edition of *The New European* weekly newspaper, founded in the wake of the Brexit referendum, pitched mainly at Europhile readers. 'CRUEL BRITANNIA', says the main headline, with a quote by the outspoken commentator Yasmin Alibhai-Brown: 'Theresa May [the British prime minister] stands as the High Priestess of integrity. But under her watch cruelty to refugees, migrants, asylum seekers and settlers has been normalised.'

Weddings and withering words – the world keeps turning.

Inside, 'The Brex Factor' column by Steve Anglesey reports on a suggestion by a caller to Britain's LBC radio station that a solution to the Irish border problem would be to 'microchip the population so you know who's in there'. Meanwhile, another item covers a comment made by Nigel Farage, lead Brexiteer and former head of the UK Independence Party, that 'we should have a Bank Holiday on the 23rd of June, Brexit Day, and we should celebrate that in all four corners of the United Kingdom'.

On these various not so spirit-raising notes I fall fast asleep.

'Hype-zig' in first class
Bonn to Leipzig

Time to move on. I have a three-train day starting at 09:23, via Cologne and Hanover to Leipzig. I am due to arrive at 15:19.

I have decided to go 'posh'. Deutsche Bahn is meant to have particularly slick first-class carriages. I shall pay the extra and travel in first. It is a long way to Leipzig and I may as well do it in style.

I am too early for the Max Hostel breakfast.

'Next time check the leaving time,' says a bossy woman holding a mop.

I hand over my key and she turns away to go back to what she was doing. As she does, I ask for my key deposit of five euros – all guests must provide such a deposit, so I had assumed she would simply hand this to me.

'May I see your key deposit card?' asks the bossy woman with the mop, bossily.

Oh yes, I had been given a piece of paper. Why this little piece of paper was necessary, I'm not sure.

I hand over the hallowed paper.

She wordlessly takes this and hands me five euros.

Not so posh at the Max Hostel this morning.

Perhaps this is just an off day.

* * *

The sun is out in Bonn. At the station a burly man with a red peaked cap, red waistcoat and a DB tie prints out today's connections. The train to Cologne arrives at 09:43, whereupon I have five minutes to catch the train to Hanover, which gets in at 12:28. At Hanover, I have nine minutes before the train to Leipzig, due to arrive at 15:19.

This print-out service is absolutely brilliant; you are given the exact train numbers and the departure platforms. It is officially called *Fahrplanauskunft* (timetable information). The first and the last trains will be IC (Intercity) trains, while the one between Cologne and Hanover is an ICE (Intercity-Express). The man in the red waistcoat recommends a breakfast stall at the station where I buy a ham baguette and a coffee before sitting to wait as I have arrived early to make sure I do not miss the first train.

Bonn Station has a large bookshop and is quiet, apart from a mysterious humming sound. I peruse the books to kill time (there's a small section in a corner with English titles, mainly thrillers) and board the 09:23, which turns up as advertised at platform two. We are soon whizzing along. It is, I am realising, really quite difficult to take a slow train in Germany. I am on the top deck in first class surrounded by business folk working on laptops. We are in Cologne in a flash and I am soon on the ICE to Hanover, ordering tea from a first-class assistant with a pinstriped waistcoat and a red tie.

'Earl Grey or English Breakfast?' he asks.

Very posh on this train.

I ask for English Breakfast, and soon discover that this is not a free service when I am asked to pay by the man in the pinstriped waistcoat.

Never mind. We are soon crossing the River Rhine on a bridge with a statue of Kaiser Wilhelm II riding a horse. The sky is perfect blue with sunlight falling in streaks through tinted windows onto the super-comfortable reclining leather seats of this spotless carriage. ICE first class really is rather fine. These seats are in a league of comfort of their own, reminding me a little of those 'man den' armchairs Americans are so fond of when watching sport on huge home cinemas while guzzling Budweisers and devouring pizzas and nachos. Except they're much classier than that, in shades of grey and black with a tasteful, modern design (not a beer-can holder in sight).

Beyond Cologne the train rises on a bridge above an autobahn with fast-moving Mercedes and BMWs before passing an enormous Bayer HealthCare Pharmaceutical factory and pulling into Wuppertal Station with its splendid colonnaded facade dating from the mid-nineteenth century. This railway has long been an important route for the transportation of German goods, hence the great expense laid out for the original station at Wuppertal so long ago. The trackside in these parts remains chock-a-block with factories, cooling towers and warehouses. Many things are *being made* and there hardly seems enough land upon which to make these things despite Germany's vast size. Take a train from Cologne to Hanover and simply stare out of the window if you want to understand the sheer scale of German industrial success.

Using an online translation site, I attempt to read *Frankfurter Allgemeine Zeitung*, a newspaper discarded by a previous passenger. A long, complicated story about 'Europe's north-south collapse in the monetary union' runs alongside another on *Das Iran Problem*. But taking pictures of the paper and then trying to read minute text about *Das Iran Problem* on my phone proves beyond me. I put the paper aside as the train rolls into Hagen Station, where a sign simply says 'HUNGER?' and points towards a McDonald's. Why mess about with fancy slogans?

The trackside factories continue after Hagen, cooling towers rising like rockets on a North Korean military parade and providing yet more evidence of Germany's powerhouse economy. A little farther on at Hamm Station, however, we pause for a while and I watch a guard watering potted plants while whistling a tune. He seems in a world of his own, whistling away as he occasionally plucks a dead leaf or prods the soil as though searching for snails. After all the grand-scale efficiency since Cologne, this gentle plant-loving station guard is quite unexpected.

But the world of business is soon bouncing back – in the form of a man wearing a suit sitting behind me who begins a long conference call. He is in charge of this call, which seems to have several listeners at the end of the line.

He has a booming voice and speaks in English.

'Shall we start?' he says. There is a murmur. 'OK, the background is the following: a project to understand what we are and understand where we go. I do not want to enter any political games. From different angles I would like people to raise their voices. What is working and what is not working? From next week I would like to see resources going where things work, not where they do not work.'

He continues in this vein for some time: 'voices must be raised' and 'things must work'. 'Routes to market' must open up. The 'market must be challenged'. He believes in 'big business models' but they must be 'good big business models'. It is 'not what I need, it is what the market needs'.

A colleague raises a point, finally.

My travelling companion considers this. I get the strong impression that he does not like the idea.

'OK, it is good to be open-minded,' he says. 'But not excessive.'

He pauses.

'What do our customers want?' he asks.

Someone else raises a point. He seems to like this one more.

'Good, good! We must not be shy!'

The employee at the end of the line ventures a few further thoughts.

'Correct! Fully correct!' says my companion.

The conference call continues for quite a while.

You do not, I reflect, get any of this in second class.

We stop at Bielefeld Station.

I try to shut out the conference call and mug up on Leipzig. It is the tenth most populated city in Germany and the largest in

Saxony with a population of 582,000. According to GfK Verein, a marketing organisation that conducts surveys about German life, it is the most popular city for single people, with 51.7 per cent of the population living on their own. This compares to a national average of 37.5 per cent. According to the World Economic Forum, however, Leipzig is the 'most liveable' city in Germany, with a strong modern industrial base that has seen BMW and Porsche move plants nearby in recent times. Unemployment, GfK Verein reports, is down and the economy is doing so well some now even refer to the city as Hype-zig. There's a well-regarded university. There's a world-class zoo with Siberian tigers, lions, gorillas and extremely rare Chinese pangolins that attracts visitors from near and afar. Bach and Mendelssohn composed works in Leipzig that can be heard at its much-loved opera house. High culture, high-tech creativity and curious creatures – the city seems to have it all.

Of course, the twentieth century was not kind to Leipzig. During World War Two, Leipzig's Jewish population was deported to concentration camps and tragically few survived. Leipzig was also heavily bombed during the conflict, with much of the city centre destroyed. Then came the dark years of the German Democratic Republic.

In 1989 the city hit the headlines for the right reasons. Key anti-government public rallies, regarded as having contributed to the fall of the Berlin Wall, were held at St Nicholas Church, not far from the train station. The protests were referred to as the Monday demonstrations as they were held on Monday evenings. They were copied across the country.

But why did they begin in Leipzig? Well, one of the key factors was the lack of a Stasi (GDR's secret police) headquarters in the city, it is said. The spontaneous protests had a chance in Leipzig.

Leipzig is a good city for railway buffs. Firstly, it is home to Bayerischer Bahnhof, Germany's oldest preserved station, which dates from 1842. Then there is the giant main station, which opened in 1915. This station is, I am staggered to learn, the world's largest in terms of floor space, covering 83,460 square metres. I am about to arrive at the world's biggest station in terms of floor space.

I order a Bitburger beer from the assistant with the pinstriped waistcoat and begin reading *A Legacy of Spies* by John le Carré; I have finished *Bruges-La-Morte* (it's only short). Reading along the way is one of the great pleasures of this trip and le Carré feels like suitable material for this part of eastern Europe, once the stomping ground of many a spook.

The assistant brings a tray of mini Mars bars. These *are* complimentary. The businessmen in first class continue to peck on their laptops. The captain of industry behind me, seemingly content with his motivational pep talk, gently snores. We arrive at Hanover Station at 12:28 precisely.

The 12:37 to Leipzig is on time, too, naturally. In my experience, there is nothing quite like the efficiency of German trains anywhere on the planet, other than in Switzerland, almost needless to say (but it's not fair to expect anyone to compete with the country that invented Rolex watches and cuckoo clocks).

I find a comfortable blue leather seat in first class and we are soon passing long transport wagons stacked with strange mummified-looking cars wrapped in white plastic. Will the industrial success story of Germany seen from our windows never end? Well, yes... for a while, at least. The line moves into rolling countryside with sunshade-bright rapeseed fields. Grain silos cast eerie silhouettes on the horizon. Haystacks on long rolling fields disappear into the distance as though they may only stop at the nearest border; Poland to the east or the Czech Republic to the south, it's about equidistant to both from here. The grand-scale production of factories along the tracks between Cologne and Hanover has been replaced by grand-scale farming. The rail-scape has turned bucolic: Big Bucolic.

A digital display at the end of the carriage says we are travelling at 131 kilometres an hour (82 miles per hour). This counts as slow in Germany; a positive crawl of a ride. Compared to ICE we are trundling along; a donkey with a limp by comparison to ICE's Derby winners.

Feeling hungry, I seek the dining kiosk, which I find is attended by a ramrod-backed assistant with a quizzical expression. I ask which sandwich he would recommend.

'I could not possibly say, sir,' he replies in perfect English. He raises an eyebrow in the manner of Jeeves and awaits my response but, before I have a chance to open my mouth, adds in a suave style as though letting me in on a secret: 'But may I suggest, sir, the *cheese and pickle*. The *cheese and pickle* is particularly popular on today's journey, sir.' He raises an inquiring eyebrow as if to suggest that this would be a very sensible choice and to make any other might be some kind of dire mistake. I buy a cheese and pickle sandwich. I had not expected to meet Germany's version of P. G. Wodehouse's fictional valet on the 12:28 to Leipzig.

It is enjoyable simply to gaze out of the window as the countryside unravels and the train 'trundles' at 82 miles per hour in a south-easterly direction towards Leipzig. For a long stretch trees with pretty purple blossom line the track blocking the view across the fields to the horizon. Then there is a break in the pretty purple trees and the never-ending landscape opens up once more, before the pretty purple trees return and this sequence is repeated many times over. These are the views in the run-up to Halle (Saale) Station; pronounced *hall-eh zall-eh* by the conductor. It sounds as if we are arriving at a remote stop-off on the Silk Road, rather than a medieval city in the German state of Saxony-Anhalt.

After Halle (Saale), out of curiosity and with plenty of time on my hands I look up IC 2441, the number of this Intercity train, on the internet. I'm surprised to discover that it has a claim to fame. A Norwegian singer named Moddi once gave an impromptu performance on this very service. The lovely tune is appropriately enough entitled 'Train Song', which he sang while playing an acoustic guitar in the company of a fellow musician on a cello. The lyrics are about a man taking a train to meet a lover and not knowing quite what to expect. The YouTube video is touching, with shots of the train rolling along this very track. Moddi performed the impromptu song for a family sitting near the dining carriage.

All on the IC 2441. How wonderfully unexpected.

As is, for me, Leipzig Station.

The IC 2441 pulls in and we disembark into the world's biggest station in terms of floor space.

Great archways and columns soar upwards. Grand staircases lead to long corridors with cavernous ticket offices and canteens. Shiny tiled floors seem to stretch forever. A marble bust of Friedrich List (1789–1846), one of the pioneers of German railways, rests on a plinth in a corner. Light filters through skylights the length of football pitches illuminating the 298-metre concourse with its 19 platforms. A mall introduced after the country's reunification lurks in the basement housing a KFC, Subway, Starbucks, McDonald's and Pizza Hut. There are banks, travel agencies, delicatessens, florists and fashion emporiums. A shop sells tickets to Leipzig Zoo.

Trains are clearly a big deal in Leipzig – and there is history to back this up.

The track between Leipzig and Dresden, about 70 miles to the south-east, was the first major railway in Germany, opening in 1839 with the backing of List and the assistance of a Scottish engineer who had helped survey the groundbreaking line between Liverpool and Manchester in 1830. List was a visionary who believed that extensive railways could bring the German states together; which they eventually did. Under Otto von Bismarck, the first chancellor of the German Empire (1871–1890), railways were taken under public ownership as part of a well thought-out plan to strengthen the fledgling nation.

Leipzig to Dresden was selected because of the mineral wealth of the region and it proved a runaway success, although there is a sad aside here. List, who did not make much money from his foresight regarding trains and who suffered from both illness and bad luck in financial crashes, eventually committed suicide. The marble bust in the corner has an unhappy tale to tell.

I exit past List and cross a street busy with custard-coloured taxis. Then I head straight for St Nicholas Church where I am soon marvelling at its extraordinary palm-tree-shaped columns and gaudy pink interior. The grandiose scale and candy-floss colours of St Nicholas Church are almost surreal in their sheer outlandishness. It's hard to imagine that this was once the epicentre of the revolt against communist rule. The original church is from the twelfth century, with striking neoclassical alterations made in the eighteenth century. Its flamboyant interior takes me completely by surprise after the IC 2441 from Hanover.

But I'm on a train mission this time (rather than a Maastricht table mission) so I do not linger long.

From the church I make my way to Bayerischer Bahnhof passing a row of shops that includes one selling mugs and hip flasks adorned with pictures of Russia's President Vladimir Putin. Some of the older generation in Leipzig look back fondly on the days of Russian influence and Putin is admired for his strong leadership. Hence the Putin paraphernalia. It is quite bizarre to see mugs with the bare-chested Russian premier clutching a rifle as he strides through undergrowth in the wild and holding up his rod in one hand and a fish in another; bare-chested once again, wearing a green cowboy-style hat and an inane grin as he poses by a lake.

Beyond the shops and a run of Soviet-era apartments – where many of the Putin hip flask buyers must live – I come to the imposing facade of Bayerischer Bahnhof. Four high arches that once led to the platforms are topped by the green and white flag of Saxony, with an old ticket hall building on one side. The working station today is below ground.

Supporters of historical architecture stepped in during the 1990s to save Bayerischer Bahnhof. They did a great job. Part of the old ticket hall has been converted into a popular pub with its very own brewery and restaurant. Inside black and white pictures on old wood-panelled walls capture the station's glory days. A wooden carriage has been turned into a special dining booth up steps near the door. I sit at the bar resting my feet on a railway track attached for this purpose, taking in the long hall with its many tables and gleaming copper beer vats.

I get talking to Lars, the barman.

'Walls,' says Lars, pointing at the wood-panelled walls.

'What about them?' I ask.

'Original!' says Lars.

'Windows,' he continues. He points at some windows and I await his next communication.

'Original!' Lars says.

'The bathroom downstairs,' he continues.

'Original?' I venture.

'Yes! Yes! Original!' he says.

Lars gives me three identical leaflets, in German, about Bayerischer Bahnhof.

'Thank you so much, but one is absolutely fine, no need to waste any,' I say.

'Ah!' says Lars. 'But when you are falling down in the water and this one is gone—' he points to one of the leaflets '—then you will have these two.' He points at the other two leaflets.

Lars gives me a look to suggest 'What could possibly make more sense than that?' He has a thin moustache, a pointy chin and a small pot belly poking out beneath his black polo shirt. He seems very much to enjoy his job.

I thank him and ask him about the railway track footrest.

'Original!' he says.

I really should have guessed.

Lars goes off to polish some glasses, and I listen to some folksy music for a while.

Glad to have gone to Bayerischer Bahnhof, I hit the streets to find my apartment for the night.

The apartment is part of a complex called the Hentschels Apartments. I find it just off Berliner Strasse, close to the main station and a series of adverts for an *Erotik Messe* (erotic fair) and a Single Party. The latter features a picture of an embracing couple and will be held at the TwentyOne dance club in a few days; evidence of Leipzig's 51.7 per cent singles scene. But there is no way to get into the Hentschels Apartments: just a locked door. I try pressing some buzzers. Nothing happens. I read my online booking. Under its Important Information section is an instruction that I must go to Kurt Schumacher Strasse, 300 metres from the apartment, to collect the key.

I retrace my steps in the direction of the station. At this address, a man with tattoos hands over the key and tells me, somewhat smugly, that I should have read the Important Information. I thank him for this advice and return to the Hentschels Apartments to enter a smart, clean blue-and-white room with an espresso machine. It is probably the best room I have had yet. Euros seem to go a lot further in Leipzig than they do in Bonn.

I am tired, but I have another mission: to buy some essentials I spotted earlier at a cheap-looking shop. I am behind with washing and I have come round to the idea that I could just buy simple new (or second-hand) clothes and discard dirty items. I realise that this is not good for the planet. I also realise, because I'm aware of this, I'll probably try and keep everything and end up with an even heavier backpack by the end of the trip.

However, this is the approach I have chosen to take.

Having purchased a large number of items from a 'reduced' rack, I eat a chicken kebab at the Ali Baba kebab shop, sitting in a booth beneath a picture of Istanbul. I am the only customer dining in the restaurant, although a few come in for takeaways. It is a spicy, well-priced kebab. Leipzig is *good value*. Then I consider watching Liverpool versus Roma at Bobby's Sports Bar. This is close to Ali Baba, but I look in and it seems gloomy inside. I walk back to the apartment past some beautiful art nouveau buildings, some awful communist-era tower blocks and Leipzig Station.

In the evening the massive station has taken on a Gothic look. The sky has turned purple and the clock face above the entrance glows yellow and orange, looking like a low-lying harvest moon. Columns on the facade shoot upwards and phantom-like figures glide in and out of the high arched entrance. Leipzig Station is both captivating and distinctly strange, a world unto itself: gargantuan, eerie and compelling.

Into Poland
Leipzig to Wrocław

In the morning I return to the station past the Erotik Messe posters, a job centre and a bar open 24 hours a day. Silver bullet-like trams glide past. Custard-coloured taxis whizz about, as ever. The air is crisp. The sky is bright. I have an intriguing day's journey ahead by train.

I am about to break east – a long way east, even further beyond the boundaries of the old Iron Curtain.

In a ticket office I inquire about the timetable from Leipzig to Wrocław in Poland. Wrocław is a large city that I have always wondered about, having seen it on the maps of various low-cost airlines. What an unusual name, I have always thought. What goes on in Wrocław? It is, I have established, pronounced Vrots-waff. Which is quite confusing as it is not spelt that way (in English, at least). Polish pronunciations have long been a mystery to me. In the past I have visited Szczecin (Shchechin) and spent a weekend in Rzeszów (Shesh-ouf). I have given up trying to guess pronunciations. They are just too tricky.

The Deutsche Bahn employee seems to understand Vrots-waff and she taps on her computer and says: 'Zis is forty-seven euros.'

I show her my Interrail Pass.

'Zis does not cover zis train,' she says.

The train company between Dresden and Wrocław has not signed up to Interrail.

So I buy a ticket for Wrocław on a Trilex express service. I can get to Dresden for free with the Interrail Pass. I have decided that I will indeed travel as far as Ukraine, probably rolling on as far as the Black Sea on the sleeper train (on Rowan's tip-off back in Calais) before trundling back through the Balkans to Venice. This means crossing Poland.

The 10:00 to Dresden is shiny and red with three carriages. It is baking today. The *Leipziger Volkszeitung* paper says that last month, April, was the warmest since records began in 1881, during the days of Bismarck and his frenetic railway building. It seems as though May could keep the heatwave going. My Interrail Pass has become tattered and the conductor struggles to stamp the document as we glide through suburbs and skirt a field of solar panels.

Through Borsdorf and Wurzen we rattle after making stops with a ding-dong-ding announcement at each station. A derelict factory with shattered windows emerges as do many a dingy, crumbling building from communist times. It's a far cry from the trackside success story between Cologne and Hanover around here. The east of the country, despite the Hype-zig nickname, clearly still has a lot of catching up to do; hardly surprising given that reunification was less than 30 years ago, while the period of Soviet influence when eastern Germany was the German Democratic Republic, a self-described 'socialist workers' and peasants' state', lasted more than 40 years after the devastation of World War Two.

Ding-dong-ding, ding-dong-ding we go, stopping at many little stations amid the tumbledown remains of communism: Dahlen, Oschatz, Riesa, Glaubitz, Priestewitz, Niederau... ding-dong-ding-dong-ding-dong-ding. It's almost hypnotic.

I am deep into John le Carré's *A Legacy of Spies*. The protagonist, a former spy, is reminiscing about Leipzig and Dresden during the Cold War, encounters with the Stasi and smuggling films out of East Berlin. Hair-raising moments in which agents meet under surveillance risking torture at the hands of the Stasi mount up, as does the sense of secrecy and mistrust: who's double-crossing, or triple-crossing, who? A lone westerner travelling by train around the former GDR might well – or perhaps probably would – have been monitored by the secret police back then. It's not that long ago.

A long car-carrying train appears in the opposite direction near Niederau. A patchwork of higgledy-piggledy allotments marks the run-in to Coswig. At Radebeul Station a little black steam train and a collection of old carriages rest on a siding (a perfect stop-off for rail enthusiasts considering a break). I slip into the rhythm of the track with John le Carré as we roll on to Dresden-Neustadt.

I have an hour here before the onwards connection. This is another interesting station, though nowhere near as big as Leipzig's. Dresden-Neustadt, completed in 1901, is on the site of a former station opened in 1844 that serviced Germany's first railway between Dresden and Leipzig. The ticket hall has an airy skylight and delicate art nouveau decorations depicting trees and flowers. A model railway is to one side of the hall, near the platforms. For one euro you can make the little trains go round a version of Dresden's city centre.

The highlight of Dresden-Neustadt is a superb Meissen porcelain artwork in green and gold showing Saxon castles and gardens on a wall above a newsagent near a kiosk selling *currywurst* and beer. This is a mesmerising work that captures a Saxon dream-world of figurines, spires and sculptures of angels.

The sandstone exterior of the station is dark with dirt. A makeshift stall near the entrance offers asparagus, strawberries and pickles. Close to this stall I notice a plaque with a message on the station wall. It begins: 'During National Socialism, Dresden-Neustadt Station was used as a starting point for many deportations of Jewish women, men and children.' During October 1938, 724 Dresden Jews were deported to Poland, the plaque says. Auschwitz and Birkenau concentration camps are mentioned. An inscription is written in Hebrew, and a brass Star of David has been fixed to the pavement in front of the plaque. I stand here for a while considering the depths to which human beings can descend. Back in Britain our understanding of the Holocaust is one step removed from the actuality of what happened: the women, men and children who disappeared along tracks from railway stations now used every day by commuters.

* * *

The Trilex express is cherry-red and splattered with adverts for destinations. The train is already quite full and I sit opposite a couple speaking Polish. All I understand of their conversation is the occasional mention of a 'lifestyle fitness club', although the word *dobra* features a lot (Polish for 'good'). The train has two levels, with steps to higher seats. We depart through woodland and I show my ticket to the conductor, while my adjacent neighbour buys a ticket to Wrocław for 35 euros. There seems to be an on-board ticket promotion (which is annoying given that I paid more).

The couple opposite do not cease chattering. On seats across the way, two women are rabbiting non-stop, too. The Polish on their way to Poland like to chatter. This is the most gibbering train yet.

Thick pine and silver birch forest is broken from time to time by hazy farmland as we roll further eastwards than I've gone yet. We reach Löbau, still in Germany, where an old-fashioned station house is painted bright orange; the most garish station house to date, but rather charming in a garish, orange, old-fashioned way. Next up is Görlitz, the last stop before crossing into Poland. This town seems larger than the others since Dresden, perhaps as it's on the border, with a tall church spire rising above avenues of colourful nineteenth-century mansions.

Polish flags fly on an apartment block across the border line and we soon stop at Zgorzelec Station, where the chatterers opposite disembark and a silent couple takes their place, the man looking remarkably similar to Lech Wałęsa, the former head of Poland's Solidarity movement, while the woman has bright pink nails and pink trousers. We traverse a sea of yellow rapeseed fields. For a while it is almost as though we have entered a yellow fantasy land. This otherworldly stretch comes to an end and we pass yet more derelict factories – it's not just eastern Germany that has yet to recover fully from the days of Soviet influence – before entering another pine and silver birch forest. Sunlight barely penetrates the trees, just the occasional beam breaking through and flickering across the passengers on the busy Trilex express to Wrocław.

A succession of station names begin with 'z'. After Zgorzelec, we pull into Zagajnik and Zebrzydowa. Then we cross a river with white rapids and arrive at Bolesławiec, a sleepy looking town famous in Poland for its ceramics. By this station a small hill of pine logs awaits transportation. Soon afterwards we stop at Tomaszów Bolesławiecki, where a man in a red military uniform is walking a dog. Chojnów is followed by Legnica, which is notable for its cobbled station platform. We clatter by another old restored steam train. Wrocław Muchobór, on the outskirts of the city, has a platform with a section of lawn. I do not think I have ever seen platforms with cobbles and lawns before.

This is my slowest train yet. There really are a lot of stops. I turn my mind to Wrocław, the biggest city in western Poland and the fourth largest in the country (population 638,000).

The city has been ruled by many empires over the centuries, returning to Polish control after a border change following World War Two. Up to 1945 the city was called Breslau and was part of Germany. In 2012 Wrocław hosted the European Championships football tournament. In 2016 it was a European Capital of Culture. The city is renowned for a charming old town, many nightclubs and bars (there is a university and a youthful population) and the Racławice Panorama. This is a gigantic circular mural depicting the Battle of Racławice, a Polish uprising against Russia in 1794. The mural is more than a hundred metres long and is reputed to be quite brilliant, a major attraction in Poland.

The other big deal in Wrocław is its dwarfs. Across the city more than 350 bronze dwarfs are to be found. Each is depicted differently, so there is the Chimneysweep Dwarf, Motorbike Dwarf, Gambling Dwarf and Horse-riding Dwarf. While this may sound bizarre – which it is – the dwarfs have a significance as they were a symbol of the anti-communist Orange Alternative movement prior to Wałęsa forming the first Solidarity government in 1990. This group embraced absurdity to lampoon the communist government. When the absurd regime eventually fell, the dwarfs arose as public art.

Pondering the city ahead, I realise that we are upon it. The shiny, cherry-red Trilex express pulls into Wrocław Główny, the main city station, where someone wearing a blue dress is waiting for me on platform five.

Knowing the trains are taking me to Poland, my girlfriend Kasia has taken time off work at the last minute and jumped on a Wizz Air flight to join me. Kasia is Polish, from a town to the east of Warsaw. For the next few days I have a companion, a translator, a guide and a plan. We are going to catch trains onwards from Wrocław to the little-visited city of Katowice, a centre of the country's coal and steel industries, and then to the much-visited city of Kraków, from where I will continue, solo once again, into Ukraine. Eventually we are to meet up again in Venice – as long as I don't get lost on trains in eastern Europe, that is.

It is great to see my 'guide' at the end of the platform. We have booked an apartment close by and are about to head off in that direction before hitting the town for a night out (Kasia has it all worked out).

But first there is the small matter of Wrocław Główny Station. It must be one of the weirdest in Europe. Stations are part and parcel of the enjoyment of this kind of train travel – and Wrocław's is a beauty.

We exit the lobby via a passage decorated with art nouveau tiles depicting swirling plants and flowers and enter a square in front of the station. We turn around... and there it is.

Unbelievable.

Wrocław Główny Station looks like a palace belonging to an Indian maharaja. Painted a peculiar saffron-yellow the facade stretches a hundred metres with turrets and towers, castellated walls and columns.

The station dates from the mid-nineteenth century and is the handiwork of a flamboyant Prussian architect named Wilhelm Grapow. It was built for the Upper Silesian Railway and is number eight on the list of tourist sights in Wrocław on a tourist map Kasia has brought with her, just behind the zoo but ahead of the history museum.

'In Wrocław we are in the region of Lower Silesia, and when we go to Katowice we will be in Upper Silesia,' she says. 'That is the differentiation.'

I love it when she uses words like that.

We take a few pictures of this unexpected station before crossing the street towards Wrocław's old town.

We are about to meet many dwarfs in one of the most beautiful, almost completely overlooked cities in Poland.

I never thought I would go to Wrocław. But that, as I have said, is the whole point of this journey: just follow the lines and see where they lead. We cross a busy, street with squealing trams. The sun beams down. It is a fine, hot day in western Poland – perhaps the warmest of the trip yet. An ancient city in Lower Silesia awaits.

CHAPTER FIVE

WROCŁAW IN POLAND TO LVIV IN UKRAINE

'I MEAN, WHAT THE HECK! IT REALLY IS A WEIRD SYSTEM'

Poland has been much in the news of late; not always for the best of reasons (and nothing to do with trains).

First of all, there's the small matter of the independence of the country's judiciary. Poland's president, Andrzej Duda, a member of the controversial right-wing Law and Justice Party, has angered the European Commission by introducing a mandatory retirement age of 65 (down from 70) for all members of the supreme court. A total of 22 of the court's 74 judges have been forced into early retirement, allowing the Law and Justice Party to make replacements, effectively taking control of the court.

The European Commission claims Poland is flagrantly breaking European Union law: 'These measures undermine the principle of judicial independence, and thereby Poland fails to fulfil its obligations under article 19(1) of the treaty on the European Union read in connection with article 47 of the charter of fundamental rights of the European Union.'

In other words, 'Stop, you can't do that!'

The Commission says it will take the Polish government to the European Court of Justice unless it reverses the policy – and Article 7 of the European Union's Treaty of Lisbon has been invoked, opening up the possibility of sanctions and loss of voting rights. Across Poland there have been protests, with liberals attacking the power-grabbing behaviour of the Law and Justice Party.

This party was formed in 2001 and has a sad recent history. It was founded by identical twins Lech and Jarosław Kaczyński, but in 2010 Lech, along with his wife Maria and 94 others, including senior military officers, the governor of the National Bank of Poland and leading politicians, died in a plane crash in thick fog in Russia. The crash was blamed on human error, although there are many conspiracy theories. Despite being neither president nor prime minister, Jarosław, something of a shadowy figure who once oversaw the burning of an effigy of the Solidarity leader Lech Wałęsa, remains the party's de facto leader.

Recent government policies have been both deeply conservative and controversial. A law to restrict abortion has been mooted, sparking widespread 'free choice' demonstrations; meanwhile, shopping on Sundays has been banned on three Sundays of every month, with a total shutdown coming soon. Both measures have proved popular with the Catholic Church, to which more than 90 per cent of the population belong. However, the Sunday shopping restrictions are hated by pro-business groups, who believe the policy will result in job losses (plus longer working hours on Saturdays), and the European Commission says the abortion law would run counter to human rights commitments: 'If adopted, the draft law would remove the possibility of terminating pregnancy in the case of severe foetal impairment, including cases where an impairment is fatal. This step would be at variance with Poland's obligations under international human rights law.'

Then there is the Holocaust bill. There has been great unrest over a proposal by the Law and Justice Party to make it illegal to blame Poland for crimes committed during the Holocaust. Jail terms of up to three years were initially considered for anyone mentioning 'Polish death camps' or suggesting that Poland was complicit in Nazi Germany's war crimes.

Were it not for international condemnation and the intervention of the Israeli Prime Minister Benjamin Netanyahu, who called the proposal an 'attempt to rewrite history', the bill may well have become law.

About three million Jews in Poland were murdered by the Nazis at concentration camps such as Auschwitz, Treblinka, Sobibór and Bełżec. This was about half of all Jews killed in the Holocaust and historians recognise some Polish complicity, despite many Poles risking their lives to protect Jewish neighbours.

The Holocaust bill comes at a time when the Law and Justice Party has gone on the offensive against immigration, failing to meet European Union migration quotas while vowing to 'protect' Poles from outsiders who might be terrorists. Of this strong stance, Anna

Materska-Sosnowska, a leading political scientist at Warsaw University, has commented: 'The anti-immigration rhetoric is fuelling Law and Justice now. Simply put, the party is managing fear. This will be continued as the party isn't changing its anti-EU course.'

This is despite Poland being the largest net recipient of EU aid.

Meanwhile, the lobbying group Reporters Without Borders says Poland has dropped to the country's lowest ever ranking in its Press Freedom Index; the nation is now at position 58 out of 180, wedged between Fiji and the Dominican Republic. The number one ranking country is Norway, while North Korea – unsurprisingly – comes in at 180. In its summary of its findings, Reporters Without Borders cites a 'tightening control' of public media by the Law and Justice Party, with some news outlets now little more than 'government propaganda mouthpieces'.

Oh, what a terrible mess, you might say. Or in Polish: *Och, co za okropny bałagan*. And don't try repeating that after a couple of vodkas.

Platform, tracks and legends
Wrocław

Wrocław Główny Station is south of the city centre. Our apartment is halfway to the market square close to Pub Szkocki (the Scottish Pub), which comes complete with a sign advertising 'HAGGIS' and a picture of a bagpipe player wearing a tartan kilt. The apartment is in a crumbling nineteenth-century building with a dimly lit staircase and tall wooden doors. An entrepreneur has converted one of the apartments into four separate en suite rooms that are like mini-apartments. They are smart, cheap and have little kitchenettes.

Going east makes a lot of sense for penny-pinching train lovers.

Wrocław is a revelation. Past Pub Szkocki and a tremendous art deco shopping mall we cross a bridge over a water channel following a row of communist-era buildings. Next to one of these houses is a stall selling a great number of Polish and European Union flags. Polish politicians may be falling out with the EU but most Poles are fans of the institution that has allowed so many to work abroad at higher wages.

More than a million Poles currently reside in the UK, so many that Polish recently became the second most spoken language in England. The 2004 enlargement of the EU – when Poland, Cyprus, the Czech Republic, Estonia, Hungary, Latvia, Lithuania, Malta, Slovakia and Slovenia joined – led to tens of thousands of Poles coming to the UK to work. Migration *out* of Poland seems to be incredibly popular (if not the other way round).

The enormous market square at Wrocław is surrounded by tall structures with gables and high windows. The feel is Germanic, as though the city is still Breslau. Towering step-shaped roofs shoot upwards. Intricate stucco depicts august figures from the Habsburg and Prussian empires. Stone lions, eagles and griffins guard doorways while wrought-iron balconies twist outwards from mustard-coloured mansions. The overall effect is flamboyant and showy. This is, our 'Wrocław Top Ten' map tells us, 'one of the largest old town market squares in Europe'.

At the heart of the square is the magnificent Gothic town hall, with parts dating from the 1270s. Its centrepiece is a splendid gilded clock below a gable with a series of gilded porcupine-like spikes and a copper-topped tower with a weathervane. A comical bronze sculpture of a bear with a long, shiny tongue is to be found at street level. It is said to give you luck to touch this tongue (hence its shine). Kasia and I do just that.

There are many 'freedom dwarfs' around the square: Laptop Dwarf, near Moped Dwarf, close to Horse-riding Dwarf, near ATM Dwarf, a few strides from Tourist Dwarf, not far from Papa Dwarf (bigger than the others). While this might sound like some kind of gnomish nightmare, they somehow seem to work. It's as though they are laughing at the communists of bygone days. I rather like them.

Kasia and I go to a restaurant/bar intriguingly named Motyla Noga (Butterfly's Leg) and find ourselves, perhaps-not-so-romantically, talking trains. Motyla Noga is down a cobbled lane and through a small door in a wall that opens into a courtyard with tables. All of these are taken – Wrocław is hugely popular with Polish tourists on breaks, says Kasia, even if few foreigners visit – so we enter an indoor room with a vaulted ceiling that feels like the type of place dissidents of old may have gathered during communist times. We find old armchairs by a film poster of Charlie Chaplin, where I drink a strong, fizzy beer and Kasia has a glass of white wine as she proceeds to tell me *all about platforms at Polish train stations*.

'You have the *peron*, the platform,' she begins, making sure I'm taking this in. I nod and make a face to suggest 'Well, of course I knew that much already' (which I didn't).

'Then you have another number, which identifies which track you are at,' she says. I nod once again as though to suggest: 'Ah, I admit I didn't know that, but it can't be that difficult. I've got it, I've got it.'

Kasia shoots me a look that I interpret as: 'Oh, really?' 'In Warsaw,' she continues, 'I have been on platform one, track twenty-seven. Sometimes it's crazy. There aren't even that many tracks used by passengers at that station.'

She pauses, seemingly to let this sink in. 'For foreigners it is confusing,' she adds. 'Even for Poles! No one gets it. I mean, what the heck! It's a really weird system. I don't know who came up with it. I'll show you how it works tomorrow.'

I'm glad Kasia has made it. Polish trains seem *complex*.

Kasia sips her drink. 'When I try to explain Polish trains to outsiders, they say: "Why do they not just have one platform number? Why do they have to have two?" We *have* to be different!'

Continuing our romantic discussion of the Polish rail system, I ask Kasia if Polish trains usually run on time.

She pauses once again and chooses her words carefully: 'I can't speak for all people, but I can speak from my experience, which is not good.'

She pulls a face that can only mean one thing: 'They're really bad.'

On a more positive note, stations have, however, improved in recent times, according to my Polish rail expert.

'Basically, they renovated a lot of the stations before Euro 2012,' Kasia says. 'That's when they began English announcements at main Polish stations and they've kept them ever since.'

Polish train briefing complete, we finish our drinks and go for a stroll to a peaceful island with a church on a bend of the River Oder. Across another bridge, on the opposite bank of the river in Ostrów Tumski, we find ourselves in the oldest part of Wrocław. This is home to the city's cathedral. Twin redbrick towers topped with copper spires shoot upwards to a height of 98 metres. The cathedral, originally completed in 1272, was badly damaged during World War Two in the Battle of Breslau when Soviet troops attacked the German stronghold. The Nazis surrendered just two days before the end of the war, making Wrocław the last major German city to fall. More than 6,000 German soldiers died in the 82-day siege as well as 80,000 civilians. Around 80 per cent of Wrocław was destroyed and the cathedral was rebuilt in the 1950s.

Its doors are shut for the evening. We walk back to the apartment along the main street towards the island. Here we find a man in a black cape and a top hat lighting gas lanterns with a stick with a flame at one end. He cuts a striking figure in this long black robe, looking like a ghost from another age. Tourists stop to take pictures as he wanders between the lanterns.

'I want this job,' says Kasia, who has been considering a change in direction in her career for a while, just as I am now (post Dover). 'This would do for me.'

It does, I have to admit, look quite satisfying.

With that, via a Kasia-selected vodka bar or two by the main square, we return to our apartment passing more trams: bells ring, wheels shudder and breaks squeal as carriages clatter by.

Wrocław is a good place for train lovers.

* * *

In the morning we visit the Big Attraction: Racławice Panorama, Wrocław's famous circular mural. Upon arrival, however, we discover you must buy a ticket in advance and the circular mural is fully booked. What a popular circular mural! Kasia is crestfallen as she hadn't realised you had to book and this had been her idea. My 'guide' looks downcast.

'There's no point in us trying to talk our way in,' she says. 'That is not the Polish way.'

I had suggested a bit of begging, but Kasia says: 'Where rules are involved, rules are obeyed.'

Ever since communist times, when rules were very much obeyed *or else*, Poles have been sticklers for regulations, she says.

But this is just one of the things you have to put up with on an impromptu train ride. As with the cathedral last night, top sights such as famous and extremely popular circular murals may be impossible the day you pass by. That's just the way it is and there's little point in worrying too much about it.

In this frame of mind, we head back towards the market square as Kasia tells me a train-related story connected to her family. Our romantic Polish railway dialogue continues, but this time it's not about platforms and tracks.

'After the war my great aunt came here,' she says. 'It was because the city was so well equipped. The Germans had been driven out and the people who moved away sold stuff. It was cheap. My great aunt came on a packed train. It was so overcrowded she had to sit on the roof. After the war they had nothing. She came across the south of Poland from the south-east to get here. She wanted to get linen, carpets, pots – whatever. I could not believe it when she told me this: that she *had been on the top of a train*. In India maybe they do that, but not here. After the war they must have been desperate.'

As she says this, we cross a square and come to St Mary Magdalene Church.

This church has a famous bridge, the Penitent Bridge, which stretches between twin spires at a height of 47 metres. Having disappointingly missed out on Wrocław's circular mural, we decide to check out this 'tourist sight', soon finding ourselves climbing many steps to the top – where we learn of a legend.

The story goes that a beautiful but vain girl named Tekla once lived in Wrocław. As she grew into womanhood she loved dressing up in finery but would reject the advances of young men as she was too 'lazy' to be a wife. She preferred simply to look at herself in the mirror. Her father was angry with her and said so. Shortly after his outburst Tekla was kidnapped and forced to sweep the bridge between the towers of St Mary Magdelene Church for eternity as a punishment for her vanity. Eventually, however, when she was 'old and ugly', she was rescued by a witch. To this day, the bridge has 'remained as a reminder to all lazy young ladies', according to an information panel.

Not perhaps the happiest of tales.

We descend the tower, pick up our bags from the apartment and return to Wrocław Główny Station, where we are catching the 13:49 to Opole Główne Station.

Peron three, Tor five
Wrocław to Katowice via Opole and Gliwice

Wrocław Główny Station has a library. For those with time to kill before a train, this is the place to go. We enter the maharaja's palace beyond a man asleep by a fountain and go up some steps to visit this sanctuary.

Inside the *biblioteka* a librarian with a jumper bearing the words *'BON VOYAGE'* says hello and we take a look around the cool, calm space, stopping to sit on a sofa in a corner. Here Kasia picks up a book of children's poetry. She begins to read part of a poem, 'Locomotive', by the Polish poet Julian Tuwim (1894–1953):

A big locomotive has pulled into town,
Heavy, humongous, with sweat rolling down:
A plump jumbo olive.
Huffing and puffing and panting and sweaty,
Fire belches forth from her fat cast-iron belly.

'It's a famous Polish poem,' Kasia says. 'We learn it at school and I love it.'

I do, too. It's charming and perfect for the location, going on to describe the contents of the carriages, including one filled with 'corpulent' passengers eating frankfurters, another with elephants and bears, and one with a 'cargo of grand pianos'. The wheels of Tuwim's locomotive are soon clattering through mountains, tunnels, meadows and woods, steam bellowing upwards as the verses chunter along.

Train travel during the age of steam... Then it really was slow trains: slow, beautiful trains that huffed, puffed, panted and sweated. Slow train travel is wonderful now, even if it is tricky at times in Germany, but let's face it, journeys must have been simply amazing back then.

The steam era, which finally puffed out when diesel and electric-powered trains took over en masse in the mid-twentieth century, was without doubt the golden age of train travel. But who's to say that, with a little bit of imagination, there can't be a new golden age now?

Down on *peron* three, Kasia and I read a memorial plaque to the Polish actor Zbigniew Cybulski. He was a 'kind of Polish James Dean', says Kasia, and he came to a tragic end here as he attempted to leap into a carriage, missed his footing and fell beneath the wheels. Nearby another plaque remembers Zagra-Lin, the World War Two Polish resistance group, which attacked Nazi soldiers at the station in 1943.

Old stations tend to have stories (and often they're bloody).

* * *

The 13:49 is from *peron* three and *tor* (track) five. With Kasia leading the way, I follow along and let her work out the intricacies of Wrocław's *peron/tor* set-up. That's what 'guides' are for, after all. The stairs to the *peron* are remarkable in that to one side of the steps is a baggage conveyor belt. You simply put your luggage on this slow-moving belt and ascend the steps. It's a fantastic idea that I can see catching on elsewhere, especially with small children. In Wrocław several are taking trips up and then running down to do it again and again as we arrive. Which is of course exactly what you would do if you were a small child waiting for a train with your parents in Wrocław.

A rush of passengers boards the 13:49 but Kasia is a wily Polish train traveller and we manage to secure two seats. Other passengers stand. The train is blue, yellow and silver with blue and grey seats designed with a natty geometrical pattern. A tubby conductor with a goatee and a red tie inspects our tickets as we potter out of Wrocław into sunny fields.

This train is indeed slow – if not steam train speed. We are sitting in a booth of four with two guys opposite us who fall fast asleep with their mouths open as though intending to trap flies.

There's no way of dressing it up: this ride is not exactly the prettiest yet. Communist-era apartment blocks soon arise and do not seem to go away much as we pass the stations at Lipki, Oława and Brzeg. As we gaze out at these, I mention the communists I met in Bonn and Kasia simply replies: 'They don't know what they are asking for.'

She pauses as we take in a particularly grim apartment block right by the track. The concrete on the walls is crumbling, with rusty satellite dishes affixed to balconies and colourful washing drying incongruously on racks amid the grime.

'My parents' lives were shaped by communism,' says Kasia, who was aged five when the old regime collapsed. 'Secret police. People informing on each other. People disappearing after arrest. People were unsure who to trust.'

She pauses as a train heading for Wrocław clatters by noisily in the opposite direction. 'Food shortages,' she continues, referring to her parents' experiences growing up, as told to her. 'All products, in fact, not just food. People didn't have toilet paper. You couldn't get furniture, washing machines, anything. Not unless you knew people. You had to know people then or have people who knew people. You had to be lucky like that.'

Another Wrocław-bound train causes another pause. 'Then there was the media,' Kasia says. 'People did not know what was going on in the West. It was all propaganda news. State news. These days there's "fake news", but that's nothing like propaganda news, when you have no other source of information.'

Kasia looks out at yet another concrete block and repeats her earlier comment about the communists in Bonn: 'They just don't know what they're asking for.'

Kasia and I have talked about this often before. She simply cannot understand how anyone could possibly want communism after its so recent well-chronicled failure in eastern Europe.

We fall into silence as the train crawls into sun-baked countryside before coming to a metal bridge over the River Oder and stopping at Opole Główne Station.

We have been travelling along a famous Polish track, the very first to open way back in May 1842. The line was initially between Wrocław and Oława, extended to Katowice in 1856 by the Upper Silesian Railway. The first locomotive, the *Silesia*, was built in Manchester by Sharp, Roberts & Co and many of the tracks were transported from Britain. The inaugural journey covering 16 miles took 42 minutes and this route was chosen in order to speed up the transport of steel and zinc that were crucial to the Prussian empire.

Opole Główne Station is another gem. We have half an hour till our next train to Gliwice, so we take a look around the ticket hall, built in 1899. By the original polished wooden ticket booths stand little polished wooden tables that must have once been used to complete forms. Now they are decorative, attached to a beautiful tiled floor with a pistachio and mauve floral pattern. Light shines through high, arched windows.

Clusters of bulbous lamps hang from beams. A mural depicts ladies and gentlemen of bygone times on a platform by a steam locomotive.

Outside is an old restored locomotive. It is big and dark green with lanterns at the front. Rail aficionados may be interested to know that it is a TKt48/2 (serial number 4490) with a boiler produced in Sosnowiec in 1955 and was stationed in Katowice and Kluczbork before moving to Opole, where it was used as a heating boiler from 1993 and turned into a 'monument to technology' in 1996.

Is this *too much information*?

After this interlude the 15:16 arrives and Kasia and I, despite being savvy to the *peron/tor* conundrum, only just catch the train as we are initially at the correct *peron* but the wrong *tor*, which is totally obscured from view at the far end of the platform. We board and find seats. A portly station guard checks the wheels using a spanner and we rattle onwards in a cherry-red carriage heading for Gliwice beyond yet more apartment blocks.

Soon we enter a thick silver birch forest. The smell of cigarettes wafts through the carriage; passengers must be smoking in the toilets. There is no air conditioning on this Polskie Koleje Państwowe (Polish State Railways) train and the air is hot and stuffy.

This is Polish mining territory. Mining shafts and factories with cooling towers arise, leading to yards filled with scrap metal and mountains of used tyres. We roll through Kotulin, Toszek and Pyskowice, the scenery changing little along the way.

'You can say that here we are truly in the middle of nowhere,' says Kasia.

'I can truly believe you,' I reply.

Not long afterwards the train comes to Gliwice. This has a modern station with a roof of white metal hoops and glass panels. Here we have ten minutes before the 16:40 to Katowice, which is due in at 17:09. I have to buy a ticket for this leg as it is operated by Koleje Śląskie (Silesian Railways), not Polish State Railways. Silesian Railways is not covered by Interrail.

Kasia and I have another one of our romantic Polish train talks. She tells me that the train system in Poland is complicated as Polish State Railways has many subdivisions with many regional railways. There was once, she says, an attempt to create a low-cost intercity brand that Polish State Railways hoped would ape the success of budget airlines. It was initially named Tanie Linie Kolejowe, which translates as Cheap Railway Lines.

'They had to change the name because it didn't sell,' she says. 'It was in the early 2000s. When it came to trains, people felt that *cheap* sounded... *cheap*. They didn't like it. So they changed the name to Twoje Linie Kolejowe.'

This means Your Railway Lines. This worked and Polish State Railways conveniently did not have to alter the logo as the letters matched.

The brand was no longer *cheap*. The tickets, however, remained *cheap*.

I am learning a lot about Polish trains.

We judder through an industrial zone of factories and derelict warehouses. Shortly afterwards we arrive in Katowice.

Music in a mining town
Katowice

Katowice is not top of most people's bucket-list of places to visit in Poland. As my copy of *The Rough Guide to Poland* says: 'Given the factory-filled appearance of [the region's] urban landscape, and the catastrophic pollution produced by its heavy industries, it's a place unlikely to appear on any but the most eccentric of tourist itineraries.' There is, the writer adds, an 'inescapable aura of post-industrial decay'. On top of this, England lost 2–0 to Poland here in a disastrous World Cup qualifier in 1973, ending the Bobby Moore era. Who would, *Rough Guide* suggests, wish to be reminded of that?

But I suppose I am quite eccentric and 1973 is a long time ago. There is something about poor old neglected Katowice that appeals to me. Also, I note, my copy of the *Rough Guide* dates from 2002. Perhaps matters have moved on since then. Perhaps Katowice is a very exciting place these days.

First impressions are mixed.

We disembark into my least favourite station yet.

Katowice Station appears to be a shopping mall. It was renovated in 2013 and handles 12 million passengers a year, being a convenient hub with links to Kraków, Bielsko-Biała and Częstochowa. The station is also, however, a maze of dull shops and confusing to navigate. For a while we do not know how to get out, eventually leaving by a back exit beside a delivery road. From here, we loop round the station past a nightclub, a kebab shop and a betting shop to a square where two young men are rapping in front of the shiny mall. Inside there somewhere trains lurk. We deposit our bags in a little apartment facing the mall above a 'Commando' shop selling T-shirts with 'PRIDE OF POLAND' messages, pellet guns, camouflage trousers, military knives and jackboots.

The apartment's inventory runs thus: a sink the size of half a sheet of A4 paper in a tiny bathroom, a very creaky bed, brown and lilac walls, a single paper napkin, four goldfish-bowl-shaped wine glasses and a slightly mouldy bathroom. In the hallway outside the apartment is a metal gate with a combination lock that regularly slams as other inhabitants move about. It is as though we are in a little prison.

We are not in the room for long.

Kasia has hatched a plan.

We are soon at the magnificent concert hall of the Polish National Radio Symphonic Orchestra listening to Beethoven and Tchaikovsky.

This is the way to do it. I have put on a powder-blue shirt and a pair of cheap slip-on shoes, both hastily purchased at a shop at the station, and we have eaten a good meal of Silesian rolled beef, dumplings and red cabbage washed down with Katowice-brewed beers at a no-nonsense restaurant on the main pedestrianised street in the centre of town. We have walked past a giant apartment block dating from the 1960s as well as Bobby Burger fast food restaurant and a giant circular arena, Spodek (which translates as Saucer, or Flying Saucer), where rock concerts are held. Pearl Jam, the Smashing Pumpkins, Depeche Mode, Robbie Williams and Elton John have all played at this extraordinary building.

Now we are at a state-of-the-art concert hall that was not around when the 2002 *Rough Guide* writers dropped by. A lot has indeed changed recently in Katowice and this multi-million złoty concert hall, opened in 2014, is an important part of the city's redevelopment.

New powder-blue shirt: tick. New slip-on shoes: tick. Could I be smarter? Yes: tick. I'm wearing jeans (but at least I've tried).

We enter a hall with wavy, caramel-coloured wooden walls, balconies and spotlights.

'I hope we don't smell of beer,' says Kasia as we enter the lobby.

Inside, sophisticated classical music lovers wearing black are quaffing coffees and champagne. Our tickets cost 15 złoty (£3). These were the most expensive available and we have great seats in the middle. The stringed instrument ensemble strikes up with the tall Spanish conductor of the guest Orchestre d'Auvergne from France waving his arms vigorously. The sound of violins, cellos and violas reverberates with precision and perfection. I close my eyes and listen to the music of Ludwig van Beethoven (of Bonn in Germany), Pytor Ilych Tchaikovsky (of Votkinsk in Russia) and Bohuslav Jan Martinů (of Policka in the Czech Republic).

Heavenly notes float across the chamber. The rattle of the tracks is forgotten. Beethoven, Tchaikovsky and Martinů have taken over. The music is sublime.

* * *

In the morning we return to the concert hall but this time walk past the entrance and go to the Silesian Museum. This museum is in a former coal mine. It opened in 2015 after relocating from the centre of town. You enter a long passage into what was once one of the main Katowice coal mines and disappear downwards along darkened tunnels not knowing quite what to expect.

At the bottom is a slick museum with displays explaining the history of coal mining in the region. With all its flashy interactive displays and endless galleries, the museum looks as though it must have cost a lot of cash. Kasia says that the European Union footed the bill. I look this up to find that the EU invested precisely 48,085,334 euros in the museum (£42.8 million). A project statement says that the museum will 'revitalise a former industrialised area by providing great new facilities for local people and tourists alike'.

'I'm telling you: get into the EU, because this is what happens next,' Kasia says.

Perhaps, if things really do take a turn for the worse as many believe the economy will post Brexit, Britain will resort to reapplying again one day soon.

It's worked for Poland. Maybe it will work for us again, somewhere down the line.

An information panel explains that the first steam engine in central Europe was introduced from England to Upper Silesia in 1788 to help 'dewater' the Fryderyk silver mine in Tarnowskie Góry. It was known then as the 'fire machine' and Frederick William II, the king of Prussia no less, and the German poet Johann Wolfgang von Goethe went to inspect the phenomenon.

This part of Poland is important. After World War One, the Allies were going to pass the territory from Germany to Poland. The premise was that Poland had little industry and needed this land, where many Poles lived, to compete in the modern world. Most of the rest of Poland was then agrarian. Germany, obviously, did not want this. A referendum was held in 1921. It was won by the Germans, although it is believed that about 180,000 former residents returned for the vote, thereby swinging the result.

Dodgy dealings in a referendum: who would have imagined it?

The newly formed League of Nations eventually intervened after various insurrections, and the vast majority of the land was given to the Germans with an agreement to allow free trade across the border. This seemed to work... until the Nazis came along.

Kasia and I enter an art gallery in another room with works with titles such as *Condensers in Chorzow (Sunday)* by Rafal Malczewski showing a woman walking a dog in a hayfield next to a factory (1934). The painting appears to represent the shock many had with the rapid industrialisation of Upper Silesia. The most striking image, however, is *Jewess with Lemons (Citrus Seller)*, an oil on canvas by Aleksander Gierymski (1881). The subject's face is plaintive and pinched. She holds a basket on one arm that is full of fruit while a basket in her other arm is empty: good times and bad times. It's a powerful picture.

Then we go up the tower.

The Silesian Museum comes with an intact mine shaft. You catch a lift to the top and then the city of Katowice stretches out below.

What is most interesting, to a non-Pole, is the architecture dating from the communist period. Straight ahead is the giant apartment block we walked past last night on the way to the concert. The building is almost 200 metres long and contains 762 apartments spread over 15 storeys. It is known as Superjednostka (Superunit) and it was designed in the late 1960s by Mieczysław Król, an architect who was much influenced by the superstar Swiss-French architect Le Corbusier. At first it's hard to know what to make of it. On the one hand, the building is impressively massive and incredibly eye-catching. On the other, it's a great big concrete slab and must be pretty awful to live in.

Across the horizon are many such concrete tower blocks, but Superjednostka trumps the lot. Kasia's 'They don't know what they are asking for' springs to mind once again. As many as 3,000 people live in that monstrosity.

Oh, what a lovely city!
Katowice to Kraków

We return to the station. We board the 12:47 to Kraków.

The 12:47 is an orange train with tinted windows. We depart nine minutes late, passing disintegrating buildings and an old water tower that must once have been used by steam trains. The service is run by the Koleje Malopolskie train company, which operates in the next region, but Kasia believes this one is covered by Interrail and the conductor does, too.

As we roll away, quotes from Pope John Paul II, the former archbishop of our destination, and Father Leon Knabit, a Benedictine monk, flash on a digital screen. We traverse silver birch forest and rattle by a strange yellow train marked 'STRABAG' that seems to be fastening a track with a peculiar metal mechanism punching the rails with metal rods. A mine shaft emerges on the right just before Trzebinia Station, where a noisy stag group joins our carriage.

Kasia reads the day's papers.

A story in *Dziennik Zachodni* (*Western Daily*) is all about the *de-communisation* of street names and monuments in Katowice. Meanwhile, an article in *Gazeta Wyborcza*, a Polish centre-left paper, says President Duda should face a tribunal over politicising the judiciary and disrespecting the rule of law. Yet another piece, written by four Polish historians, draws parallels between the rise of fascism in Europe before World War Two and now: 'Fascism and populism need to have enemies of the nation, preferably internal, but the choice of enemy is not always crucial. Today extremist right-wing movements can choose: refugees, liberals, Muslims, the elites, Brussels. And, of course, always Jews.'

Depressing stuff. Even more depressingly another article reports on a strong earth tremor, almost four on the Richter Scale, that hit a coal mine about 35 miles south-west of Katowice a few days ago. There were 11 miners working 900 metres below the ground; four were evacuated by rescue teams, two bodies were found and there has been no contact with the remaining five. The rescue has been badly hampered by billowing methane gas.

The stag group gets even noisier. This may have something to do with the bottles they are passing around.

'If it wasn't for those jerks, I'd be enjoying this ride,' says Kasia.

We move to the next carriage.

Cargo wagons full of gravel jolt by. Peculiar wooden huts on stilts cast shadows on fields of potatoes and corn.

'Hunters use them to shoot wild boar that eat the crops,' says Kasia, who was brought up in the countryside and knows such things.

The sound of singing rises in the adjoining carriage. The stag group seems to be in full swing.

Listening to their songs we arrive at Kraków 13 minutes late at 15:03.

* * *

Our third apartment in Poland is close to the station and comes with a peculiar but completely fantastic hammock attached to a beam in the lounge, a huge, extremely comfortable bedroom on a mezzanine level, a model of Buddha, oriental art and a retro leather swivel chair. These online bookings can be so hit and miss. The pictures can look incredibly good (the one in Katowice appeared to be a palace) or not so great (we were not sure about Kraków) but then turn out to be actually quite brilliant.

Kasia tests out the hammock and I give the swivel chair a quick spin. Then we go for a walk through a small park back to the station.

Kasia wants to show me the old part of Kraków Główny Station – just the start of her 'guided tour' of the city (I am glad to be with my very-well-organised 'guide' in Poland).

Earlier our train arrived at a modern section of the station with lots of shops, but on one side there is the old station house from the 1890s.

The first station here opened way back in 1844, says a panel, and was in neo-Renaissance style. The current building is in an 'eclectic style' with grand columns and arched windows. Now it's home to History Land, a museum with models that explains Polish history. An elegant passageway from the museum curves by the tracks with wrought-iron support columns, nineteenth-century lanterns and a lovely old clock.

Railway stuff *done* we wander to Rynek Główny, the main square.

This giant medieval square is bigger even than the one in Wrocław. At its centre is a huge cloth hall with a long row of arches with bars and cafes. Inside are long corridors of handicraft stalls but we head to the famous Noworolski cafe, an art nouveau delight with a magnificently decadent interior with caramel curtains, wood-panelled walls, oval mirrors and ruby-red carpets. A pianist tinkles in a corner as we find a leather booth and order coffees. Noworolski opened in 1910 and Vladimir Lenin would read the papers here during the two years in which he stayed in Kraków after being exiled from Russia (1912–1914). At that time the revolutionary-to-be apparently very much liked the cake and would entertain both his wife and his lover at the cafe. It was during this period that he indulged one of his passions: ice skating. His favourite rink was at a botanical gardens very close to the station.

During World War Two occupying German soldiers demanded that Mr Noworolski supply biscuits and cakes for a restaurant that was opened in adjoining rooms. As an act of protest Mr Noworolski delivered 'bad quality cookies' (so says a little history of the cafe in a leaflet). The Germans got wind of what was going on and Mr Noworolski had to go into hiding. Then in 1945, when it was clear the war was almost over, Mr Noworolski returned with his pre-war staff and 'took over the premises and chased away the Germans who were afraid and in panic'.

It's a very nice cafe – and quite a lot has gone on here.

We mingle among the crowds and explore the fortifications of the elegant Wawel Castle, built on the orders of Casimir III the Great in the fourteenth century, then we pass synagogues on little lanes in Kazimierz, a neighbourhood that has been for centuries home to the city's Jewish community, and cross a river to visit a former factory.

Oskar Schindler's enamel factory is now a tourist attraction that sheds light on the horrors of World War Two. The German industrialist employed more than 1,000 Jews so they would not be placed on Nazi deportation lists. In the museum sickening pictures show men being hanged after capture by SS guards. Rooms display possessions seized by the Nazis. Photographs show children huddled on street corners – and testimonies describe many war atrocities. One given by Stella Muller, aged eight, is gut-wrenching: 'The horrible screams of the children come from the street, their cry for help to the disgusting guffaw of the amused Germans; they are throwing children out of windows on to lorries, sometimes they miss.'

This is a description of a 'displacement' from Kraków in October 1942 during which 4,500 Jews were deported to the Belżec death camp and 600 were murdered in the ghetto. The Auschwitz concentration camp is a 90-minute drive from Kraków.

We do not go there but we do catch a taxi a short distance to Nowa Huta. Built on the eastern outskirts of Kraków by the communists, Nowa Huta translates as 'the New Steel Mill'. It is home to a massive steelworks and vast housing estate built in brutalist socialist realism style. The idea was that the city, begun in 1949 and now with a population of 200,000, would create an industrial, technology-driven counterbalance to the strong Catholicism and tradition of scholarly learning in Kraków's old town, which represented a threat to the regime. This challenge took its ultimate embodiment in the form of Pope John Paul II, elected Pope in 1978 when he was the city's archbishop. His strong presence was a thorn in the side of the authorities.

'Their plan didn't work,' says Kasia as we walk along a huge avenue off what used to be Josef Stalin Square, now simply Plac Centralny (after a short period as Ronald Reagan Square).

Ironically, Nowa Huta became a hotbed of resistance and, along with the Gdańsk dockyards, an important centre for the Solidarity movement.

* * *

We catch another taxi back to Tytano, a vibrant neighbourhood just to the west of the main square.

At Tytano a former tobacco factory has been transformed into a series of hipster restaurants and bars. We eat Thai spring rolls and pizza at an outdoor restaurant, before going to a cocktail bar and doing what a lot of people do in Poland on a Saturday night: drink vodka.

Time slips by in a delicious blur.

As we walk back to the apartment across Rynek Główny, tipsy, I admit, we get a taste of the type of tourism that has blighted so many eastern European cities of late.

A fat man wearing a pink polo shirt and chino shorts waddles by clasping a can of beer.

'Oi! Oi! Oi!' he yells. 'We are! We are! We are Brits!'

Locals cross the square to avoid him.

'Oi! Oi! Oi!' he repeats. 'We are! We are! We are Brits!'

Just in case anyone didn't get his message the first time.

He disappears down a lane with his mates, 'Ois!' echoing amid ancient buildings.

Perhaps not the best advert for shiny new Britain plc.

A close shave
Kraków to Lviv

To reach Lviv in western Ukraine I need to catch an hour-long rail replacement bus from Kraków to Bochnia Station in Poland, then a train from Bochnia Station to Przemyśl Główny Station, also in Poland. From there, a train departs to Lviv Station in Ukraine, arriving at 18:37. I am going to spend the best part of my day travelling.

I had hoped to avoid all replacement buses but there seems no way round the one to Bochnia. Kasia and I part with a hug and a 'see you in Venice' before the bus moves on, driven by a man wearing jeans and a T-shirt with a slogan saying 'PSYCHO'. As though living up to his clothing he pulls away with great speed. We cross the River Vistula, fast, and traverse a series of factories, breweries, scrap yards and warehouses, even faster.

At Bochnia Station, I wait at a long platform with a handful of fellow passengers watching a display announce that the train will be 15 minutes late, then 20 minutes late, then 25 minutes late. This is worrying, as there is an 18-minute connection time for the train to Lviv.

Dogs bark. Time ticks by. A cargo train rolls past slowly enough to jump on board. Eventually the 12:58 service to Przemyśl, a blue and grey train run by Polish State Railways, turns up. It is 20 minutes late. Perhaps we will make up time and all will be OK.

On board I go to the bright orange dining carriage where I meet Dave and Robert. They are middle-aged backpackers and are the only other people in the dining car. Hearing me talk to the waiter they invite me to join them; they seem a gossipy pair.

Dave is American. Robert is from near Newcastle. They live in Berlin. They have flown to Kraków and intend to take trains across Ukraine, the highlight being an excursion to visit the site of the 1986 Chernobyl nuclear disaster. They have booked a full-day tour of the exclusion zone.

Dave, originally from Napa Valley in California, explains why.

'We're laughing about it now,' he says. 'But it's serious if you think about it. We live in a technological era and there are greater disasters in mankind in this era: social and environmental.'

They want to see the centre of the disaster close up for this reason.

'We benefit from nuclear energy on a daily basis and don't think of the moral or ethical considerations,' Dave continues. 'Germany is slowly closing its plants. I want to see a piece of history. Tour guides take you round with a Geiger counter.'

Dave has worked for the English website of a German newspaper, while Robert is a Deutsche Bahn employee, a signalling design engineer. They have close-cropped hair and wear similar green T-shirts. Dave has glasses and is slightly pudgy. Robert does not have glasses and is very thin and has a well-trimmed goatee beard. Other than these small differences they are almost identical.

They both order schnitzels.

Robert tells me about his work in trains.

'I'm involved with the European Train Control System,' he says. 'It's an EU idea that you basically run trains on the same signalling system – a unified train protection system. It's got to reach a critical mass.'

Robert advises me to look at the website Openrailwaymap.com, which he says is a very good train website.

Dave discusses his involvement with the Paradise Papers, the leaked set of confidential electronic documents that detailed offshore investments of many corporations and individuals and made world headlines in 2017.

'I was a behind-the-scenes editor,' he says casually.

Then he adds: 'I also worked with reporters who dealt with Julian Assange. That was interesting.'

Dave pauses and eats some schnitzel. 'The NSA-Merkel story,' he says. 'You know, the US National Security Agency spying on Angela Merkel's mobile phone. That was another one.'

He seems to have been at the heart of all sorts of intrigue.

We stop at a long platform at Rzeszów Główny Station, where Robert asks me about my ticket to Lviv. I show him the Interrail Pass.

'That won't work in Ukraine,' he says.

He explains that we will be catching a Ukraine Railways train, not a Polish State Railways train. He seems to know exactly which trains are covered by Interrail. If I want to get to Lviv on the 15:45 service, I must go to the Ukraine Railways website and buy a ticket, quickly, or else there will be a three-hour wait till the next train.

I look up the Ukraine Railways website while Dave and Robert continue to eat their schnitzels. By some absolute miracle I manage to buy a ticket.

The train moves slowly onwards through forest.

We cross a river after Jarosław Station and stop at Munina Station, which has a pretty station house with a garden with pink flowers. The train creaks around a bend and over another river. Churches with copper spires emerge on a hill ahead. An announcement in Polish mentions Przemyśl.

We have arrived.

We are beyond the departure time for the Lviv train.

As we pull into Przemyśl, Dave, Robert and I, along with a woman wearing a jumper that says 'GO SIT ON A CACTUS', wait by the doors.

We hit the platform running – in completely the wrong direction.

I follow Robert. Dave follows me.

Robert bellows: 'There's a blue train! That is Ukrainian!'

Other passengers join our charge towards the blue train, convinced we know what we are doing. The blue train ahead is indeed a Ukrainian train – a completely empty Ukrainian train with the lights off.

Not the right Ukrainian train. A man who appears to work at the station says: 'Keep going down that way.'

He points down the platform.

We take his advice and come to a sleek orange and grey train with a row of guards standing by the doors. This is the correct Ukrainian train. I show the electronic ticket and am let on board and we pull away almost immediately.

I am on my way to Ukraine.

* * *

This is an exciting moment for train lovers: we have changed gauge. Oh yes! We are now on 'Russian gauge', which is precisely 4 feet and 11 27/32 inches, rather than the standard-gauge of Polish railways, which is 4 feet and 8 1/2 inches. This was the gauge (the width of the tracks) that George Stephenson settled upon in the 1820s. The Russians chose a different width for their line between Moscow and St Petersburg in the 1840s simply because they felt like it. Why follow what Stephenson dreamt up in another country?

Dave and Robert are nowhere to be seen. They must be in another carriage. Kids at a railway crossing wave at the train. Przemyśl's copper spires fall into the distance. A Polish border guard in a khaki uniform inspects my passport. We move through a huge railway yard. Words in Cyrillic appear on a television screen at the end of the neat blue carriages. We enter wild woodland. A very long train with cargo wagons filled with logs sits at a siding. A 'WELCOME TO UKRAINE' text message appears on my phone.

A slender Ukrainian border guard with a crew cut, a revolver and a camouflage uniform checks my passport. The document is in order. He stamps it. And I ask the Polish man next to me whether there is a dining carriage. He has some English. He says 'no' and offers me a sandwich. I thank him and explain that I am after a beer. He replies: 'Ah! I don't drink beer.'

We discuss Polish politics for a bit.

'I am disappointed,' he sighs.

'About what?' I ask.

'The people,' he says. He is not initially as forthcoming about his political views as he is about his sandwiches.

'What about the people?' I ask.

'The people, society. I cannot believe that people in Poland have given up democratic values for some populist promises and social benefits,' he says, referring to the recent shift towards the right in Poland.

'What do you mean about social benefits?' I ask.

'The government is handing out "free lunches" in many social benefits to win popular support. The country cannot afford this in the long run,' he says.

He goes on to explain that each family after their first child now receives 500 złoty (£100) a month for each additional child; an amount of cash that goes a long way in Poland. The idea, he says, is both to gain popularity and to reverse the trend towards an ageing population.

'It won't work!' he says, reaching a crescendo. 'The long run! Not in the long run! People are getting used to having too many things for free.'

My companion gesticulates vigorously as he makes these last points. Then he comments: 'There you have it.' And he returns to reading a magazine.

As he does so we are crossing a wide plain stretching as far as the eye can see. Long perfectly straight dirt tracks taper into the distance. It is a mesmerisingly vast landscape and does not feel like Europe at all, even though it is.

We reach Lviv at 18:39 – and passengers file down the platform into a cavernous station.

I am, I realise, straying a long way from Venice. From one complicated country I have reached another, with plenty of complications of its own.

Gondolas and Aperol Spritzs by Rialto Bridge feel pretty far away right now.

I have, it dawns on me, *deviated somewhat.*

CHAPTER SIX

LVIV TO ODESSA IN UKRAINE, AND BACK

SLEEPER TRAINS AND BEAUTIFUL PEOPLE

Lviv

UKRAINE

MOLDOVA

ROMANIA

TRANSNISTRIA

Odessa

THE BLACK SEA

I intend to deviate further still. From Lviv it is possible, as Rowan way back in Calais said, to catch a sleeper train to Odessa, the Ukrainian city/beach resort on the Black Sea. At booth number three in the giant ticket hall at Lviv Station I attempt to buy a sleeper ticket for tomorrow night. As I explain myself by writing down the destination and date I realise I am holding up locals. Behind me a woman says *'Americano!'* I am sent to booth number eight, which has no queue and is apparently for foreigners. The assistant speaks a little English. She charges 500 hryvnia (£14) and hands over a ticket.

Lviv Station is another fine example of European railway architecture. It dates from 1904 during the Austro-Hungarian Empire, when Lviv was known by the German name of Lemberg, and has an OTT art nouveau style that includes elements of later introduced Soviet grandeur. Cornices and green-marble columns are adorned with decorative swirls. Wagon-wheel-shaped chandeliers flicker above. Caramel curtains with long tassels hang by windows the size of garage doors. Corridors and winding staircases disappear in mysterious directions. It's all a bit *Alice in Wonderland*.

As well as the VIP HALL, there exists somewhere a HALL FOR OFFICIAL DELEGATIONS and a HALL OF ENHANCED COMFORT. Excellent. What could be better? I decide to inspect these tomorrow. This is a veritable treat of a station. I step outside and take in the grand exterior with its Italianate columns, sculptures of heroes and high metal dome topped with the yellow and blue Ukrainian flag.

The time is 7 p.m. It's about two miles to Hotel Plazma, my abode for the night (the furthest I have had to venture to digs from the tracks yet); Lviv Station is on the western edge of the city. With extravagance I have booked the suite at Hotel Plazma for the price of a couple of sleeper tickets. Hotel Plazma is right in the centre of town near the main square and the opera house, and it 'happily opens its doors for Lviv guests', according to the website.

Sounds good to me. I follow a long dusty road lined with food stalls, take a left and descend a hill to reach a long square by an ornate opera house. On the square smartly dressed elderly folk are singing traditional songs in a gathering of some sort. I stop to listen for a while. This is all quite pleasant.

Hotel Plazma is nearby. A faded yellow sign announces the establishment. You enter an alleyway by the sign and then press a buzzer with a yellow sticker by a small door. From here you ascend a chipped staircase for four floors. Feeble light illuminates the stairs and you must cross landings with bolted doors.

At the top you enter a door with a yellow sign to be happily greeted by a receptionist in the middle of filing her nails. She smiles, hands over a map of Lviv, gives you the key and points to a wooden staircase.

Rooms are up this steep wooden staircase, which leads to an attic with a narrow corridor. The suite is at the very end of the corridor.

It's the best room yet – on a corner with gold and green curtains, matching gold and green wallpaper, a floor with gold and green tiles and a black leather sofa with cushions depicting Tower Bridge, the Colosseum and the Statue of Liberty. A kettle sits on a side table although no cups, coffee or teabags are to be found. From a small terracotta terrace I can see other balconies in a courtyard upon which housemaids and a chef are smoking and gossiping. Trams rattle by on a street below.

Pleased with my choice of accommodation, I walk around the block, home to a shop selling fur coats and a 'creative dining place' (so says a sign) with a DJ. On the corner a bride and groom, just married, appear to be stranded waiting for a driver. A man on a moped performs a wheelie along the road that leads to the Kork Irish Pub, where I sit outside with *A Legacy of Spies*.

Lots of young adults are walking about – everyone seems *millennial*. A waiter brings me a foaming pint of eastern European lager. I sit with this pint on this balmy evening on this pleasant terrace pinching myself that I have somehow reached Ukraine after leaving my flat and catching a train to Clapham Junction. I order a hamburger. It's an excellent burger. Another foaming pint of eastern European lager is delivered. I know I should maybe be more imaginative in my choice of venue than the Kork Irish Pub, but I am simply worn out – you might say: completely knackered – by the long journey today and the run across Poland. Perhaps I should be pounding the streets to seek a traditional Ukrainian restaurant on a hidden little square and sampling Ukrainian culture up close and personal. Perhaps that's what *travel writers* are supposed to do in such situations. Perhaps I should be ruminating on the nature of Ukrainian culture and other such matters right now. I'm just too tired for all of that. Besides, I like it at the Kork Irish Pub in Lviv.

Sufficiently fed and watered I return to my green and gold suite and watch Barcelona play football against Real Madrid on a television screen with so much interference that it appears to be snowing in Spain.

'Gareth Bale!' yells a commentator.

The Welshman has just scored in the snowstorm: 2–2.

From the open door to the balcony shrieks of millennials on nights out rise and more trams scuttle by.

It's been a good day on trains travelling so far east, right to the very edge of Europe.

Very nice ladies
Lviv

How do you get to know a city where most of the signs are in Cyrillic and you do not have a guidebook? You take The Best Free Walking Tour, obviously. A leaflet for this tour is in the reception of Hotel Plazma. You meet the guide, who will be holding a yellow umbrella, by the statue of Neptune in the market square at 11 a.m. The tours last two hours and you do not have to pay a single hryvnia unless you feel like offering a tip at the end.

Which is how I become acquainted with Maria, who is leading The Best Free Walking Tour. She is indeed by the statue of Neptune holding a yellow umbrella. She is in her twenties and has a *Mona Lisa* smile. She wears pink-framed glasses and a blue-and-white top and carries a handbag with tourist information, I presume, poking out.

I introduce myself and mention that I have never been on a free walking tour before. 'Do some people not even tip at the end?' I ask.

'Oh yeah, sometimes,' she says. 'Very rarely, though.'

We talk as a group of tourists assembles.

She tells me that she is still learning English and that she 'gets a little worried when native speakers are on the tours'. Group sizes can be as big as 60 tourists 'but when it's minus fifteen degrees Celsius: nobody'. She has been a guide for four years and has a motormouth style that keeps everyone on their toes.

The time ticks to 11 a.m. and Maria tells everyone: 'I'm sorry, I broke my microphone so I will speak louder than usual.' The dozen or so in our group form a semi-circle and each person says where they are from: Luxembourg, Belgium, Germany, Scotland, Lithuania and America.

Then we head across the square, admiring the fine stone city hall and being told that '*lev*' means 'lion' and that more than 4,500 images of lions, the city symbol, are to be found in Lviv. This is the very first information Maria imparts – and, as we are soon to discover, it's a key part of the tour.

First, though, we listen to a potted history of the country. 'We were for a long time Polish,' Maria half yells. 'Then Cossack. Then here comes the Polish troops! Then we were under Poland and Lithuania for some time. Then Austria. Then we declare independence. Then Soviet Union. Then here comes the Nazis! Then the Soviets again! In August 1991 we declare independence.'

All told in just about one breath. It's a remarkable feat of brevity that leaves us all a bit goggle-eyed and reeling. Yet, that said, all the bases have been covered and we're clearly not going to get bogged down with *historical stuff*.

'Now we have a dispute with Russia over Crimea!' Maria exclaims, almost as an afterthought. 'But everything will be OK!' she says, almost challenging any of us to deny it.

She seems pretty optimistic about all of this, despite Russia having become well entrenched in the region on the north coast of the Black Sea since seizing Crimea from Ukraine in 2014. President Putin's disregard for the country's sovereignty has had many, American generals included, fearing catastrophe. Could this be a prelude to World War Three? Will the Baltic states and Scandinavia be next? That's what some people think and these remain very real fears. Since the Russian invasion leaflets and manuals have been distributed in Latvia, Lithuania, Estonia and Sweden explaining what to do if the worst happens. Troops have been drilled in readiness for an attack. Meanwhile, Russian battalions have gathered near borders and gone on intimidating training exercises.

Peace in Europe really does seem fragile, as Père Xavier Behaegel said back in Lille. Visiting Ukraine, whose very name means 'borderlands' and which has suffered so many invasions during its history, you sense this straight away. This is indeed the edge of Europe. This is a partially occupied country. This is where Russian muscles have been flexed and new rules apply.

Maria seems pretty cool about things, though, and merely shrugs when one of the Germans in the group asks when the war is likely to end.

'It is what it is – and it will end when it ends,' she half yells once again, before shrugging as if to suggest 'These things are run by forces beyond our control'. Then she ushers us onwards. There are sights to see! No time to waste talking about Crimea and World War Three.

A series of stalls sell trinkets in the shape of lions, fridge magnets in Ukrainian flag blue and yellow colours, shot glasses (this is eastern Europe), as well as toilet paper depicting Putin's face next to the words in Cyrillic 'USE ME'. Putin is definitely public enemy number one in these parts. You've got to admire the ingenuity of the stallholders: things may be bad in the east of the country, but you may as well cash in on the crisis.

Lviv's city centre is a treat: an explosion of colourful, elegant buildings from the mid-nineteenth-century (many Hapsburg) and earlier. Labyrinthine lanes twist off in all directions to secretive courtyards with fountains and ancient churches with ornate interiors dripping in gold and decorated in shades of pastel pink and blue; Maria takes us into a few, explaining the histories in her rapid-fire style. We stop by the imposing stone facade of the Latin Cathedral, which we learn dates from 1360, with a foundation stone laid by Casimir III the Great; Pope John Paul II visited the church in 2001.

'You like?' booms Maria – this, we have quickly picked up, is Maria's catchphrase.

'We like!' we reply, like good dutiful tourists on a free tour.

We inspect an unusual bronze 'beer belly' that has been fixed to the ground in a cobbled courtyard. Locals, Maria says, love beer and this monument to overindulgence has been the starting point for many a night out. We take pictures of the bronze beer belly. Then we are marched to the 'smiling lion'; a stone lion with a curious grin attached to a house on a side street. As Maria said in her opening gambit, lions are to be found throughout Lviv. Spotting them becomes a game on our tour. As we wander between the sights, with the tourists beginning to chat to one another (there is a lovely informality on a free walking tour, even if the pace is frenetic), Maria occasionally stops to point at a rooftop or a facade and yell: 'Lion!' The chatter ceases and we, the tourists, follow her gaze to the relevant stone lion. Maria seems to require acknowledgement of each such spotting. So we nod and say things like: 'Got it! That's a good one!' It's as though we're on a safari in Kenya searching for the real thing on a game drive.

'You like?' booms Maria at yet another lion, watching our reactions closely.

'We like!' we reply.

Our group stops by a statue of the local writer Leopold von Sacher-Masoch, after whom the term 'masochism' is named. In his book *Venus in Furs* (1870) Sacher-Masoch fantasises about being controlled by women wearing fur coats; a dream he turned into reality in his private life with various mistresses to whom he acted as a slave, once even signing a contract handing over his freedom.

'If you want you can put your hand into his trouser pocket you can feel something interesting,' Maria says.

The statue has a hole in one trouser pocket.

Some of the women in the group do this to feel what is below – giggling as Maria looks on approvingly. What an unusual man. What an unusual statue.

Maria presses on, urging stragglers in the group swapping stories about their travels in Ukraine to hurry up – in a nice, if loud, way.

An old-fashioned pharmacy that is part working pharmacy and part pharmacy museum, with all the old wooden shelves and bottles still in place, is next on the tour. We take pictures of the old bottles. Afterwards we pace onwards along little cobbled lanes and emerge near a shiny red tram from 1912 that has been converted into a tourist information office next to the beautiful baroque opera and ballet house, built at the end of the nineteenth century above a small river that flows beneath the stage. The facade is all Corinthian columns and grand arches, with figures representing comedy and tragedy by the entrance. The building is featured on the back of the country's 20-hryvnia note.

'You like?' booms Maria.

'We like! We like!' we reply. We're well used to the routine by now.

Our final stop is in the old Jewish quarter, where we stand in silence – for once – by a memorial to those from Lviv who died in the Holocaust, many sent to the Belżec concentration camp in eastern Poland. More than 150,000 Jews resided in Lviv in 1939, a third of the population; now just 1,200 live in the city. It's estimated that only one per cent of the pre-World War Two Jewish population survived.

It's a staggering statistic. The horrors of World War Two are a constant backdrop to any visit to these parts of eastern Europe – and, with each reminder, I cannot help thinking back to Churchill's words about the need for a 'kind of United States of Europe', with which I began this adventure by rail. It is only 74 years since the war of all wars ended.

Subdued, we return to the square with the statue of Neptune.

Here, Maria announces that the free walking tour has concluded. It's certainly been a whistle-stop couple of hours. She says goodbye and we all give her tips. Maria has been absolutely great, one way or another, whizzing us around without holding us up with the type of tedious commentary that some guides – fearing they are not offering *value for money* – bore tourists to death with. Perhaps that's because none of us paid a single Ukrainian hryvnia to start with.

That seems to be the joy of these 'free tours', even if this is my first one and maybe I'm jumping to conclusions. Less is more: we've seen some of the principal sights of Lviv; we've got a rough idea of the layout of the city centre; no booking was required; there's been no fuss; and a few of us tourists have got to know one another. We now know what we *like*, if not what we *don't like*, in Lviv. On an impromptu jaunt round Europe by train a 'free' tour or two seems like a very good idea indeed.

* * *

A few of the tourists hang around afterwards. Gail from Edinburgh, who told me during the tour that she had taken the train from Kiev to reach Lviv and is 'just ticking off the country' (Ukraine), and John, from New York City, are the last stragglers to leave the square by the opera house. I have already asked John from New York City if he feels like going for a quick drink after our sightseeing exertions. He does. I ask Gail from Edinburgh if she would like to join John and me but she seems a bit alarmed by this suggestion and declines.

So John and I go back to the market square to a bar near the statue of Neptune that we had noticed earlier. It serves cherry wine and has a picture of a topless woman with curly ginger hair and a suggestive look clasping large cherries before her breasts by the entrance. This is not as risqué as it may sound; it's one of a long row of cherry wine bars busy with tourists on the square.

John buys me a glass and proceeds to tell me all about a date with a Ukrainian woman that went wrong two days ago in Odessa. In fact, it did not so much go wrong. It did not happen. He sighs.

'She was a very nice lady – I mean *nice*,' he says, pausing to let the sheer extent of her *niceness* sink in. 'We arranged to go out. But then there was the cognac festival.'

He sounds terrified even mentioning this cognac festival as it appears to bring back bad memories.

'The cognac festival was at lunchtime and I met some people and we got talking and I totally forgot about her. When I woke up the next day, I called her to say sorry but she didn't want to speak to me. Pity. She was *very nice*.'

John extended his stay a day in the city to overcome the cognac festival. He shakes his head at the memory.

John took the sleeper train from Odessa to Lviv and got talking to another woman in his compartment. She was *very nice*, too. 'We stayed up till one thirty. She was the mother of children in a professional dance troop.' John did not arrange a date with this woman.

We sip our cherry wine, standing by a high table outside the bar. I buy a small bottle as Kasia has mentioned she likes it. When I do, John says: 'I would buy one, too, but I haven't got any room in my bag. I've got bottles from all the places I've been.' He likes to try out the local booze and take samples home.

John is spending a few weeks touring Europe. 'I'm in the middle of getting divorced,' he says after a while. He has two children and has already moved out of the family home to an apartment block in Queens where 'eighty per cent of the other people are Chinese, it's like Shanghai'. He was brought up in Kazakhstan 'in a tiny village in the middle of nowhere'. His father emigrated to America in the early 1990s. He is in a confiding mood.

John has a job in technology. 'I have got to the stage where I can work anywhere on the move,' he declares. He twitches slightly. He is tall with wide shoulders, short grey hair and has a bit of the suave George Clooney about him, which might explain all the *very nice* women. 'I usually travel business or first class,' he says. 'I have millions of air miles. I just fly about using them. You see I know how to play the system.'

'What do you mean?' I ask.

He leans forward as though letting me in on a secret and explains how he simultaneously opens 'multiple accounts with airlines at the same time on different internet browsers. The airlines know about this and they try and catch up with the methods. So you have to keep ahead of them. There's a community of us [an online community] and we keep each other informed. It's becoming very popular, but it is getting more challenging.'

His business-class flight from America to Europe cost him $200. This was simply the taxes, which you have to pay whatever happens. 'My wife and the kids and I have been to a lot of places: Thailand, Japan, Europe – many times.'

John plays the same game with hotels.

'I either stay at a top-end hotel or at a hostel,' he says. The latter is when the 'game' does not work. It is a strange method of travel.

John does not reveal the exact tricks of the trade regarding air miles and hotel points. Which is a pity. He recommends that I go to Transnistria, an autonomous region in Moldova close to Odessa. He visited there on this trip and has contact with a guide. He gives me his contact's email and number: 'It's an interesting place, it doesn't even exist on the map.'

These parts really do feel like an edgeland.

John leans forward once again, bends and shows me a part of the top of his head that has no hair at all, although the rest of his hair is bushy and thick. 'Kazakhstan,' he says. When he was a boy he went out in heavy snow in the countryside and got lost, eventually returning to civilisation and being taken shivering to a nurse who warmed him by a fire. But he was put too close to the flames. His hair was burnt and the lifelong hairless patch was formed.

'She had good intentions, I'm sure,' he says.

We finish our second round of cherry wines. John departs. I go to a cafe on a cobbled square by the Jesuit Church for a bowl of *bograch* soup; beef on the bone with bacon and a hunk of bread. A busker by the Jesuit Church plays the song 'Bad Moon Rising'. A striking blonde woman, possibly *very nice* and just right for John, teeters past wearing a mackintosh and red high heels. She looks the sort who might just have attracted Sacher-Masoch's attention, too.

I walk up a hill to a medieval castle with a large Ukrainian flag and a vista across the old town and Soviet-era housing estates on the outskirts. Lviv is another excellent city for simply wandering around. I collect my bag from Hotel Plazma and potter to the station.

On a Ukrainian sleeper
Lviv to Odessa, with a visit afterwards to Transnistria

The train to Odessa departs at 22:12. I am a couple of hours early. Sometimes on this type of trip this is just going to happen and I am quite OK reading a book to kill the time. Anyway, it looks as though it's about to pour down, and I want to have a good poke around Lviv Station.

The VIP HALL turns out to be dreary, with a few folk on low-slung sofas in a first-floor room with yellow walls and someone in a uniform who is about to ask what an interloper is doing there. The HALL OF ENHANCED COMFORT, if I have got the right place as everything is quite confusing, appears to require a steep entrance fee. Another uniformed official prevents entry and requests 115 hryvnia (written on a piece of paper). In the free, regular waiting hall, two pigeons court one another near a kiosk selling sandwiches. Passengers are slumped on chairs, many half asleep. I never do find the HALL FOR OFFICIAL DELEGATIONS, which is hidden well away from nosy parkers such as myself. Soldiers, heading east perhaps, are to be found in the shadowy ticket hall. They gossip and laugh and seem in a good frame of mind given recent turns of events.

Outside Lviv Station is an intriguing circular Soviet-era cafe that looks plucked from a *The Jetsons* cartoon. Inside I find a long, slow-moving queue. Instead, I go to a stall with Coca-Cola sunshades where I purchase a *piva* (beer), from an assistant with pink hair who gives me a complimentary boiled sweet to accompany my drink. Heavy rain begins to fall (I was right). But it's dry beneath the Coca-Cola awning as I finish off *A Legacy of Spies*.

A priest with a black cassock, a backpack and a green plastic bag scurries through the rain. A pair of bag ladies greet one another with cries of delight and kisses (looking like luvvies on Oscar night). Orange, yellow and purple trams pull into a stop to my left. Bells ring. The trams come and go. A man in a tracksuit spits into the gutter near a pizza kiosk. Taxis judder over the potholed road. The temperature is 17°C, says the digital display above the station entrance. Further soldiers, these ones wearing green berets, appear and proceed towards town.

Kevin from Stratford-upon-Avon sits at my table.

We fall into conversation, as backpackers tend to. I ask how long he is travelling. He looks as though he is pretty hardcore and in for a long haul. He wears a black T-shirt, a black beanie and black jeans. He has an angular, canny face with thoughtful eyes.

'Till the money runs out, basically,' he says. 'The best thing is not to check the bank account.'

He is a freelance illustrator. He is, he says, 'avoiding life, I think this is my fifth midlife crisis'.

Lightning flashes, followed by a rumble of thunder. Rain pelts down. Kevin explains that his current journey began when he flew to Madrid, as this was cheaper than getting a train from Stratford. After this, he took a train to Barcelona and another to Toulouse. In Toulouse he found it was less expensive to fly to Paris than take a train. So he flew, and then boarded a train to Bruges, from where he travelled by rail to Brussels and then Cologne before catching a plane to Moscow. Kevin took a train to St Petersburg from Moscow, then another to Helsinki and a ferry to Tallinn in Estonia, where he enjoyed the 'hippy blues music scene'. From Tallinn, he took further trains to Tartu, also in Estonia, and Riga in Latvia before boarding a bus to Vilnius in Lithuania that had free coffee and Wi-Fi – 'it was amazing: free'. Kevin flew from Vilnius to Minsk in Belarus and from there to Kiev.

Previously he has conducted similar jaunts in Cambodia, Vietnam and Hong Kong. In the latter he ran out of cash and slept rough for four nights: 'I was squashed in a seat in McDonald's one night – then I slept in a park with a bag over my head to keep out the light at dawn.' He managed to secure a working visa in Australia, where he stayed for almost two years using 'supersaver tax' (which he explains, although I do not understand). Then he flew to Germany, going to Dresden, Munich and Nuremberg, before hanging out in the Czech Republic and flying to India for six months followed by two months in Nepal. Later on, he went to Johannesburg for a while, China and Japan. Along the way he sketches the places he visits. He shows me a pad with some skilful drawings.

Boy does Kevin get around. 'My parents, I think, had two holidays in their lives: both to Tenerife,' he says. He pauses, pondering this. Then he says: 'You have to go out of your way if you want to find somewhere interesting.'

Thunder crashes once again. Rain falls in hosepipe streaks. Kevin notices his rucksack is getting soggy. He grabs it and puts the rucksack on a seat. He is going into Lviv and is taking shelter. The rain relents and off he waddles. 'If you ever need an illustrator, give me a call,' he says as he departs.

Back in the station I have half an hour to kill and I discover that the entrance to what I take to be the HALL OF ENHANCED COMFORT is in fact 15 hryvnia, not 115 hryvnia. I go in and eat an awful chicken sandwich next to an urn overflowing with plastic tropical plants. School mistress-like announcements ring out in Ukrainian, echoing across the varnished wooden bar/sandwich kiosk.

I board the 22:12 sleeper to Odessa.

My carriage is royal blue with a lemon yellow line and the numbers '044 10445' on the side (for anyone who is interested). This is carriage nine and I am in berth 31, which has two bunks and one other occupant, Natalia, aged 26, who is on the top bunk opposite my lower bunk.

She has straight dark hair and an inquisitive manner. She wears a white top and skin-tight black trousers. She immediately introduces herself and tells me in English that she is going to Odessa to seek work. 'I am a psychologist,' she says. 'But I think I will get a job in hotel cleaning room. Service. Restaurant help.'

After saying this she asks: 'Do you have wife or girlfriend?'

I explain my romantic situation.

'I am not married and I have no boyfriend,' she says matter-of-factly. Natalia has a deadpan manner and would make an excellent poker player.

The train moves out of the station into pitch-black Ukrainian countryside as Natalia says she intends to work for a few months in Odessa, save money and return to Lviv. Getting a job as a psychologist is difficult in Ukraine.

Laughter breaks out in the next-door compartment – a party is going on. I ask if Natalia minds if I have a beer; I bought an extra one at the kiosk in the rain. She nods that this is fine. I open the can and place it on a little table with a ruby cloth.

'I don't drink. I don't smoke. I don't do anything interesting,' says Natalia, watching me owl-like from her bunk. If she joined the professional poker tour, The Owl might make a good playing name.

She tells me there has just been a festival in Lviv and she shows me pictures of celebrations in a square on her phone. Natalia's friends are dancing with their arms in the air, appearing to have a very good time indeed. She flicks through these for a while as I finish my drink. Some of the other photos show her parents smiling by a table with shot glasses laid out, as well as her home village and some of the sights in Lviv that we saw on the free tour earlier today.

Then we make our beds. Mine requires turning the seat down so the mattress is revealed. Natalia and I say goodnight – and I fall swiftly asleep to the rhythm of the track, only waking once in the middle of the night, somewhere in the middle of Ukraine, when the train stops and the two vacant places on the bunks are filled.

* * *

The morning is grey and dull as the train travels through thick green forest. Natalia and I order green tea from a carriage attendant wearing a blue uniform with yellow lapels. These arrive and Natalia kindly offers me a chocolate biscuit, which I accept.

There are many ranks for Ukrainian Railways employees and the symbol on our attendant's lapel shows that he is the second lowest in the pecking order, a junior chief. Below him there is the rank of private while the ranks above in ascending order are medium chief, senior chief, higher chief, deputy director, first deputy director and director. More than 400,000 people work for Ukrainian Railways. To put this in perspective, the population of Lviv is 723,000. The entire population of Ukraine is 42.4 million. So roughly one in every hundred people in Ukraine works on its railways if I have done my sums right.

Natalia and I eat our biscuits – the other two occupants of the compartment remain asleep – and I calculate from my smartphone that we are near Koshary, about 70 miles from Odessa. This is a long way east of Calais (about 1,500 miles as the crow flies).

Our carriages pass through wide-open countryside with emerald and biscuit-coloured fields. The sky is increasingly leaden, not looking promising at all. Yet squint your eyes and the view from the window turns into an abstract Mark Rothko painting: green and yellow squares (the fields) blending into a high rectangle of moody grey (the sky). As the train moves on, the artwork subtly mutates: bold lines of black emerging here (trees on the horizon), long thin rectangles of brown there (recently ploughed fields), with splashes of red (fields of poppies) or explosions of gold (the glinting onion domes of remote churches) adding to the delicious mix.

We pull into the Black Sea city/resort of Odessa at 08:43. The journey has taken ten and a half hours covering 515 miles, which works out at just 49 miles per hour. Natalia and I say goodbye amid the melee of disembarkation and all the passengers of the 22:12 sleeper service from Lviv traipse down a long, slippery platform in a downpour.

Classical music plays at Odessa Station, a Soviet-era construction with a domed hall, brass depictions of soldiers clutching guns and a television screen showing current Ukrainian army soldiers in training. We are just 100 miles or so across the Black Sea from Crimea and the Russian troops that invaded the country not so long ago are *over there*.

It is not far from the station to the Black Sea Hotel past a beautiful onion-domed church. In one of the low-slung black leather armchairs in the reception I take stock – and hatch a plan. I want to visit Transnistria. John's talk of the autonomous region has got me thinking; just as Rowan had of Ukraine. It is apparently possible to catch a train there, from Odessa to Tiraspol. I approach the hotel manager, Dmitri, to ask his advice.

Dmitri is tall and beanpole thin with dark-framed glasses, loafers and a slick blue suit; he reminds me of the singer Jarvis Cocker. He joins me at my coffee table in the hotel lounge and, before discussing Transnistria, we fall into a general conversation about this and that.

After describing my journey, which I'm finding to be a handy way of breaking the ice this far into my *Slow Trains to Venice* trip, I ask how he feels living so close to an invading army.

'What we have is a very difficult situation,' he says, lighting a cigarette. 'It is depressing. I want to think that the future will be good. We want peace and I want Ukraine to be part of Europe. I would like to visit the cities of Europe, but the situation in our country is very bad. I don't have...'

He rubs his fingers together to indicate money, peering intently at me as he does so.

'We want to live better off. We want to work more, but it doesn't pay. We are angry because of our situation. If you go to Kiev you can see by people's faces that they are very dark. I want to learn English better. I want to go to Europe and work, maybe in Poland or Italy. Pay is better. We have strong army and good police. We feel safe. But I want more money.'

He rubs his fingers and peers again.

Dmitri believes that the Russian invasion has had a bad effect on the Ukrainian economy, particularly on tourism. 'We want to be closer to Europe. We want cars with European registration plates. We want more money.'

More finger rubbing and peering. He finishes his cigarette.

Dmitri arranges for me to take a day tour by taxi to Transnistria; going by train is impossible for a few days, he says, as the service is only occasional.

Which is how I find myself shortly afterwards bumping along in a clapped-out old banger on a potholed road to Ukraine's border with Moldova and its mysterious (to me) autonomous region. The driver speaks no English and smokes continuously as we clatter through farmland with Madonna playing on the car stereo. I call John's contact in Transnistria and remarkably another Dmitri answers and says he would be pleased to show me the sights and that he has a special interest in the autonomous region's train stations. He gives my driver instructions on his location. We soon cross the border, pass a series of downtrodden Soviet apartment blocks and stop at a smart two-storey brick house with a security gate.

My new Dmitri springs through the gate wearing sunshades and a polo shirt. He has a side-parting and a clean-cut look that reminds me of the character Richie Cunningham from the television series *Happy Days* (as played by the actor Ron Howard). I seem to be meeting a series of doppelgangers: Clooney, Cocker and Cunningham, the three Cs. He grins widely and tells the driver to head for Bender Station.

Dmitri and his wife Maria began a tour agency in Transnistria last summer, Go-Transnistria.com. 'I am local,' he says. 'I lived here twenty-seven years, then I studied in Russia and lived in Angola for four years.' He still has interests in Angola as well as in Mozambique. 'We organise long tours in Transnistria but sometimes people get held up at the border. We are trying to develop a government strategy for tourists – nostalgia tours to see the Soviet way of life.'

Transnistria, Dmitri explains, is an independent state within Moldova on a strip of land along the eastern bank of the River Dnister. The region declared independence in 1990 and there was a bloody war with Moldova in 1992. The state is aligned with Russia and Russian is the main language. Its red and green flag comes complete with a hammer and sickle. Transnistria, population 475,000, has its own passport.

'We even have our own currency, the Transnistrian rouble,' says Dmitri, as we park in front of Bender Station.

This station is a throwback to the Cold War. Cyrillic letters run above the entrance with grand columns opening into a hall with sweeping staircases with ornate balustrades and pictures of trains in socialist realism style. The first station here opened in the 1890s but was destroyed by Stalin when the Red Army retreated so the Nazis could not use it. The current station dates from the 1950s and there are very few services. Russia's Nicholas II once visited Bender. Dmitri shows me a few old steam locomotives and carriages in a park to one side of the station. Within one of these is a rail museum (closed).

We go for lunch in a Soviet-style canteen in a bus station. A hearty dish of rice, meatballs and red cabbage alongside a bowl of spicy soup is served by a woman wearing a red Soviet-style uniform. A red painting on a wall depicts Russia. Red flags with hammers and sickles hang by the windows. A meal for two costs a grand total of three euros (£2.69).

Dmitri takes me to a statue of Lenin in a nearby park.

'In Ukraine they destroyed all the Lenins,' he says. 'But we still have him. There is always a place for Lenin in the world. If there was no Lenin, someone would have to invent him.' A visit to the statue, close to an old Soviet cinema, is a key part of his tours – so perhaps he is biased.

Driving onwards we take in the parliament building in Tiraspol and the Great Patriotic War Tank Monument (a Soviet T34 tank from World War Two). Russian flags flutter on lamp posts along the main street. We stop at Tiraspol Station, a long honey-coloured building from Soviet times that lists trains to Moscow in another grand ticket hall. Outside a bar not far from the station's car park, a wobbly-looking man with a Russian flag draped over his shoulders smokes a cigarette.

We jump back in the car and pass the wobbly smoker and more Russian flags on lamp posts. Dmitri departs at his house, where I am introduced to his wife Maria, who kindly gives me a packet of Angolan coffee as a gift. Then my driver hurtles at enormous speed to the border, where we are held up in a queue before zooming in torrential rain, at even greater speed, along the potholed road to Odessa. This is probably the worst drive of my life. A terrible grinding sound emanates from the back suspension. The windscreen wipers don't work properly. We bounce through craters. We slide in mud. No seatbelts work on the back seats. It feels as though we could, at just about any moment, end up a wreck in a ditch.

I vow to stick to trains from now on. They're so much nicer.

Back from the Black Sea
Odessa to Lviv and onwards

In the deluge in Odessa I make a snap decision. Dmitri, the hotel manager, has explained how difficult it will be to take trains south into Romania or west across Moldova. The only border crossing by train with Romania, according to the useful website Rail.cc, is a place called Vadul Siret in Ukraine and Suceava in Romania. However, according to *Europe By Rail: The Definitive Guide* by Nicky Gardner and Susanne Kries, this journey is part of an intimidating ultimate challenge suited only to train pros between Lviv in Ukraine and Belgrade in Serbia and is not one for those pootling about (like me). There are peculiar connections and possible bus journeys. Moreover, the daily trains between Romania and Serbia were axed last summer at short notice. It sounds a nightmare.

Getting to Odessa had seemed such a good idea. Getting out of Odessa to Venice poses problems I should have anticipated. From the Black Sea Hotel I walk through the downpour to Odessa Station and buy a sleeper ticket back to Lviv for tonight. From Lviv I will catch a further sleeper to Budapest in Hungary (at least, this is what I'm hoping). I will have, if all works out, taken three sleeper trains on consecutive nights. I will have become at one with the rails.

I will also be in the right direction for Italy.

While I am in the station the rain miraculously stops and I go for a long walk through the puddles of Odessa.

It is fair to say that a higher percentage of beautiful people live in Odessa than in most cities. Beautiful people who know how to be beautiful. The rain has barely stopped and out they have come in skin-tight clothing, women and men alike. They have perfect poise and perfect grooming. They promenade down Prymorskyi Boulevard towards the sweep of the Potemkin Steps (site of the famous scene in the 1925 film *Battleship Potemkin*), looking effortlessly wonderful. They hang out in cafes and parks and *sushi nightclubs*. They wander into the Sexy Fantasy shops as though intending to purchase groceries. People do not do such things with such grace and glamour in other places such as – for example and completely at random – Milton Keynes or Basingstoke. Not in my experience, anyway.

Even the buildings are beautiful: great baroque and art nouveau edifices from the nineteenth century in shades of pale pink, apple-green and aquamarine. Angels flutter in elaborate stucco above doorways. Nymphs, maidens and muscle-bound gods peer down from rococo facades. Yes, a few buildings here and there are crumbling with neglect, but they are crumbling in a somehow beautiful manner that is tricky exactly to explain.

In a park near the beach by the Black Sea, naval officers in white uniforms with ramrod straight backs walk with their sweethearts. I dip my hand in the jade-coloured water on an almost empty beach as peach light bathes the horizon. Then I go back through the park, buy a cheeseburger from a cafe near the Black Sea Hotel and return to the station.

* * *

The 22:05 to Lviv purrs on a platform. Rain has begun to fall yet again and it feels right to be leaving this beach resort, even after such a short visit. As Robert Louis Stevenson once wrote: 'I travel not to go anywhere, but to go. I travel for travel's sake. The great affair is to move.' In this instance, in Ukrainian Railways style. I have splurged on first class and a female guard wearing a cap at a jaunty angle and bright red lipstick points me to compartment number six saying: 'One, two, three, four, five, six. Six!'

Inside are two beds with crisp linen and pale blue/lilac blankets. There is an oriental-style carpet, a little table with a ruby tablecloth, an oval mirror, a tiny television (which I cannot work), and a plug for charging electronic devices. It is extremely comfortable and, I soon discover, I have it to myself.

We depart a minute late, sliding out of Odessa Station as classical music echoes from speakers.

The female guard asks: *'Chay? Kava? Miloko?'* (Tea? Coffee? Milk?)

I decline and she asks: *'Billety?'* Ticket?'

I show her the ticket, which cost 1,200 hryvnia (£36) and is already, I can tell, going to be worth every penny. The guard goes away and comes back with a bottle of water, pausing in the doorway to eye my possessions. On the table I have placed two bottles of Staropramen lager, *From Russia With Love*, a wash bag and a map of Odessa. Satisfied that I am not breaking any rules she departs. However, she clearly has her eye on me.

Rain streams down the train as we roll through darkness. I turn off the light and look out, catching ghostly shadows of trees and buildings. Sodium lights on empty roads flash by. This is remote landscape. We stop at Podilsk just after midnight. A neighbour starts snoring. Sleep comes fast as the train creaks on.

It is a very good night's sleep and I awake to find the female guard looking into my berth and asking: *'Chay? Kava? Miloko?'* Somehow she has opened the door despite my having locked it; she must have a master key. I say yes to *kava*. She regards me with great scepticism and distrust. She eyes my possessions once again. She is the boss in this first-class carriage; I have no doubt whatsoever about that. She brings the *kava* and I hand over some notes. She nods, apparently satisfied with me for once.

We pass a series of Hapag-Lloyd and Maersk containers by a station where people are walking along old tracks with possessions in plastic bags. How on earth they got there and what they are doing I do not know.

Shortly afterwards, at 07:55, we arrive at Lviv.

* * *

After inquiring about tickets to Bucharest (not available) and Belgrade (impossible, it would seem), I purchase a sleeper ticket from Lviv to

Budapest. It will depart at 21:00 and arrive the following morning at 08:20. I am certainly doing a fair bit of Stevenson-style *moving* now.

A yellow number six tram rattles along to the centre of Lviv, where I have a mission: to see Lychakiv Cemetery. I had completely overlooked one of the city's main tourist attractions, which happens to be a graveyard, the last time I was here.

Lychakiv was created in 1786 and covers 100 acres with more than 400,000 graves. I reach the cemetery up a hill and buy a ticket (the cemetery has official museum status). A map is provided with your ticket, leading you around the many artfully constructed gravestones with sculptures of those buried alongside angels, eagles, lions, urns and towering crosses. Recent pop singers lie alongside artists, historians, composers, politicians and writers spanning the centuries. It's a sunny morning with the sound of birdsong, the occasional peal of church bells and a bewitching sense of serenity.

Back on Market Square near the statue of Neptune I drink coffee and read a tongue-in-cheek article from *The Economist* that explains the intricacies of Lviv, capital of the region of Galicia. It is all quite complicated. If you refer to Lviv as Lviv you may be accused of being a 'Ukrainian fascist who bayonets Polish babies for fun', while if you call the city Lwow you might be called 'a Polish nationalist who bayonets Ukrainian babies for fun'. Spell it Lvov and you open yourself to the accusation of being 'a Soviet mass murderer', while people who refer to the city as Lemberg are Nazis. Quite a lot of controversy over a name, all in all, though I do not think the journalist is being strictly serious.

Candy sellers wearing flowery dresses with old-fashioned corsets and frames walk by the cafe. Plenty of beautiful Odessa-style people are about. More church bells toll. A woman with angel-wings attached to her back glides by on roller skates with a sign advertising a tattoo parlour. Down by the opera house I eat sausages with potato wedges and very hot mustard at a stall. Nearby another stall sells Ukrainian football scarves and a doormat bearing a picture of President Putin. A message in Cyrillic on the doormat says: PUTIN: SHOE CLEANING. I go to Hotel Plazma, where I negotiate a room for a couple of hours rest and to use the shower. I do like Hotel Plazma.

Afterwards, I try to buy a copy of *Venus in Furs* but cannot find a bookshop stocking the unusual work in English; *Venus in Furs* has just got to be an interesting read. Then I return to the station with a copy of *The Ukrainian Week*, an English language magazine, and sit at exactly the same seat at the stall outside the station where I met much-travelled Kevin. I wonder where he has got to now. For all I know he could be in Poland, Peru or Papua New Guinea. Just as long as the money holds out during his fifth midlife crisis.

The editorial in *The Ukrainian Week* calls on the country to prepare itself for a fully-fledged attack from Russia. A 'powerful guerrilla army' is required to stop President Putin if he decides to move on from Crimea to other parts of Ukraine. The nation must be put on an emergency standing. 'Enemy agents' need to be rooted out and preparations made for cyber warfare. Already the National Guard of Ukraine has co-opted a group called Azov Battalion, a radical Ukrainian militia run by volunteers that lead attacks on pro-Russian rebels in eastern Ukraine. It's all going on, not so far away down the tracks.

What a world we live in.

I cross the concourse to Lviv Station, with which I have become quite familiar of late. A red, white and blue train awaits by platform two, close to the HALL OF ENHANCED COMFORT. The 21:00 is ready to roll and so am I.

Ahead lies a journey west with a changing of the bogie (altering the width of the train's undercarriage so its wheels match a new track gauge) at a station named Chop, before entering Hungary at a place called Záhony. It is with a feeling of great anticipation that I find my sleeper compartment and meet a new travelling companion.

CHAPTER SEVEN

LVIV IN UKRAINE TO BELGRADE IN SERBIA, VIA BUDAPEST IN HUNGARY

DODGY POLITICS AND A FEW DRINKS

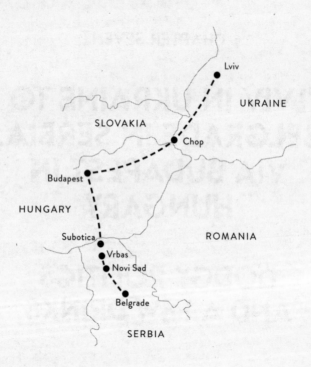

The cabin on the 21:00 sleeper service to Budapest has a three-tier bunk, wooden panels, and a burgundy faux leather seat. This seat converts into what will be my bunk bed. A sink is hidden beneath a small table and there is a cabinet with a mirror, cup holders and a socket for electric shavers. At the end of the burgundy seat sits Leila, an assistant at a solicitor's office in Dublin specialising in personal injury and debt. She is originally from Cape Town. She has an Irish accent, blonde hair and hazel eyes. She wears a black T-shirt and jeans. She drinks a bottle of Pepsi.

Leila has a story to tell.

'I was detained at the Russian/Ukrainian border,' she says, matter-of-factly. 'In Russia everyone needs a visa. I had one but when we got to the border it was half an hour after midnight. The visa had ended at midnight. I got woken on the train from Moscow by Russian border officials who checked my passport.'

The irregularity was discovered.

'I didn't know what the guard was saying. I only know one word of Russian: *spasibo* [thanks]. I had to collect my things and get off the train. I was taken to a hut with loads of officers and detained. They had a debate between themselves and I was held for a few hours. Then a female officer came and said they could extend my visa but that it would cost a thousand roubles.' This is about £12. 'She asked me if I had that and I said I would have to pay by card. Then they all discussed my card for a while. They said they couldn't scan it. So I was walked to a cashpoint and made to take out a thousand roubles. Then I went back to the hut and another officer said I would have to pay a fine of two thousand roubles. They said I had seventy days to do that. Then they made me sign all sorts of documents and give them my bank details. I did what they said.' She pauses. 'I didn't want to be blacklisted from Russia.'

The ordeal ended at 5 a.m. and she had to wait until 5.40 p.m. for an onwards train. She arrived at Kiev at 1 a.m. Leila does not seem too fazed by what happened, even though she only has ten days away and she did not get a chance to see Kiev properly.

Train travellers, I have noticed, like to talk.

I bought two beers at Lviv Station. I open one can and offer Leila the other.

'Actually, I have vodka in my Pepsi,' she says.

She takes a sip.

She talks about Brexit: 'Everyone in Ireland was shocked about that.'

She discusses President Trump: 'I hate him. I really hate him.'

Then Leila asks: 'You don't mind if I vape?'

I say I don't.

Leila begins to vape.

She says: 'I sleep with this under my pillow. If I have a horrible dream, I have a vape. It takes the edge off.'

Leila tells me that she left South Africa for Ireland when she was aged 18. 'Basically, I wanted to get as far away from South Africa as I could.' She took a three-year photography course and worked in a pub for a while.

The train rattles and creaks through the darkness. We must be deep in countryside. No sign of civilisation. No sign of anything.

Leila says that on the train from the Russian border to Kiev the guard made advances towards her. 'He was a greasy guy and he pinched my shoulder and laughed at me. Then he sat next to me and asked if I had a boyfriend. I said I did and he said: "But he doesn't mind that you go on your own to Ukraine?" Then he made a hole with his fingers on one hand and put a finger from the other through it.' She pulls a face. 'I had to tell him that my boyfriend would not like that. He just huffed and went away.'

We pull into Chop and a clanking sound begins beneath the train. It appears that the changing of the bogie has begun.

The noise makes it impossible to sleep. Leila says she once travelled by train from Kashmir to Goa in India: 'I had a few experiences there. Men stared at me the whole time, but that was just normal. If you're on your own, they think they have permission. In one carriage it was awful, though. A man talked to me in Hindu in a deep whisper. I didn't understand him and I felt cornered. The window of the train was so dirty I couldn't even see out of the compartment. Then he started touching himself where he should not be touching himself and I didn't know what to do. I did not want to make a scene. I was stuck. He kept touching himself for quite a while and when we got to a station he got up and went to the bathroom. After that a colonel from the Indian Army came into my carriage and sat down next to me.'

She pauses and has a vape.

'He was OK,' Leila says. The colonel acted as her 'protection' for the rest of the trip. 'I always find something happens to me when I travel. You have to trust people, though, when you're on your own. Something might happen that's bad, but then your faith in humanity is restored.'

Leila has a sip of Pepsi-vodka.

A border official collects our passports. I walk along the corridor and look out to see glimpses of bogie-men beside the track. The banging continues for a long time, at least 90 minutes. Doors slam. Passports are returned. There is a station announcement and we move through the darkness on our new bogie across the River Tisza. We stop in Záhony, where Hungarian border guards check passports and one pokes about in my backpack with great interest as though expecting to discover a gun or goodness knows what. Disappointed by my lack of criminality – and nonplussed by the books and various accumulating city maps – he grunts.

He leaves us and Leila says: 'We could have had a dead body under your seat.' There is a wide space for bags at the bottom of the bunks that the guard did not examine. At around 3.30 a.m., we move on. The border has, finally, been crossed. Documentation and train wheels are in order. We are on our way once more.

The Locomotive Hostel, a spa, bridges and a pub crawl
Budapest

In the morning I fetch tea for Leila and me. We are crossing the Hungarian plains; cowboy-land with tall yellow grass. Leila is going on to Vienna where she has one day before her flight back. She allocated little time at each destination. 'I did this trip for the train rides,' she says. 'I didn't have enough holiday for the Trans-Siberian Express, so I got it into my head to fly to Moscow and head south.'

We move into woodland. Orange light shines across treetops as though the woods are ablaze. Leila asks if she can take my picture. She has an old-fashioned camera with black-and-white film. She prefers this to digital as 'you develop it and half the time you don't even remember what you took'. We exchange emails and the train rolls into Budapest-Keleti Station where I get off and Leila stays on for the rest of her ride.

At the station I visit a ticket office set aside for foreigners where I try to work out *where next*. I am staying overnight in Budapest at the intriguing Locomotive Hostel near the station and have a whole day in Hungary's capital. But I want to keep on the move, perhaps to Belgrade.

This ticket office is manned by a man wearing a florescent jacket and jeans. He introduces himself. His name is David and he is a paramedic student working in the office to earn money to cover his exams. He seems at a loose end. He also seems to be very switched on about Hungarian trains. He quickly establishes that there is a 07:57 service to Belgrade tomorrow that arrives at 16:26. He uses Deutsche Bahn's website to look up the train time. 'It really is the best, we always check with Deutsche Bahn,' he says. This journey will be on a train named after Ivo Andrić, a famous Yugoslav writer.

'It is not a fast train,' he says.

I reply that this is OK with me.

I thank him and say that he was much more approachable than the incredibly grumpy assistant at the regular ticket office, where I had gone first before being directed to the ticket office for foreigners.

'Hungarians are quite rude,' David says. 'They're depressed because of the economy. We are in the top five for suicides and there is a lot of alcoholism. Almost every day there is a train hit.'

I ask him what he means by that.

'A train hit. A suicide,' David says. 'If a train is a hundred minutes late, we know the police are investigating the scene.'

He plans to emigrate: 'A lot of young people want to move abroad now. Here you pay rent and get food and your pay-cheque is gone in one day.' He laughs about this. 'I am planning to go to another country, somewhere I can establish a family and have a nice life. I can't see a future here. You get about four hundred euros a month for a full-time job. It's not enough. I'm going to be twenty-five soon but my parents had a house and a car and me by that age. I am so far behind. My sister says: "When are you going to get a house?" She's much younger so she does not understand. I have no choice. A lot of friends of mine are in their thirties and still living at home. I don't want to be rich. I just want to be able to go to a supermarket and not have to worry about what to buy. Now people get to the counter and have to take things back as they don't have enough. It is awkward and embarrassing.'

David gives me a Deutsche Bahn printout of my route tomorrow. He is the most talkative and friendly ticket assistant I have ever met. I thank him and wish him best of luck.

Then I look around Budapest-Keleti Station. It is one of the grandest stations yet, dating from 1884 with a jaw-dropping entrance flanked with neoclassical columns and rows of figurines. On either side of the high, arched glass-panelled doorway are statues of George Stephenson and James Watt, the Scottish engineer who made great advances with early steam engines. Railways took a while to develop in Hungary as leaders during the Austro-Hungarian Empire were not as keen on trains as in other countries. It was in the late nineteenth century around the time Budapest-Keleti Station was built that interest began to take off.

Inside, rose-coloured marble columns arise alongside murals of classical scenes. Corridors with art nouveau ceiling-lights peel away in long lemon-yellow side buildings. To the left of the entrance is Baross Étterem, a dimly lit restaurant with more neoclassical columns and pink walls. 'Strangers in the Night' is playing when I enter and I am the only customer. A white grand piano stands to one side below a chandelier with many broken bulbs. Budapest-Keleti Station is a bit worn around the edges: crumbling plaster, tattered curtains, pollution-stained stone... quite splendid but also quite shabby.

My Hungarian sausage omelette is first rate, served swiftly by a cheerful waiter in a waistcoat. Other dishes include fried goose-liver, beef stroganoff, goulash (of course) and stuffed cabbage served Transylvanian style.

The waiter begins to lay a very long table close to mine. I ask him if a party is in the offing. Yes, he says: the Hungarian women's water polo team is coming for lunch. They are stopping by on a train after a tournament. They are, he says, ranked second in Europe and much loved in Hungary.

Baross Étterem is the perfect place for a post-train meal.

I cross a square to find the Locomotive Hostel. This is tough, at first. However, after a bit of walking up and down the street (and around the block), I eventually locate a tiny sign above a doorway that says 'LOCOMOTIVE HOSTEL' in small red letters on a piece of gold paper. It's next door to a women's high-heel shoe shop and a short distance from SEX SHOP. I press buzzer 14 as instructed by a message on the gold sign and climb a staircase to a balcony overlooking an inner courtyard. Here, a man with a whiskery face emerges and opens a door into a little apartment with pictures of ancient locomotives covering the walls. A couple of Israeli backpackers are lounging on a sofa. I am shown to my room, which comes, rather surprisingly, with a four-poster bed adorned with strips of red fabric that remind me slightly of those hung on a butcher's door. Unusual. It is not en suite; there is a communal bathroom. From my room I have a view straight across to Budapest-Keleti Station.

The man with the whiskery face, I learn, resides at the top of wooden steps on a makeshift mezzanine level. He is usually, I find, sitting at a computer on the mezzanine level with the sound of his tapping keyboard fluttering down to the little reception below. Maybe he is writing a Hungarian novel. Maybe he just likes to send lots of emails. The man with the whiskery face is not the owner. When I ask who is, he tells me that the owner is away and that he 'likes trains very much', hence the hostel's theme. Which is a pity. It would have been interesting to talk to a Hungarian rail enthusiast who is so keen on trains he has opened one of the world's two such locomotive-themed hostels. The other? Near the station back in Wrocław.

* * *

From the Locomotive Hostel, I go down a hill heading for a famous Budapest attraction.

When you have spent three nights in a row on sleeper trains in eastern Europe it is a good idea to do what I am about to do: go straight to the River Danube to visit the Gellért Baths thermal spa for a long soak.

It's a long walk along a straight road lined with elegant nineteenth-century buildings to the river, where I come to a suspension bridge and a line of luxurious cruise ships moored by the riverbank. I turn in the direction of the sleek ships with their tinted windows, aft deck pools and cocktail bars; I need to pass the moorings to reach the Gellért Baths. As I cross a road to get to the riverbank a thirty-something American couple joins me. They appear to be heading back to their ship.

They have just gone jogging (rather than see the sights) and appear to be in a foul mood (despite their fancy, no doubt jaw-droppingly expensive, cruise ship holiday).

She: blonde, toned, tanned and in gym gear. 'I wonder what the population of Budapest is,' she snaps at her partner.

Her partner: blonde, toned, tanned and in jogging shorts. 'Google it!' he replies with a deep sigh.

She, snappily again, but this time also angrily: 'What?'

He, sounding as though she is bugging him: 'Google it!'

She, sounding sarcastic: 'Oh, yeah.'

They cross the gangplank to their ship, ready to be whisked in a plush cabin to another historic European city to go for a run and bicker after their all-inclusive breakfasts, lunches and dinners.

Train people are so much better than cruise ship people.

The population of Budapest is, for the record, 1.7 million.

More fabulous nineteenth-century mansions with ornate stucco and grand towers line the riverfront by the ships. These must be some of the best places to live in the whole of Hungary. Beyond the dream boats, apricot-coloured trams rattle across an elegant green metal cantilever/suspension bridge. I follow the trams westwards, crossing the glimmering river on this fine bright day. On the other side, straight ahead, is Gellért Baths.

These baths are connected to the Gellért Hotel on the Buda side of the city. The entrance is through a spectacularly ornate, totally OTT doorway with stone carvings of bathers in various states of undress. Inside is a beautiful hall with tropical plants, long burgundy-leather banquettes, high arched skylights and multi-coloured stained glass. The atmosphere is humid from hot water emanating from pools in chambers deep within the basement. Art nouveau lamps with brass fittings illuminate hidden alcoves in which marble sculptures of partially dressed maidens lurk. The motif on the mosaic floor is of little blue fish nibbling at what look like coral reefs.

You enter the bathing area via a turnstile flanked by pink marble columns. A long corridor leads to changing rooms and a kiosk selling swimming caps (which must be worn in the pools). If you have booked your own changing booth, you simply leave your clothes there, don your swimming costume and cap, and lock the door to return later; no locker required.

Inside the pool area are a dozen or so pools with temperatures ranging from 26°C to 38°C. All around are Roman-style columns and art nouveau decorations: panels decorated with tiled floral arrangements, golden cherubs and swirling geometric patterns in aquamarine and lilac. Fountains shaped like lions and figures from Greek antiquity spurt water from their mouths in the shallows. This is not your average municipal swimming bath.

I swim a few lengths in the main pool, about 25 metres long and presided over by a rotund bald man who sits on a chair at one end and keeps an eagle eye out for any digression from rules. He spends little time in this chair as about every two minutes or so a fellow bather has the temerity to enter the pool cap-less. 'Eh, eh!' the rotund bald man says, waving his arms in the direction of the offender, who may not notice at first. 'Eh, eh!' he repeats, patting his head to indicate 'Where's your swimming cap?' The offender (most cap-less bathers appear to be aware of their guilt), feigns innocence in a 'this can't be anything to do with me' manner. Eventually, however, the offender is shamed out of the pool and the rotund bald man briefly takes his place once more on his chair before repeating his routine.

After a while, I enter a side chamber glittering with golden decorations and dazzling pink and apple-green tiles. The water here is in the high 30°Cs and contains sulphate, magnesium, calcium and many other minerals that are said to be good for you. This is, I can vouch, the perfect place to loll about for a while after a series of long train rides in Europe. Muscles loosen. Aches ease. The rattle of the track seems a distant memory. You need moments like these on a long, slightly crazy rail extravaganza like mine.

The Gellért Baths first opened in 1918 and have been recently restored to their original design following patch-up work to damage caused during World War Two. They are simply brilliant. Whether you visit Budapest by train, plane or even (Lord forbid) cruise ship, make a beeline for Gellért. Just don't forget your swimming cap.

* * *

Feeling refreshed, I do a bit of gentle *train investigation*.

My first destination is Budapest-Nyugati Station; *'nyugati'* means 'western' in Hungarian while *'keleti'* translates as 'eastern'.

To get there I do one of the most wonderful things you can do in central Europe: I take a slow stroll in the sunshine along the River Danube in Budapest. This is especially marvellous if you are in a Zen-like zone after a session at Gellért, as I am.

The reason it is such a great experience is Budapest's bridges. There are 14 in all and they are of course crucial to the city's identity. With Pest on the side of the Gellért Baths, and Buda on the other, the bridges of Budapest provide the cohesion that make the city one, although the origins of the oneness of Buda and Pest date back to before the bridges.

A symbiosis between the settlements on the two banks of the Danube has existed for centuries, but the first permanent bridge across the river was constructed in 1849: the famous Chain Bridge, which has become a symbol of the city. I'm heading that way, but first I re-cross the elegant green metal cantilever/suspension bridge by Gellért. This is now known as Liberty Bridge, although it was once Emperor Franz Joseph Bridge; the ruler of the Austrian-Hungarian empire inserted the final silver rivet upon its opening in 1896.

I don't make it to the other bank, at first at least. Halfway across I pull myself up on the low-hanging metal suspension chain, easily done, and sit amid the rivets to have a picnic. On the way over I had seen others doing this and more have taken their place. At a stall near Gellért I bought a sandwich and a small bottle of chilled white wine (a tipple of some sort or other, I had noticed earlier, seems de rigueur among the Liberty Bridge picnickers). On a good day such as today, this is highly recommended.

To the left are the tree-clad hills of Buda upon which medieval rulers and later Ottoman invaders built palaces and fortifications; the latter particularly enjoyed the local hot springs and some of the baths in Buda (though not Gellért) date from the period of Turkish control between 1541 and 1681. To the right is the sprawl of art nouveau and neoclassical loveliness along the riverbank leading to the centre of Pest. Straight ahead is a dazzle of light on the olive-green Danube, the bridges in the distance arching across the surging river, each seeming to underline Hungarian determination to conquer this mighty waterway. Sitting between the rivets of Liberty Bridge is a good place to consider the incredible feats of engineering required to tame the Danube. Despite being one of the shortest of the city's bridges, Liberty is still a remarkable 333 metres wide.

It is also a vantage point to consider bygone times: the times of the Celts, the Romans, Magyar tribes, the Tatars and Turks, before the Hapsburg and Austrian-Hungarian days and the post-World War Two communist influence with the infamous 1956 uprising, when Soviet tanks crushed the revolt, rumbling down the streets beside the Danube. The country's first independent elections were held in May 1990 after the fall of the Iron Curtain the previous year; Soviet tanks and troops eventually withdrew in July 1990.

Like a good bridge picnicker, I eat my ham sandwich, drink my chilled white wine and relax by the rivets, which were blown away where I'm sitting during World War Two. All Budapest's bridges were destroyed by the departing Germans then but Liberty Bridge was the first to be repaired and reopened, in August 1946. With the sun blazing down and wine flowing, it is eerie to remember that this very point was once laden with dynamite by a German sapper. I watch as a dream boat with a busy cocktail pool slides beneath us heading southwards. A day-trip tourist vessel churns north towards Chain Bridge, a muffled microphone commentary rising. Above, mythical Hungarian falcons gaze inscrutably upon the scene from masts above the suspension towers. This must be one of the best picnic spots in central Europe, if not anywhere.

The river walk to Chain Bridge takes me back past the tinted windows of the fancy cruise ships to Elisabeth Bridge, which was finally rebuilt after World War Two in 1964. Long swoops of white suspension sweep across the river, which is just 290 metres wide here; Elisabeth is the shortest of Budapest's bridges and is a key link for the city, with six lanes for vehicles. Its suspension cords are held in place by two giant white arches that look somehow megalithic: metal reincarnations of prehistoric stones, on a giant scale.

Next up is the real biggie of Budapest bridges. I walk on along the banks past moorings for tourist boats, with the spidery, ethereal outline of Chain Bridge rising ahead. The sleepy little Thames-side town of Marlow in Oxfordshire may feel a million miles from a central European city that was once the co-capital of mighty empires. Yet there is an unlikely connection. William Tierney Clark, the British engineer who designed the 72-metre suspension bridge across the Thames at Marlow, which opened in 1832, was much admired by the local Count István Széchenyi, who called upon Clark to create a version for the Danube. This he duly did and in 1849, after nine years of construction, with parts made in Britain shipped to Hungary, the bridge opened to great fanfare. This was a highly charged moment at a time when Hungary was asserting its national identity, attempting to break free of the Austrians, and it was also a turning point for its capital. Just 24 years later, Buda was officially merged with Pest and Budapest came into being. To this day Clark, a Bristolian who lived much of his life in Hammersmith in London (he designed the original Hammersmith Bridge across the Thames), is revered in the Hungarian capital.

The result of his work was one of the modern wonders of the world when it opened and remains an iconic European landmark to this day, stretching 375 metres with stone lions guarding each end. It's crowded with tourists taking pictures when I arrive, and I join them snapping away for a while – wondering, as I did back in Lviv at the Irish bar, whether this is really what *travel writer*s ought to do.

But enough about Hungarian bridges!

I cut inland past a Four Seasons hotel and a modern sculpture of a tall, thin woman wearing high heels and a miniskirt in the direction of Budapest-Nyugati Station. The streets around here are lined with well-to-do houses with espresso cafes on corners, hair salons, upmarket restaurants and Mr. Funk doughnut shop (which seems particularly popular).

Before reaching the station, however, my attention is diverted once again. It's hard not to notice a series of protest placards on the edge of Liberty Square.

A little bit of politics in central Europe... to add to all the other issues swirling about along the train lines of the Continent I've encountered so far.

The controversy here centres on the statue's depiction of the Archangel Gabriel (representing Hungary), with an eagle (representing Germany) harassing Gabriel from above. It was, I learn from the placards, secretly installed overnight in 2014 despite opposition from those who believe it fails to recognise Hungary's complicity with the Nazis during World War Two. One says: 'Hungary was a faithful ally of Hitler during the Second World War, being the first in 1940 to join the Axis powers. On March 19, 1944, the arriving German troops were received with bouquets rather than bullets.'

Hungary's prime minister Viktor Orbán, leader of the Fidesz-Hungarian Civic Alliance, is blamed for allowing the monument to be erected – and this is not the only criticism the controversial politician has attracted since gaining power in 2010.

Orbán's fierce anti-immigration policies, which have included the erection of electrified razor wire with heat sensors and cameras along Hungary's southern border, have drawn international condemnation, while his grip on the country's media has strengthened to such an extent that one prominent journalist, Balazs Lang, has said: 'I've been doing this for twenty-five years now but I've had enough. I'm going to quit because there's no point in being a journalist in this country any more.'

As in Poland, Orbán also acted to politicise the judiciary by removing critical judges, and financial irregularities at elections, as well as possible vote rigging, causing some independent observers to question how fair recent parliamentary elections have been. In a further move he has made it a criminal offence for lawyers to assist asylum seekers. Orbán claims that he is creating a new kind of politics: 'illiberal democracy'. Independent observers prefer the description 'authoritarianism'.

Yet more stirrings of discontent in Europe. Yet more disturbing times.

A long train journey across the Continent is eye-opening, and it is not all about what you see from your carriage window.

* * *

Nyugati Station, when I finally get there, is a bit of a let-down: slightly older than its sister station, built in 1877 on the site of the terminus of the country's first railway line between Pest and Vác in 1846. It's another grand affair that could pass for a presidential palace, but it's really rundown, with pigeons seemingly having taken over these days. The station is connected to a dimly lit modern underground station where a woman approaches me and asks: *'Seeeks?'*

At first I do not understand.

Then she leans forward to show me her breasts. *'Seeeks?'*

She potters away asking commuters one after another the same question. She is obviously high on something and desperate to raise some cash to buy something to attain further elevation.

After this encounter I take a tram from Nyugati to the city's railway museum in the suburbs to discover that it is only open at weekends (my mistake). I look over a fence at some carriages from the mid-twentieth century before being told to go away by a plump woman who appears to be an official of some sort.

Train investigation complete, perhaps not as satisfactorily as hoped and with many diversions, I go back to the Locomotive Hostel, where the whiskery man is tapping away and no one else is around.

It's early evening now and I still feel full of energy after Gellért. A leaflet on the table in the empty reception says that a tour of Budapest's 'ruin pubs' will depart from the Lion Fountain on Vörösmarty Square at 8.30 p.m. and that shots are included, although the tour is *so much more than a traditional boozy pub crawl*. This is not a free tour, the price is a few forints, but it sounds promising, even if I'm not quite sure what a 'ruin pub' is.

So begins my Big Night Out in Budapest. A small group has formed by the Lion Fountain. A guide named Rita is in charge. She has a theatrical, flamboyant manner – and says she's about to take us to four former warehouses and meat-processing plants that have been converted into pubs.

As we head off on our way to 'ruin' I meet my fellow comrades in search of good times one by one. It's all very social – and rather random. I never quite know where conversations will go next. Which is how it should be on a good boozy, who-cares-what-happens night out.

On the way to Ruin Pub Number One, and continued within it, a bearded man from Portland, Oregon tells me that there is an 'educational crisis in America: it's gonna kick the US in the ass in ten years' time'.

'Why's that?' I ask.

''Coz there won't be anyone to run anything anymore,' he replies.

'Who's to blame?' I ask.

'Inequality, man. Inequality's to blame. If you ain't got nothin', you ain't goin' nowhere. And more people these days ain't got nothin', man,' he says.

We all drink bright green shots in a courtyard of what looks like a former mechanical garage discussing inequality in the US and elsewhere for a while. A few of us, me included, buy beers on top of this. We down our drinks pretty quickly... and move on.

On the way to Ruin Pub Number Two, down a twisting lane leading to who knows where, another American, from Florida, talks about his favourite holiday spots. He is gargantuan and works in some capacity in the airline business (I never quite find out what capacity). He clearly gets about a bit.

'My number one place for food? Guess!' he challenges me.

'France?' I suggest, with the entire globe at my disposal.

'Wrong! Wrong! Argentina!' he exclaims, before challenging me once more: 'My number one place for scenery?'

'The Grand Canyon,' I tentatively try.

'Wrong! Very wrong! Positano in Italy!' he replies. We reach Ruin Pub Number Two where we are all delivered bright red shots and a few of us, me included, buy beers on top of this. Ruin Pub Number Two is the former meat-processing plant, now draped in tea lights and with a DJ spinning discs.

'My number one for atmosphere?' asks my new gargantuan American friend, who seems to be full of such questions and quite certain of their answers.

I down my bright red shot and take a punt on Venice.

'Wrong, wrong, wrong! How very wrong!' he says with great aplomb, flailing his arms to demonstrate my answer's complete and utter wrongness.

'Rome!' he thunders.

'But of course!' I reply.

'Rome for atmosphere. Oh, Rome!' he says, drinking a great gulp of beer to mark the finality of his opinion.

We move on to Ruin Pub Number Three. On the way to this one, set in a former warehouse of some description (I believe it once housed rope), Elizabeth from Maryland – there are a lot of Americans on the pub crawl – says that she and her husband sold their house to go on a round-the-world trip that has lasted two years so far. She advises me, as though letting me in on a secret on a par with who really killed JFK, not to book any rooms in Europe described on the internet as *cosy*.

'Cosy just means small,' she says dismissively. 'Never, never trust cosy! That much I can tell you.'

At Ruin Pub Number Three, we are given bright blue shots and a few of us, me included, buy beers on top of this. Spencer, yet another American, tells me he has decided to continue from this point onwards with a drink in each hand at all times. He is aged 19 and travelling in Europe with his father, who felt unwell this afternoon and ducked out of going on the tour at the last moment, allowing Spencer the freedom of Budapest's ruin bars.

For quite some time Spencer bewails the minimum age limit of 21 for drinking in most US states. 'I mean, come to Europe, man,' he says, 'and you've really gotta make the most of it, man!' He appears uncertain at times whether to drink from his left hand or his right, such is the marvellous freedom of the drinking laws for 19-year-olds in the European Union.

Spencer confides after a while that he is named after Winston Churchill's middle name (Churchill cropping up again). His parents, he says, made the gesture as a nod towards Britain and America's special relationship.

Spencer's timing as far as drinking is concerned is impeccable. Just as we are about to head off to Ruin Pub Number Four, he finishes the last drops of both his left- and right-hand beers... and we all move on, again.

On the way to Ruin Pub Number Four I talk to my first non-American, Christoph, a mechanical engineer from Germany. He is discussing the European Union.

'The EU, oh, the EU! I like it as a concept, but oh, the EU!' he says.

'What do you mean?' I ask.

'Where does the money go? Where?' Christoph asks rhetorically. 'We don't know where the money goes. Do you know where it goes?'

'In Britain, farmers and areas of economic disadvantage do quite well...' I begin, but Patrick, also from Germany and who has been listening to us, cuts in: 'The EU is good for the new members building roads, trains and stadiums: Poland, Romania. That's what the EU is good for. Is it good for the big countries?'

At Ruin Pub Number Four, another warehouse (I believe this one once held spices), I get talking to Rita. We are all given bright pink shots this time and a few of us, me included, buy beers on top of this (Spencer, naturally, has two). As hip-hop blares from the sound system, Rita tells me that tour-guiding is only one aspect of her employment. She also teaches dance and works as an IT headhunter. In addition, she is a political science undergraduate and the leader of a Catholic youth group.

'This must be the world's only pub crawl led by a Catholic youth group leader,' I suggest.

'These are not pub crawls!' Rita replies as though affronted by such a suggestion (but not really). 'They are pub tours!'

The Americans, Christoph, Patrick and I keep going for a while in Ruin Pub Number Four after saying goodbye to Rita at the official end of our 'pub tour'. Unofficially, the pub tour goes on.

My *Lonely Planet* guidebook for Budapest warns about 'drop-dead gorgeous women' in Budapest who approach and suggest going to nightclubs where drinks can cost a fortune. No such women come anywhere near us during our unofficial extension to the tour. Maybe, by this stage, we simply do not look as though we have the euros (or are just not worth the bother).

At some hour, somehow, I return to the Locomotive Hostel.

It's been a good night out.

Spur of the moment
Budapest to Vrbas in Serbia

In the morning I get to know the German rail enthusiasts.

They are at Budapest-Keleti Station and have travelled to Hungary from Nuremberg by rail as part of an organised group. They are about to board a train with a red and yellow 1960 locomotive made by NOHAB, a Swedish company. The engine is, however, the work of

General Motors in America, with no fewer than 16 cylinders and 560 cubic inches per cylinder.

All of this is relayed to me – not that I quite understand – by another Christoph, who tells me: 'I don't like travelling by train. I like trains.'

He is gangly and jolly and has a camera with a long lens hanging around his neck. He is with his gangly, jolly companion, Tina, who also has a long-lens camera. The entire platform is full of similar folk, of varying heights. The mood is euphoric.

'I like to go places and take pictures of trains,' he says. 'I love trains!'

He pauses and ponders what he said earlier.

'Actually, I do really like travelling by train – I was just being silly,' Christoph says.

'What do you like most?' I ask.

He contemplates this for a moment or two. 'The best thing is that you can't change direction,' says Christoph. 'You go where the train goes. You can't go anywhere else. You don't have to *think* too much.'

Tina has been listening to us. 'I like to hear the sound of the engine,' she pipes up, 'that *powerful* sound.' She gazes fondly at the NOHAB locomotive. 'Here it is! The loco is here just waiting to show us her strength.'

They cannot take their eyes off the loco – and it is indeed a handsome locomotive, with its bulbous driver's compartment, smart yellow lines and headlamps. Charmingly, the loco even has a name: *JEANETTE*.

'Like the legendary Santa Fe F-units. Just look at it!' says Christoph, before explaining that the locomotive was sold to Norway and then onwards to Hungary, which bought 20 such locos. How he knows all this stuff, I haven't a clue.

I leave them at their platform and board the 07:57 to Belgrade. My carriage is grey and blue and empty. A whistle blows. The horn hoots twice. We pull away and the swarm of German rail enthusiasts turns to take a look, beaming broadly and waving. The horn hoots once more. The German rail enthusiasts cheer. What a jolly send-off from Budapest-Keleti Station.

It's not always been so cheerful around here of late. During the summer of 2015 a large Syrian refugee camp grew up around the station, which was evacuated and at one point all trains to the West were cancelled. Syrians waved tickets and toddlers in the air, chanting 'GERMANY! GERMANY!' to express their annoyance with Hungary and their appreciation of the immigration policy of the German chancellor, Angela Merkel, who said she would accept refugees in the country. When trains had been running Austria was angry; and when Austria let trains continue to Germany many German politicians (not Merkel) were angry, too.

At the time, Merkel said: 'Germany is a strong country and the motive must be: *we've managed so much, we can manage this*. If Europe fails over the refugee question... it will not be the Europe we imagined.'

Budapest-Keleti Station became a symbol of the refugee crisis. One Syrian woman gave birth to a child in front of the station. Sanitary conditions were dreadful for those huddled by the lovely crumbling facade featuring Stephenson and Watt. Just eight squalid portable toilets were supplied for the hundreds stranded there. After a lengthy wait for a train north many resorted to walking or hitching lifts to cover the 125 miles to the Austrian border, despite having paid for expensive tickets. Eventually the camp cleared.

In response to world scorn, Viktor Orbán said that he was defending Christianity against a Muslim influx: 'Everything which is now taking place before our eyes threatens to have explosive consequences for the whole of Europe. Europe's response is madness. We must acknowledge that the European Union's misguided immigration policy is responsible for this situation. Irresponsibility is the mark of every European politician who holds out the promise of a better life to immigrants and encourages them to leave everything behind and risk their lives setting out for Europe. If Europe does not return to the path of common sense, it will find itself laid low in a battle for its fate.'

Stations have stories, as I have said previously, and this one is fresh in the memory (and it stinks).

The *Ivo Andrić* Budapest–Belgrade service spins south along the track taken by Leon Trotsky in 1912 when he was working as a reporter for *Kievskaya Mysl*. Of this journey he wrote that 'although the railway line proceeds mainly in a southerly direction, from the cultural standpoint one moves eastward'. The landscape is flat as a pancake with emerald fields beneath a pale sky. We stop to let on an elderly woman with a shopping trolley at Kunszentmiklós. Then comes a series of stations: Fülöpszállás, Soltszentimre, Csengőd, Tabdi and Kiskunhalas.

Tabdi Station has neat beds of pink flowers and a station controller with a red peaked cap. A fierce-looking conductor with an almost completely shaven head, other than a peculiar warrior-like ponytail, sits opposite me and regards me wordlessly (and offputtingly). A yellow field speckled with crimson wildflowers leads to a copse of spindly trees with white blossom. A burly Hungarian border guard enters the carriage, requests my passport and asks: 'Thomas Doyle?' Doyle is my middle name.

'Yes,' I reply.

'Where are you going?'

'Belgrade,' I say; at least I think I am.

'OK, have a nice trip.'

Border movement *in this direction* is possibly easier than in the other.

After the razor wire we arrive at Subotica Station in Serbia. Here the conductors change. Police sit at a table on the platform gesticulating to one another as though discussing heated politics. We draw out of Subotica past a train shed with broken windows and crumbling walls. Graffiti says 'SMILE'. This is a very slow train indeed. We stop at Bačka Topola, where passengers disembark and step across the tracks. After this the train startles a deer in a field, the creature racing away as though chased by a wild cat.

At Vrbas Station, next up on this route, I do something I had not expected to do.

I get off.

I want to be lost for a while.

It is not difficult in this part of northern Serbia to do just that. I cross the tracks with a couple of other passengers and watch the graffiti-covered carriages of the 07:57 to Belgrade roll into the distance. That is that. I enter a lime-green ticket hall. I regard a little station bar at which people are talking with great animation. I ask a man cleaning his car in the parking lot how to get to the centre of Vrbas. He points to the right and says: 'Two kilometres.'

I set off in this direction past houses with picket fences that remind me of small-town USA. Kids play basketball. A silo appears with 'VITAL' written on the top. The road bends towards the centre of town, sycamore trees providing shade. Vrbas seems a well-organised, nice place to live. The sound of a manual typewriter taps from the window of an office. A MAXI supermarket and a BALKAN BET bookies are open for business. I draw some Serbian dinars from a cashpoint. Then I wonder what I am going to do in Vrbas.

Serendipity, serendipity – I must remember the wise train words of the masters, Gardner and Kries.

The Panorama 15 cafe looks inviting. A terrace opens into a bar with pink and lime-green chairs. A tall waiter with an orange T-shirt approaches. He speaks English and asks in rapid-fire style: 'Where have you come from, Budapest? How did you get the idea to come here? Where are you from, London?'

He seems to know most of the answers ahead of the questions. I fill in a few gaps.

His name is Alexander. 'I have been to Felixstowe,' he says. 'I was a seaman: chief of staff of the stewards and cooks on a cargo ship. For two years I conducted this role. Then the salary came down too much. They were employing people from Indonesia, China and the Philippines for one thousand one hundred dollars a month. I had been getting one thousand nine hundred dollars. It was too much of a pay cut. So I left.'

These are his first, and final, words to me as he calls over to the cafe's owner, Peter Vujicic, who is clearly the official spokesperson of the Panorama 15 cafe.

The waiter departs. The owner and I sit beneath a tree in a courtyard – and we talk about this and that.

Peter is a former professional basketball player. He wears a NIKE AIR: AIR FORCE T-shirt and trainers. He has a goatee and a chunky diver's watch. He seems to want to hang out and chew the cud. 'I left home at fifteen to play the game,' he says, referring to basketball. 'I went to play for Hemofarm in the city of Vršac in the north-east near Romania. That was one of the best clubs in Serbia.' He says that Michael Jordan, the American basketball player, is one of the best of all time. He discusses basketball greats for a bit. Serbians, Peter says, like basketball.

Vrbas was once one of the 'biggest industrial cities in Yugoslavia with the biggest sugar refinery, mayonnaise company, and sausage and ham company', Peter continues. There is also a trucks business and a healthy sector of retail clothing shops. Wheat, corn, soya, apricots, apples, strawberries and raspberries are also produced locally. I hope I have got all of this right. The population of Vrbas is 24,000 and the name means 'willow' in Serbian. During the dictatorial regime of Josip Broz Tito (1953–1980) the town was named Titov Vrbas (the Vrbas of Tito).

The Socialist Federal Republic of Yugoslavia, run for much of the time by Tito, existed from 1945 to 1992 covering six republics: Serbia, Slovenia, Croatia, Bosnia and Herzegovina, Montenegro and Macedonia. Belgrade in Serbia was the capital. These republics achieved independence in the 1990s after a civil war and a further conflict broke out in 1999 when Serbian forces emptied the province of Kosovo of its Albanian population. The result? NATO strikes, the withdrawal of the Serb Army and the creation of the autonomous Republic of Kosovo, which is now recognised by more than 100 countries within the United Nations and which declared official independence from Serbia in 2008.

This is, of course, a complicated region. Just look back to 28 June 1914, when Archduke Ferdinand of Austria was assassinated in Sarajevo in Bosnia, prompting the Austro-Hungarian Empire to declare war on Serbia and beginning World War One. Many dreadful deeds have happened in these parts, quite recently. More than 8,000 Bosnian Muslims were killed by Bosnian Serb troops in 1995 and as many as 30,000 expelled from the country. This ethnic cleansing led to a United Nations resolution and convictions for genocide.

Peter is just old enough to remember the NATO attacks. 'They broke down the bridge here. I was four years old and I did not understand. I don't hate anyone. I did not know what was going on. My mother said: "Let's go to the basement again." We'd go down with the grandparents and watch TV and do PlayStation. For kids it was really fun. Adults knew what was happening, but not the kids.'

He pauses and adds: 'The real truth is not in the newspapers. Factories and bridges, they said they did not bomb, but they did.' By *they* he is referring to NATO.

He talks about the train to Belgrade that I intend to catch tomorrow: 'Oh, that train! I meet many women on that train. It was very good for me. I have been to Italy and to France and have travelled by train. Yes, there are good-looking women in those countries. But there is something about the women round here: ah!' He gives a look that suggests that it is impossible to put into words the great qualities of the women of northern Serbia.

I ask Peter if the Panorama 15 cafe has any rooms, but there are none. Instead, Peter walks me round the corner to Hotel Bačka. Peter requests that the receptionist gives me a good price and then we shake hands and part. He has been great company; serendipity in Serbia seems to be in full swing.

Hotel Bačka, it has to be said, is not much of a looker. It's a Tito-era concrete construction that might pass for a multi-storey car park. That's what I had thought it was when I walked past on the way to Panorama 15. Inside is an almost comically grim lounge with grey sofas, faded orange curtains and a bar at the far end. No one, other than the receptionist, is around. She hands me a key and a leaflet for the hotel with a picture of a room with two small single beds. I go up to a room with one small single bed, beige walls and a gold-coloured armchair. Actually, it is quite comfortable. A booklet on a desk says: 'It is not allowed to take explosive weapons, inflammable materials or other dangerous chemicals into the hotel.' Fortunately, I am not breaking any rules. Another instruction is that 'linen is changed once a week, used towels are changed daily'. There are four pages of similar announcements. All fine by me.

I walk along the sycamore-lined street to another cafe at the far end of town, passing a half-built church, a pimped-up purple BMW and a street stall selling strawberries. Here I meet another man from Vrbas, who is quite opinionated.

He is tall and tattooed with a shaved head and shades. He wears black shorts and a black T-shirt. He might pass for a member of a Los Angeles rap group. 'During Yugoslavia,' he says, 'we had one leader under one flag. When he died, a fascist organisation, Croatia, wanted to be separate.'

The man goes on to talk about Kosovo and its Albanian population. He draws a map of Europe and says: 'See, Albania did not exist!' He says: 'Imagine if they came to England and live for a hundred years and have ten kids and did not pay for anything? Now they want this land!'

Bad words are spoken about Tony Blair, Britain's prime minister during the time of the NATO campaign. Bad words are spoken about Croatia. 'If a Serbian goes to Croatia with Serbian number plates, they will have trouble with car, but not the other way round.' Bad words are spoken about Muslim refugees in Europe. England, the man says, will be better off leaving Europe so the country does not have to take any Muslim refugees.

I walk back to the centre of town and go for a kebab at a restaurant Peter recommended earlier and for a drink beneath a tree at Cafe Biblioteka next to the Bambi ice-cream shop. This is a peaceful, relaxing town if you do not talk politics to tall men in black T-shirts.

I return to my room at Hotel Bačka, where I notice that a noisy engine has started up outside my window. Not so peaceful: it sounds as though a plane is about to take off. I go to the reception to complain and the receptionist says that it is a refrigeration unit for the kitchen. 'The meat! The meat! You understand? The drinks can go warm, but not the meat!' He moves me to another room.

To the capital
Vrbas to Belgrade, via Novi Sad

Breakfast at the Hotel Bačka is served in a hall that might seat 300 people.

'You want omelette?' asks the waitress.

'Yes, please.'

'You want tea, milk, yogurt, coffee?'

'Yes, please.'

She nods and departs. Another woman begins to mop the floor. The waitress returns with a well-made omelette with two hunks of bread alongside the other promised food and drink. Not bad. I buy some strawberries from the street stall and purchase some socks from a market near the VITAL silo before heading to the station to catch the 09:26 to Novi Sad.

The train appears on time and I join a carriage filled with students. We enter farmland, where the tracks are lined with banks of poppies. After passing through Stepanovićevo and Kisač, where the train waits for quite a long time by a platform with scurrying lizards, Tito-era apartment blocks mark the edge of Novi Sad, where I disembark at a Tito-era station with a pointy roof with triangular shapes and a ticket hall with Tito-era art depicting railway tracks.

I walk down a long Tito-era street, cross a bridge over the River Danube and ascend a hill to Petrovaradin Fortress. This is Novi Sad's big attraction. It is high on the hill with sweeping views of the Danube, which is big and wide and full of eddies. Petrovaradin Fortress, from the seventeenth century, is the venue for the annual EXIT music festival, which has run since 2001 with Fat Boy Slim, the Beastie Boys and Morrissey having played here over the years. I fall into conversation with a tour guide who is with some Chinese tourists.

Her name is Slada. 'I went to London and to Edinburgh once and there was no rain whatsoever for the whole three weeks,' she says. 'Then I got on the plane to come home and it began to rain that very moment. This is true!'

I ask her about the EXIT music festival. 'During the festival many of the people who come are British,' she says. 'They are very young and very drunk. All day long. Some of the older people in Novi Sad look at the British youngsters and go: tut, tut, tut. There are twenty-five stages and about two hundred thousand people attend over the four days. It is a very positive atmosphere.'

I have a coffee at a cafe by the castle fortifications before returning across the river to go to Museum of Vojvodina. Slada has told me: 'We are keeping three golden Roman helmets at the museum. There are only eleven such golden helmets in the world and we have three of them. It is a miracle. Serbia is full of miracles!'

On the bridge on the way back it is impossible to miss graffiti that has been scrawled in red paint on the walkway: 'SERBIA YES, NATO NO. YANKEE GO HOME.' Then I see the golden fourth-century helmets at the museum. They are dazzlingly beautiful but there only appear to be two of them. I ask an attendant what happened to the other one and he says it has been leant to an exhibition in Milan. The museum also displays various Serbian costumes dating from centuries past and glittering religious icons. It's a good little stop-off. As is the city of Novi Sad. I eat a tasty tuna salad lunch at a cafe with red geranium boxes overlooking the station and catch the 14:56 to Serbia's capital.

* * *

The train, filled with students once again, crosses a metal bridge over the River Danube. We arrive at Beška, where two teenage skinheads disembark, and continue to Inđija, where a long train with cargo wagons piled with railway sleepers occupies the neighbouring platform. At Stara Pazova, a man is curled up on the platform fast asleep. We go through a tunnel and past factories and industrial depots, moving slowly. At 17:17 we arrive at Belgrade Station, 25 minutes late.

My accommodation, Hostel Play, is across the way. Belgrade Station is about to close, to be replaced by a new station in a development known as the Waterfront. The move is not without controversy. Quite a few consider this a mistake as there are doubts the Waterfront will cope with passenger numbers. The station I have arrived at was opened in 1884 and has a classical facade painted yellow. Apparently when the trains stop it is to be turned into a museum. From my tiny room at Hostel Play I can see the entrance across a square busy with trams.

Belgrade is another fine city; the tracks are taking me to some of the finest sights in Europe. I go to the castle on the hill, dropping by at a tourist office where an assistant wearing pearl earrings recommends restaurants on Skadarska Street, where the best Serbian food is to be had. I must try *cevapi* (diced grilled meat) and *lepinia* (a type of bread), and wash it down with *rakija* (plum brandy). She says: 'You will like it here. We are quite literally between East and West. There is Turkish influence. There is Hungarian and German influence. This makes our history so interesting. In the nineties what happened was not so nice. Neighbours destroyed our beautiful country. I would say that sixty per cent of people like the old Yugoslavia in preference of what is here now. The European Union is a copy/paste of the old Yugoslavia. It's very interesting to see how it [the EU] has grown.'

The views from the castle across the River Danube are gorgeous. The food at Tri Šešsira restaurant on Skadarska Street is delicious. I try all the tourist office recommendations. The *cevapi* are like little sausages served sizzling with chopped onions and *ljute papricice*, roasted hot peppers. The *lepinias* are fluffy white buns. The *rajika* is fiery and good. This is a popular joint with tall white candles on the tables and musicians playing folk songs as guests sing along. People smoke and chatter; Serbia is a good place for smokers. An elderly woman dining alone taps her hands to the music, orders *rajika* and begins to sing. Neighbours clap along as she closes her eyes and loses herself in the music.

Serbian serendipity, yet again.

I stroll through streets with nineteenth-century buildings leading down the hill to the soon-to-close Belgrade Station. It is a balmy evening. I go to bed early. Tomorrow I'm heading even further west.

CHAPTER EIGHT

BELGRADE IN SERBIA TO LJUBLJANA IN SLOVENIA, VIA ZAGREB IN CROATIA

'THANK GOD WE DON'T LOOK LIKE WHAT WE'VE BEEN THROUGH'

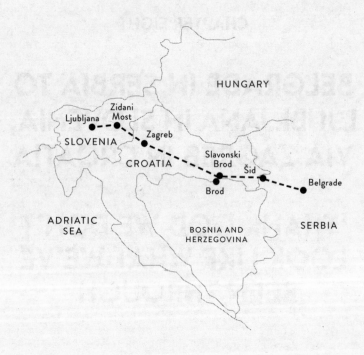

In the morning I am feeling lucky. So I go to the Slot Club next to Hostel Play, opposite Belgrade Station. It appears to be open and I am curious. Who goes to the Belgrade Slot Club on a Sunday morning? At the entrance there is a picture of a brunette woman with a plunging top flicking chips in a seductive manner as though in the chicest casino in Monte Carlo. Inside a couple of potted plants are next to a row of flashing MULTI MAGIC CLASSIC fruit machines. The centre of attention is a mechanical roulette wheel at which a stubbly man and a skinny blonde woman wearing a T-shirt saying GUESS are gambling. These are the only other gamblers. No croupiers are in evidence. I sit opposite and struggle to work out the machine for a while. Then I place 500 Serbian dinars on a few numbers and lose. I am £3.83 down. I place a further 230 Serbian dinars, including 30 Serbian dinars on the number zero. The number zero comes in and I am up 1,480 Serbian dinars (£11.34). Then I lose 280 Serbian dinars and find that, after ten minutes – which is about enough at the Belgrade Slot Club – I have a profit of 700 Serbian dinars (£5.36). A blonde assistant hands over my winnings.

Sometimes on a long train journey in Europe you have to make your own fun.

Outside, I walk up a hill to a bomb site from a NATO attack in 1999. On the map given to me by the tourist office woman a few places are marked with little black bombs and described as 'buildings bombed during NATO bombing'. At the first site, a soldier with cold grey eyes is patrolling the pavement by a crumbling building. I ask him why the building has not been demolished.

'So people remember,' he says.

If I have this right, we are at the former headquarters of the country's ministry of defence. A large mural bearing a slogan in Serbian and a picture of a glamorous female officer in the Serbian Army is on one of the walls of the decrepit building. I ask the soldier what the slogan means and he replies: 'If you know fear you may not be afraid.' He walks away. Outsiders asking questions are not, I sense, the favourite part of his job.

At a second NATO bombing site next to a church, which may be a former television centre, I inspect the half-destroyed structure. I am finding it hard to establish exactly what is what, so this may be the former television centre or it may be somewhere else altogether. The site is close to the neoclassical National Assembly of Serbia, where posters say: 'KIDNAPPED AND KILLED CIVILIANS BY ALBANIAN TERRORISTS 1998–1999, WAR CRIMINALS PROTECTED BY NATO, FAMILIES OF MURDER VICTIMS WANT JUSTICE.' Beside these messages are many pictures of the deceased. Another sign says: 'PERSECUTION OF SERBS. USA, NATO AND EU PROTECT ALBANIAN WAR CRIMINALS.'

I mention all of this to point out that tension regarding this recent war in Europe clearly remains high in Serbia. That much I already understood from the tall man in the black T-shirt in Vrbas.

'They killed the cow for a steak'
Belgrade to Zagreb in Croatia, via Slavonski Brod

It is tricky boarding the 10:25 to Slavonski Brod. For a start there does not seem to be a departure board. Queues at the ticket office are long and slow. After reaching the window and having written: 10:25 CROATIA – PLATFORM? on a piece of paper, considering this the easiest way to get my message across as it does not seem likely the kiosk assistants speak English, all I am told is 'International' by a bored-looking woman with glazed eyes.

I make a gesture that indicates 'I don't understand'.

The woman with glazed eyes fixes her glaze on me and says, a little more assertively this time, 'International.'

The man in the queue behind me, a local, witnesses this.

'So unbelievably rude. This is just the Balkan way,' he comments deadpan.

Then he tells me that the 10:25 to Zagreb will depart from platform one.

I thank my neighbour. Then I go to the train and show my Interrail Pass to a guard.

'You must have a seat reservation,' he says.

'Why?' I ask.

'I don't know why – my boss tell me,' he replies.

So I return to the ticket queues, where I notice there is a special one for International. I wait in this for quite a while, buy a seat reservation and just make the train on time.

Belgrade Station is due to close in a month's time. I won't, I am afraid to say, miss it all that much.

With a loud whistle the filthy, graffiti-splattered train departs. We crawl across a rusty metal bridge. A woman with blue hair, a nose ring and a tattoo of a skeleton sits opposite me. Next to her an elderly woman in black whispers into a mobile phone. The woman with blue hair falls asleep. Rain pelts on the roof. It is a dreary day in the Balkans. The sky is moody grey and damp eucalyptus trees line the track.

At Šid Station a lot of passengers get off, as well as several Serbian police officers. We are close to the border with Croatia. New policemen in blue baseball caps enter and check passports. Clanking comes from the front of the train; it would appear that the locomotive is being switched. After about half an hour we move on and a sign says 'REPUBLIKA HRVATSKA'. A Croatian flag flutters next to a European Union flag; Serbia is a candidate for EU membership, while Croatia is already a full member.

This railway has two literary connections. It is the track taken by James Bond in *From Russia With Love*. It is also on this line, somewhere between Vinkovci and Slavonski Brod, that the train breaks down in *Murder on the Orient Express*.

The smell of cigarettes wafts into the carriages. We pass a concrete bunker that seems to date from the 1990s war. I get off at Slavonski Brod – one of a handful to do so – and enter a silent Tito-era ticket hall. The floor is beige, the windows are tinted. The only other occupant is a woman wrapped in a blanket wearing a Sherlock Holmes-style hat. She appears to be a permanent resident of the Tito-era ticket hall. I try to work out train times for tomorrow, before walking to the city centre in bright sunshine and wondering what I am doing in Slavonski Brod.

As in Vrbas, I have decided to go off piste. Slavonski Brod is a city with a population of 60,000 known for its metal works (trains are, apparently, made here using metal produced in this works). There is also a brewery and good farming in the surrounding countryside. Slavonski Brod is on the River Sava and visitors can cross to Brod in Bosnia, a corresponding city on the opposite bank.

From the station it is about a mile-long walk into the city centre past Tito-era apartments and a tennis club. I find my guest house near a square with many cafes by the meandering river. Hardly anyone is about. Slavonski Brod feels like a place to disappear into for a while: off the map, a complete hideaway.

I ask the guest house owner how long it takes to walk to Bosnia and she says that it is best to take a taxi across the bridge.

I ask if the local Croatians and Bosnians get on well.

'All my family are born *here*. I have no family born *there*,' she replies.

Her implication is clear. She does not *need* to get on with the Bosnians across the river.

'When you go over there you will see it's pretty poor in parts: *anachronistic*,' she says. 'If you ask for some help, they will rob you.'

She pauses. 'I don't have nothing on them. They have enormous problems. I feel sorry for them. My husband was in the army. He was fighting for Croatia. Bosnian people are so nostalgic for the old days of Yugoslavia as they could come here and work. But not now.'

She talks about Serbian strikes during the 1990s civil war that killed local children. A monument to 402 kids who died in Croatia is in a nearby park.

'It was very, very opposite to UN rules,' she says. 'The war did not happen in Serbia. The war happened here.'

By this she means that the on-the-ground fighting happened outside Serbia, which was of course attacked directly by airborne NATO strikes during the Kosovo War of 1998–1999.

It does not take long, at all, for the subject to turn to war and politics in this part of the Balkans.

* * *

The bridge over the River Sava was destroyed during the 1990s civil war. We drive across the car-less new structure. On the other side my taxi driver tuts a great deal when he sees the queue of vehicles waiting to cross in the opposite direction. Drivers are being held for long checks. He will be stuck for quite a while on his return.

'Can you please take me to the centre of Brod?' I ask.

'This is it,' he replies.

I get out and look about.

There is not much going on in Brod.

I am by a burnt-out apartment block by the Sava that seems to be a remnant of the war. At the base of the tower someone has painted an Israeli flag, and another person has written over this '**** ISRAEL'. A solitary fisherman stands by the water's edge near a weeping willow. Nobody else is around. There is a pharmacy, a hair salon and the Fish Bar. In the latter the majority of the population of Brod seems to be lounging in purple armchairs drinking coffee and smoking. A football game flickers on a television. No one watches the game. Quiet conversations and darting eyes are the order of the day. It is as though I have entered someone's living room.

I cross the road and take a seat at Caffe Pizzeria Aleksandria. This has a view of the border crossing by the bridge. I cannot pretend that Brod, which was under Serb control during the 1990s conflict (hence the continuing animosity in Slavonski Brod), is full of exciting tourist sights or especially charming; the Bosnian town fails on both counts. All I can say is that the town does not feel remotely as though it is part of Europe. Brod seems cut off and forgotten: within Europe but somehow another place altogether, as if in a time capsule of 20 years or more. Nothing much seems to have moved on here for a long while now. The damage caused in the conflict remains clear to see and the tensions of the war are apparent in the strict border checks across the River Sava.

The ham-and-cheese pizzas at Caffe Pizzeria Aleksandria are, however, excellent. I sit by a window facing the bridge, watching vehicles slowly passing across after lengthy encounters with border guards. Yes, this may not be a typical tourist destination but it is *interesting* to visit Brod: to see the effects of a recent war in Europe up close and personal. Yet another reminder of the fragility of peace on the Continent that Père Xavier Behaegel back in Lille was talking about.

I return by foot to Slavonski Brod.

On the other side of the River Sava, a rail enthusiast has restored two steam locomotives, a tram and a steam roller in a little park. The oldest loco is from 1926 and is narrow gauge and was made at the First Yugoslav Wagon, Machinery and Bridge Factory in Slavonski Brod. Little noticeboards give all the details: maximum speed, weight, exact track gauge and so on. A very thorough Croatian rail enthusiast lives hereabouts.

Back in the main square at the delightfully named Navigator Cafe Bar Disco Club, I knock back a *rakija*. Almost everyone smokes and almost no one else is drinking alcohol; coffee is the order of the day. The cafe-goers are young, student-aged. There are not a great many, but it's lively with caffeine-fuelled gossip, laughter and tinny pop music. Gentle pink and lilac light fades over the Sava as evening sets in. Couples wander arm in arm through the square and along the waterfront as the sun drops on the horizon and streaks of crimson rise above distant hills before darkness envelopes the landscape. The river flows sedately by, seemingly in no hurry, its olive surface alive with eddies and swirling currents. Of all the places the trains have taken me since leaving Mortlake, to Clapham Junction, Dover and beyond, this is the most peaceful. The troubles of recent times on the Croatian side of the river may be far from forgotten, but a calm way of life has returned that seems at odds with the anxious border at Brod, the broken buildings and sense of desolation I felt across the bridge.

After a nightcap at the Navigator Cafe Bar Disco Club, I return through empty streets to the comfortable little room in my guest house.

Like Brod, Slavonski Brod is also a backwater, so incredibly quiet, if not nearly as cut off as its neighbour across the river – and it reveals an aspect of membership of the European Union that countries in western Europe sometimes fail to consider: *emigration* is as big a problem here as *immigration* is in other places. The youngsters I have seen hanging out in the main square this evening, many of whom will have been taught at the first-rate local college, may not be sticking around for long. The pressure to move away to earn better pay abroad is creating, as the guest house owner sadly says when I return from the Navigator Cafe Bar Disco Club, a brain drain that many believe threatens to cripple backwaters in the Balkans for decades to come. After I mention the students in the square, she ruefully comments: 'Yes, we have them *now*. But for how long? When they go they rarely come back.'

The city's deputy mayor, Hrvoje Andrić, put it succinctly in a recent interview: 'These young people are a strategic resource of the Croatian republic. I tell them: "Each one of you is worth more than a freshwater spring or a beach on the coast." It's hard to look at these people and think that at least half of them will be gone in months.' Andrić was making his comments at a graduation ceremony. 'We are doing our best to improve the town. But central government has no idea how to stop this happening. We have to have some return value on these people or it's not fair.'

Slavonski Brod is an odd place to stop on the train from Belgrade through the Balkans, but an intriguing one with a sense of tranquillity down by the Sava – and the shadows of recent history heavy in the air.

* * *

The monument to the children who died in the 1990s civil war, referred to locally as the 1991–1995 Homeland War, is in a playground in a park on the way to the station. It is poignant and arresting, shaped like a puzzle with a few pieces missing. In Slavonski Brod 28 children were killed in May 1992, hence the decision to unveil a national monument to the children who died in the war here. When I asked the guest house owner if she knew the parents of any of those who died she replied quietly: 'Yes, of course.' At the unveiling of the statue in 2016 the city's mayor, Mirko Duspara, said: 'After so many years, nobody has yet been held to account for the death of twenty-eight girls and boys.'

With this on my mind – a late twentieth-century tragedy in a country that people visit for beach holidays these days – I return to the train station in time for the 09:35 to Zidani Most.

I am totally winging it now, as I suppose I have been ever since I left Mortlake and took the tracks south into Europe. I am curling in some kind of crazy, elongated backwards 'C' to Venice, heading whichever way the rails seem to lead, never quite sure where the next day will take me.

Today it is Zidani Most in Croatia; at least, that's the plan.

The 09:35 Sava service is due to arrive at Zidani Most at 14:21. People waiting for the train at Slavonski Brod Station are smoking on the platform and one passenger is walking across the tracks to take a shortcut, followed hot on her heels by a station guard wearing a peaked cap, doing likewise. He blows a whistle. We pull away and emerald fields open up on the way to the stations at Nova Kapela-Batrina, Nova

Gradiška and Novska. The smell of cigarettes wafts down the carriage, though the guard does not seem to mind in the slightest (I am well used to cigarette smoke by now in the Balkans). At Novoselec Station, another woman – lighting up as she does so – casually wanders across the tracks and boards the train, cigarette still in hand.

Health and safety back home might have something to say about Croatian rail travellers.

We keep going into Moslavina Voće, where strange tank wagons that look as though they hold chemicals are resting by a platform. Culinec is home to a Fitness Factory gym. Meanwhile, the highlights of Maksimir include a derelict office block and a Pet Center depot.

We arrive at Zagreb, where I decide to get off.

I seem to have become increasingly rash.

But how could I pass a major city, the capital of a country, without taking a look?

Zidani Most can wait. Instead, I find myself inspecting Zagreb Glavni Kolodvor (Zagreb's main station). This is yet another neoclassical triumph, built in 1892, with Grecian columns, figurines, stone balustrades and arched doorways. The walls are painted a peculiar beige-peach and are filthy. To the left-hand side an old locomotive (1891) has been restored, although it appears as though someone homeless has taken to sleeping in the cab, judging by a piece of cardboard and possessions in plastic bags. Nearby a man in an anorak is urinating against a wall; maybe he is the owner of the plastic bags.

I return to the ticket hall via the main platform. At the end I have not yet visited I come to a little chapel. Inside, religious icons are locked behind metal bars and someone has lit a candle. This railway chapel is a first for me. What a great idea.

Get down on your knees and pray the 12:36 to Ljubljana turns up on time. Perhaps this is something that might catch on back in the UK.

* * *

It is pouring once again. Drops leak through a hole in the roof of the platform near the chapel. Two homeless figures huddle in a corner of the ticket hall by a shop selling Croatian national football team shirts. Outside, a long square with a few stalls offering strawberries are draped in plastic to fend off the downpour. For a moment or two I consider getting on a train, any train, and leaving Zagreb.

But I don't. Beyond the long square I come to a cathedral with tall twin spires. Opposite is Hostel Kaptol in an alley with a small courtyard. I ask the price of a room, explaining that I am not sure I will stay the night in rainy Zagreb (I still haven't made my mind up). The receptionist has quizzical brown eyes and a ballerina's poise. She says: 'Actually, I like it when it rains. I don't like the summer.'

'Well, you should get out there, then, as it's really pouring,' I reply.

'I'm looking forward to it when I go home,' she says.

I am not sure whether this is Croatian humour.

Anyway, I book a decent room with a double bed and a skylight, and go outside and sit on a bench beneath an awning in the courtyard. For a while I just stare at the rain splattering a large puddle. Then I tell myself to get a grip and explore this capital city.

The Zagreb City Museum is across an empty cobbled square. 'Closed on Mondays' says a sign. The nearby Meštrović Pavilion art gallery is also closed. The Mimara Museum is around a corner. Closed, too. Rain streams down. I walk somewhat disconsolately up a hill and stumble upon a museum that is actually open.

And what a museum it turns out to be. The Museum of Broken Relationships may not, on the face of it, be the most likely place to spend an hour or two on a dull day in the Balkans. However, it is quite unexpectedly fantastic.

Inside is a series of objects with explanations written by the former owners of the objects, detailing why each object brings back memories of a broken relationship. The owners of the objects appear to have sent them to the museum as an act of romantic exorcism. OK, this may sound pretty downbeat, but the stories are captivating.

One object, near the entrance, is a book of poetry by Bob Dylan entitled *Tarantula*. The explanation written by an anonymous person living in Sleaford in Lincolnshire, runs thus: 'Given to me by an American "boyfriend" when I was 17 and inscribed for "... who charmed the savage wolf". I didn't know he would hound my parents for years, and would eventually have a sex change and steal their name for his new persona.'

This captures the tenure of many of the objects and explanations: frankly weird but full of curiosity. Another is about a Dutch woman who lived with a Peruvian man for two months after meeting him at a disco. One day he disappears, leaving a little statue of the Virgin Mary alongside a parting note. He says he bought the statue especially for a 'new love' before he left Peru. However, the Dutch woman had once looked in his suitcase and discovered a plastic bag full of the statues. Her Peruvian beau was clearly in search of many 'new loves'.

Another is a little more worrying: an axe used to chop up the furniture of a lover who ran away. This is described as 'an ex-axe'.

The museum works – it is the busiest in Zagreb – because people are simply nosy about such matters. By the entrance, I am lucky to meet Dražen Grubišić, who set up the Museum of Broken Relationships with his former partner Olinka Vistica 'in 2004, I think'.

He is aged 48, with a broad smile and the attitude that life is a series of unlikely mishaps and we just need to roll with them.

I ask if he is the owner of the museum.

'I'm the author of it. Not the owner. Along with Olinka,' he says.

'How did you get the idea for the museum?' I ask.

'Of course, before we split, Olinka and I talked about what to do with the objects we had to do with the relationship. Wouldn't it be good to have a space to leave them. It was painful to see the objects. In the twenty-first century we burn things and throw things away and forget everything and start anew. For us it sounded like a kind of rude thing to do. We created this museum and then something happened: a reporter from the Associated Press came.' The story about the museum was picked up and written about across the globe. 'We've had one hundred and ten thousand visitors. We've become the most popular museum in Zagreb, which is really insane. For me this is a true take on love. For me it is really a love museum – love after love has gone. People think love is Cinderella, forever after. It is better to look at love from a more realistic point of view.'

Dražen asks what I am doing in Zagreb and I explain.

'Trains suck here,' he says. 'We build highways but really don't invest in trains. When I was a kid I took a train to Istanbul, Bosnia and Macedonia. I think half the railways there once were don't exist any more.'

I mention Slavonski Brod.

'Oh, Slavonski Brod! That used to be an industrial hub – thirty-five thousand people employed building trains and tanks. That was before the war. Now it's way down – nothing like that.'

'What happened?' I ask.

'It's called privatisation,' says Dražen. 'That's what happened. Everything was privatised and it was closed. Same as in Russia. Things were sold on. That's why there are oligarchs in Russia. Here it was just the same. Friends were given it by friends and they sold it off for nothing. They killed the cow for a steak. There is a big problem with depopulation in Slavonia.' This is the eastern part of Croatia. 'People are moving to Ireland and Germany. From my point of view it's our own fault. Joining the European Union was an excellent idea but we had to implement rules. We had large taxes: fifty to seventy per cent. People would rather go to Ireland than pay these. It's our problem. It's a sort of socialist thing. Before there was the mentality that the government will just take care of it all. That attitude is still there.'

Once Dražen gets going words spill out.

I thank him for being so open, we say goodbye and I go back into the rain – heavier than ever – and up the street to the Museum of Naïve Art, which Dražen has recommended. This museum is also open and contains a fabulous array of paintings in a simple yet vivid, strikingly original style that took off in Croatia in the 1930s. Harvesters are pictured by fields, villagers play musical instruments, men chop trees and peasants dance by fires. My favourite is the one of the tree choppers: three men in white costumes and red hats hang precariously in treetops wielding axes as two women in colourful shawls collect felled branches and a cow looks on as though wondering how peculiar human beings can be and a peacock struts in a corner showing off its finery. In the background the sky is a delicate blue and full of storks. My second favourite simply depicts rolling hills dotted with identical pea-green trees, the hilltops unrealistically rounded as though each is one half of a tennis ball. The works in the Museum of Naïve Art focus on countryside scenes and have an uncomplicated, compelling perfection.

Two great museums in one day.

Slowly along the River Sava
Zagreb to Ljubljana in Slovenia

The rain continues. After the museums, I mooch about the cobbled lanes in the downpour and return to the hostel. The BBC is reporting that David Miliband, Britain's former foreign secretary and member of the Labour Party, is calling for Britain to remain within the European Economic Area and adopt a similar position to Europe as Norway. Britain would leave the EU but remain in the EEA, which includes all EU countries as well as Norway, Liechtenstein and Iceland. 'I don't take the referendum result as the end of the story,' Miliband says. 'Democracy cannot be allowed to end on 23 June 2016, debate cannot be allowed to end.' About 60 per cent of British trade, he points out, is 'under the European aegis'.

Meanwhile, Jacob Rees-Mogg, chairman of the Conservative Party's pro-Leave European Research Group, says that this proposal is a hopeless 'last gasp effort' to prevent Brexit.

The debate rumbles on and the answers and outcomes remain unclear.

It is frankly depressing.

The rain seems to be affecting my mood. I mooch about the cobbled lanes once more, dropping in at the cathedral, where a line of people is waiting for confession. Stained-glass windows shoot upwards in the gloom. I go outside and find a simple cafe where I eat a bowl of goulash (which helps improve my frame of mind a bit). On any long train journey there are going to be highs and lows, especially in a rainstorm in the Balkans.

* * *

The train I am aiming to catch onwards departs at 12:36, arriving at Zidani Most at 14:22, where I will have a stop-off before taking the 16:00 to Ljubljana, Slovenia's capital, arriving at 17:01. Outside the hostel the next morning I go to Dolac Market and take shelter from the continuing downpour in another cafe. The square is busy with fruit and vegetable stalls, each with matching red sunshades that act as umbrellas today. A little bronze statue of a woman with a basket balancing on her head is to one side of the square. Lots of transactions are going on despite the rain. Strawberries, cherries, apricots, lemons and apples are being bagged up. Great yells are being made about the many great deals to be had.

The place I am at is, in fact, not just a cafe. I am at Caffe *Bar* Zagorka, which turns out to be the perfect spot for watching the action on the square. A group of elderly men wearing flat caps, perhaps former traders, has gathered drinking white wine and beer at 9.45 a.m. They seem to know everyone and have a rank of seniority in the square. With a wave of a hand or a yell, various folk are called over to exchange gossip. It is as though they are the unofficial committee in charge of proceedings.

I order a coffee from a waiter with bushy eyebrows and read a bit of *The Bridge on the Drina* by Ivo Andrić; I could not resist picking up a copy of the novel from a bookshop in Belgrade. The author after whom the Budapest–Belgrade train was named – who won the Nobel Prize for Literature in 1961 ahead of John Steinbeck and E. M. Forster – captures life in the town of Višegrad, now in Bosnia and Herzegovina, as told through the history of its bridge. It is gripping and bloody at the beginning as the ancient stone bridge is built, overseen by a psychopathic foreman, and full of juicy tales. If I had not caught the 07:57 from Budapest to Belgrade, I doubt I ever would have heard of the writer despite his obvious fame in these parts.

Go on a train... then read its book.

The old-timers order more drinks. Why should I stick to coffee if they are having wine? I order a glass from the waiter with the bushy eyebrows and realise that this really is a pleasant way to kill some time before a train to Zidani Most. I put on a fleece to keep warm and consider what I would be doing at this time on a Tuesday morning back home (settling into a series of tasks in what will soon be my former office, is the answer). The sun comes out. The sun goes in. A bow-legged man pushes a crate of strawberries past the cafe. The wind picks up and the stallholder directly in front of Bar Zagorka pats down his cherries to prevent them blowing away. An ancient man shuffles into the bar and shakes the hand of my neighbour. A group of deaf friends meets up and communicates with hand signals. Not a whole lot seems to be going on, but quite a lot is actually.

After a while I walk to Zagreb Glavni Kolodvor to catch the 12:36.

A drink at the Train Caffe by the chapel on platform one now seems to make perfect sense. So I have another wine sitting at a table next to two train employees with HZPP badges on their jackets, the insignia of Croatian Railways.

The graffiti-covered 12:36 comes on time and the creaky train pulls out of Zagreb Glavni Kolodvor, passing graffiti-covered buildings and the cooling tower of a factory. The sky looks marbleised in shades of grey with streaks of peach where the sun breaks through, while the green rolling hills beyond Zagreb remind me of the beautiful naive art back in the museum yesterday (it's as though some of the artists came here for inspiration). Soon we are following the gently-flowing olive-coloured River Sava. Maybe because I had drinks with the old-timers and at the station earlier I am feeling particularly at peace with the world as we pull into Dobova, a border town in Slovenia, where guards check our passports.

A whistle blows and we follow the meandering river once again. At 14:35 the train arrives at Zidani Most, just a few minutes late.

I have no particular reason to get off at Zidani Most; like Vrbas and Slavonski Brod, it is simply *there*. It is also, apparently, an important railway hub in Slovenia, so why not? If Zidani Most looks like a convivial place to spend a night I may stay here to complete my Balkan trio of out-of-the-way spots.

The station is by the confluence of the River Sava and the River Savinja, with the track continuing alongside the Sava in the direction of Ljubljana. For this reason, it is an especially picturesque station. To add to this, the main platform is home to a cosy-looking cafe/bar with tables on artificial grass behind a picket fence. I intend, naturally on this day of many cafes and bars, to check it out later.

But first I take a look around Zidani Most. By the station, as I have been finding so often, is an old steam locomotive. This one has a metal plate stamped 'VULCAN-WERKE, STETTIN, 1913'. Slovenian rail enthusiasts evidently exist, too. On an empty bending road beyond the old loco is a closed bakery, an open bakery and a cafe; just about the extent of the town, as far as I can tell. At the cafe, a bottle-blonde waitress with tight black leggings and a black leather jacket has various workers in overalls paying her a lot of attention. This is currently the main event in Zidani Most.

I return to the station and go to the platform bar. This comes with a curious white cat with a very long tail. Across the river trees in a woodland look like pieces of giant broccoli. The sky is still a marbleised grey, now with small patches of blue as well as golden streaks that break through from time to time, lighting up the surface of the Sava.

The waitress at the station bar wears a T-shirt bearing the message: 'THANK GOD WE DON'T LOOK LIKE WHAT WE'VE BEEN THROUGH.' She swiftly serves me a decent 'Prague ham and cheese sandwich', which I eat contentedly at this pretty spot. Zidani Most has a lovely station that will appeal to many a rail aficionado.

* * *

But I'm not hanging around. The 16:00 to Ljubljana draws slowly but surely away along the River Sava with me on it. I have decided, on the evidence of the closed bakery, open bakery and the cafe with the handful of workers and the waitress, that the Balkan trio of out-of-the-way places is perhaps better staying as a Balkan duo, for the time being.

A conductor in a green-striped shirt checks my ragged Interrail Pass. Currents swirl in the muddy river and then rapids churn over rocks. The train stops at Zagorje followed by Sava. Hills with pine trees materialise. The sky darkens as heavy rain begins again. The train chugs through the appropriate (for me today) town of Laze.

Ljubljana Station dates from 1848. Railways came early to Slovenia as the Austrian Empire wanted a connection between Vienna and the important trading port of Trieste. It was on the way to Trieste that an unexpected visitor stayed overnight at the station in October 1904. James Joyce was travelling to Trieste but mistakenly disembarked believing he and his partner Nora Barnacle had reached their destination. A small plaque marks his mistake on platform one. When it was unveiled in 2003, the Irish ambassador to Slovenia read an excerpt from Joyce's novel *Ulysses* (which had yet to be written when James and Nora passed through).

After inspecting the plaque I go to the ticket hall with its beautiful tiled floor with a depiction of a green dragon. The dragon is the symbol of Ljubljana and connected to the legend of Jason and the Argonauts. Legend has it that Jason returned with the Golden Fleece to the source of the River Ljubljana, where he killed a dragon. All over Ljubljana there are depictions of dragons, most famously on Dragon Bridge, where it is said the copper dragons at each end wag their tails whenever a virgin crosses.

You do pick up all kinds of obscure information on a train ride round Europe.

I have booked a room at an apartment called A Writer's Place, close to the station. I circle a hospital and get thoroughly lost before finding the apartment on a street corner daubed with graffiti. The buzzer is answered by a woman with cropped red hair named Katarina. She shows me into the four-room apartment, with a kitchen at one end where she is feeding her children. I ask her about the apartment's name and she says 'our great great grandpa was a famous writer'. She writes down his name for me: Janko Kersnik, who was a politician and a leading writer of Slovenian realism (1852–1897). A street is named after him, not far away. 'We had to read his works when we were at school,' says Katarina, who goes on to tell me that she is a singer at an African jazz club and visited London in 2009.

I leave my backpack in a room with a low-slung bed. I go to the street named after my amiable host's famous ancestor. I follow streets down to the river to see the art nouveau Dragon Bridge and also the Triple Bridge, a clever bridge with three parts over the River Ljubljana. This is at the centre of the city, with grand churches soaring upwards, inviting riverside restaurants and cobbled streets leading to cobbled market squares.

Slovenia's capital is serene in the early evening. Of all the cities so far, Ljubljana has the most fairy-tale feel. The river winds through the centre with art nouveau and art deco buildings on each bank mixing with neoclassical, gothic and modernist structures; the city has a delightful blend of influences with surprises just about every which way you look and is famous among architecture lovers for its wide variety of styles. Light from the many jolly restaurants and bars dances in delicious shades of purple and gold on the surface of the calm river.

Many of the hostelries have joyful little terraces facing the water; at one, I devour a delicious soup with Carniolan pork-garlic sausages, plus mustard and horseradish served on the side (you dip the sausage from the soup in these).

From the river, a lane leads up to a medieval hilltop castle, at the spot where the Romans once had a settlement. The fortifications can be tantalisingly glimpsed from below, making the walk up enticing and speeding your step the closer you get and the more you see. I reach the battlements, at 376 metres, just before sunset with the city spread out below like a map. The Triple Bridge is the best point of orientation, overlooked by the glorious pink facade of the seventeenth-century Franciscan Church of the Annunciation. Spires punctuate the rooftops of the compact city centre, while the train line leading to Ljubljana Station, where Joyce spent the night, clearly marks the northern boundary of the old town. It's also easy to make out the looming redbrick and stone national library, beyond which rises the broad green expanse of Tivoli Park. What strikes me most of all, though, is how important the narrow, meandering River Ljubljana is to the city; so much of the Slovene capital seems to be turned inwards on this enchanting waterway, very much the focal point of matters.

One man above all others has influenced the city's appearance. The architect Jože Plečnik was born in Ljubljana, then known as Laibach and part of the Austro-Hungarian Empire, in 1872. He is responsible for the eye-catching National and University Library of Slovenia, with a design based partially on an Italian palazzo yet shaped in a giant square, the central market near the river, with its arches opening onto the river, Cobblers' Bridge (a lovely pedestrian bridge flanked with Ionic and Corinthian pillars) and – of course – the mesmerising Triple Bridge, the city's architectural symbol. His style is a unique take on art nouveau known as the Vienna Secession that broke classical rules of architecture, allowing for flamboyant flare while at the same time taking inspiration from ancient Athens. Architectural tours can be arranged (though none is available during my visit). Plečnik's influence is strongest felt in

Ljubljana, although his work is also to be found in Vienna and at Prague Castle. He is, understandably, a national hero and much of the city's fairy-tale atmosphere is due to his leaps of imagination.

After my tasty soup dinner close to the Triple Bridge and walk up the hill, I do something I had not expected.

I attend a knees-up at the Slovene Ethnographic Museum.

I am about to call it a day, but I hear music coming from the ethnographic museum close to my guest house. So I go over and enter a crowded room where locals have congregated to drink wine and beer while listening to a man with purple velvet flares playing guitar solos in the manner of Jimi Hendrix beneath a pink disco light. The room is humid and full of chatter, as though the party has been going on some time. Perhaps wisely, it would appear, all Slovene ethnographic displays have been removed to a backroom to make way for the electric-guitar-loving crowd.

Slovenians, I am soon to discover, are both extremely friendly and enjoy a good natter.

Not long after arriving I am in conversation with Janko Rozio, a Slovenian architect behind a project to transform a nearby former military barracks into an art centre with a hostel. I stayed at this hostel a decade ago and I ask him why it has shut down (I had tried to book a room there originally).

'Renovations! Renovations!' he says. 'It is a great challenge to make it work. The first time it was not right. But if we had not taken over the place in 1993, it was going to be destroyed.' He gives me the names of all the others involved, which he writes down meticulously on a piece of paper.

He is with a poet named Zalka. 'I'm a socialist,' she says as a starter, adding, 'but the madness of Yugoslavia has taken a while to sort out.' That is, socialism will take some time to come as the country settles (I think, although I possibly have that completely wrong).

Slovenia broke free of Yugoslavia in 1991, declaring independence after a ten-day war with the Yugoslav People's Army. This was a clean break compared to other events in the Balkans during the 1990s, partly due to the state being predominantly Slovene, with just two per cent of the population Croat, two per cent Serb and one per cent Bosniak. The result was that there was no major internal backlash. The new state's economy began strongly with many pointing to Slovenia as an example of one of the most successful new European Union countries – it joined in 2004 – but has suffered since the Eurozone debt crisis of 2009.

Zalka believes art could be the answer. 'Poetry is the way,' she says enigmatically.

She has dark hair and infectious enthusiasm about her writing. With the music blaring across the ethnographic museum, Zalka says: 'I understand the poetry as a solicitation in two forms: first I experience it as an opening of that early experience of the world, the basic way in which the world has called me. The traces of this are still alive today; even more, it seems to be more pronounced if I just give them a chance to show that they come to the word. At the same time, the source of the poetry is a constant, constant need for translation, as precisely as possible of what I am concerned about in the fundamentals.'

She sips her drink. The guitarist launches into a soaring Hendrixian solo.

'It is not so that the funds move in us,' she says, losing me a bit. 'If we run into violence with our forehead, or such a stir awakens in ourselves; that we tremble at the sight of beauty; that something squeezes us in our chest if we face the injustice before us; that we are shaken by the experience of love? That initial "thing", which may possibly become emotion, I carefully metabolise and try to maintain as a sensitivity. This means the readiness to detect, feel, experience and think through the internal sensor, and also weigh the smallest vibrations in the world and yourself, and then, if given, is the gift of the poem.'

I nod as wisely as I can. It's great meeting all these new people with so much to say. The guitarist in the purple velvet flares hits a high note.

'I take poetry very seriously,' Zalka tells me, 'and each of the poems, even when written in the first breath, from inspiration, is ultimately the result of a filigree work, which is not necessarily outwardly visible; and I even hope it is not: perhaps, the readers will be able to say something about it. I leave my songs to mature: first in me, they usually settle when walking or running, then repeatedly written with a very soft pencil or pen on paper, only later copied and stored on the computer.'

I am now completely lost, but Zalka says everything so nicely that it's pleasant just to hear her stream of words.

I drink another beer.

The guitarist croons for a while longer and dancers wiggle beneath the ethnography museum's disco ball. It's been another peculiar day.

The Railway Museum of Slovenian Railways
Ljubljana

Katarina and I discuss politics in her breakfast room. A recent parliamentary election has seen the anti-immigration Slovenian Democratic Party win a quarter of the vote – more than any other party. The group, whose leader has ties with Hungary's Viktor Orbán, would need to cut deals with other parties to gain power. A total of nine parties are in parliament, including the far-right National Party. The Slovenian Democratic Party is firmly against plans for the European Union to create a quota system for asylum seekers.

Across Europe, as I have found at just about every stop along the way – from London to Ljubljana – the question of what to do about immigration seems to lead the political agenda.

To take my mind off politics I do what every good train lover visiting Slovenia's capital should do: I go to the Railway Museum of Slovenian Railways. It may be one of the worst cliches in travel writing to refer to 'hidden gems', but this is indeed such a lesser-known jewel – not even listed on the tourist office map I picked up at the station. Katarina put me on to it (thank you, Katarina).

The museum is just to the north of the station in a former boiler room. Upon entry into a little ticket office I am hit by the smell of oil and diesel. An assistant named Mr Dusan says the boiler room 'emerged' as a museum in the 1960s. He takes me inside and shows me a row of steam locomotives. Clanks come from a section where an engine is being restored. Some of the locomotives are in working order.

'I am just a rail enthusiast,' says Mr Dusan. 'Have you met the professor?'

I say that I haven't met him.

'Let me take you to the professor! Mr Bogić! He can explain everything!'

We ascend some stairs to an office and I am introduced to Mr Bogić, a cheerful man with wispy grey hair and spectacles.

Mr Bogić proceeds to tell me all. Although the museum began to *emerge* in the 1960s, it was *established* in 1981 and *officially opened* in 2004. 'We are part of Slovenian Railways and we have about sixty locomotives but they are not all here.' The one I saw at Zidani Most is one of the 60.

Mr Bogić has worked on the railway all his life, beginning his job in 1977. He is disappointed that youngsters these days have less interest in trains as this makes it tough to find people to restore the engines. 'Youngsters are over-interested in mobile phones and computers,' he sighs.

The professor walks me around the various engines. The line from Vienna to Trieste was completed in 1857, Mr Bogić says. Meanwhile, the line in the region of Bohinj runs through the most beautiful scenery in the country, in his opinion. We go into a backyard with yet more locos. 'Just now you must understand why I don't go for my pension,' he says, looking at the locos with great affection.

We enter a room with dusty old station clocks – and then, back in the old boiler room, Mr Bogić shows me how his technicians can use 'white metal to make bearings'.

The professor and I shake hands and I go into the backyard for a final look. Mr Dusan is here and he calls me over.

'Did you find Mr Bogić?' he asks.

I say that I have now met the professor. Mr Dusan is pleased about this. He is in the middle of setting up a little narrow-gauge steam locomotive and has already heated up the engine. 'Look see here,' he says, pointing into the engine. 'You need soft water: rain water. Any other type of water: trouble!'

He is covered in coal dust. He turns a cog and there is a hissing sound.

'Come on, let's go!' he says, pointing at a tiny carriage at the back.

I sit on the carriage.

'Let's go all the way around. It's seven hundred metres,' says Mr Dusan.

The loco makes a whistle and away we roll around the old boiler shed at Slovenia's Railway Museum of Slovenian Railways. This is my slowest train yet and we chug peacefully about for a while.

Thank you, Mr Dusan.

* * *

Feeling strangely elated, I go to the main station where the ticket assistant uses Deutsche Bahn's website to check the time of my train to Innsbruck. I have looked at the map and thought this would make a good ride. I can then drop down through the Alps and stay in Verona before taking the final train eastwards to Venice. We establish that the next service is the 15:27 via Villach in Austria, arriving in Innsbruck at 21:44, which is rather later than hoped.

Oops. But I decide to stick to the plan. To celebrate going on such an extremely slow steam train, I drink a honey-flavoured beer at the Kratochwill brewery, not far from the station, while reading a copy of *The Coronet: The Journal of the Friends of the Slovenian Railways Museum* given to me by Mr Bogić. This edition includes a description of a journey from Yugoslavia to Jerusalem in 1977, a discussion about 'major boiler repairs', a further debate about railway names, and links to various YouTube videos of rides. It is written in English by John Gulliver of Barnstaple in North Devon. Mr Bogić, when handing me the journal, told me: 'John Gulliver is a gentleman of the first grade.'

Yes, there are keen rail enthusiasts across the globe, but British rail enthusiasts really are very keen.

From platform ten, I catch the 15:27 to Villach, only just making it after letting time slip by at the brewery.

CHAPTER NINE

LJUBLJANA IN SLOVENIA TO VERONA IN ITALY, VIA INNSBRUCK IN AUSTRIA

GOULASH, STATIONS AND GRUDGES

On board the 15:27 to Innsbruck I settle into a compartment with six wide lilac seats with blue headrests set at various heights. Passengers, it appears, must select a seat with a suitably corresponding headrest. I do so. A woman with plastic bags and a small panting dog is the only other occupant. The dog sniffs my trainers and resumes panting. There is, I notice, a smart motif depicting mountains stitched in a slightly different shade of lilac on the seating; appropriate as we are heading in the direction of some. Our compartment is cut off from other passengers by a grimy sliding glass door. The train looks bedraggled, as though it dates from Tito times.

We pull away past an advert for McDonald's – 'I'M LOVIN' IT'. A guard in a blue jacket inspects tickets. Beyond the city limits we move through tree-clad hills, pausing at Škofja Loka, with its potted plants and station cafe. The scenery becomes more rugged. Pyramid-tipped mountains wrapped in smoky-grey clouds arise to the south. With a steady rattle we negotiate long bends through pine forests and little farms. I feel as though I am re-entering western Europe, which I suppose I am around about here. When was the last time I was in it? Somewhere between Bonn and Leipzig. Which seems a long time ago.

At Lesce-Bled Station there is unfortunately no view of the beautiful lake for which the town is so famous. Beyond are more misty mountains: the edge of the Julian Alps. Churches with thin spires poke out of tiny villages with houses with A-shaped roofs. A factory pumps steam on the outskirts of Jesenice, close to the Austrian border. We enter a long tunnel, the little black dog panting and rasping in the gloom. The tunnel opens into fields dotted with yellow and purple flowers followed by forest with telegraph-pole pine trees beside mountains with snow-clad peaks. We must be in Austria by now. Indeed we are. The train stops at Faak Am See (a place-name to be pronounced carefully) in Carinthia in the far south of Austria. 'WELCOME TO AUSTRIA' says a text on my mobile phone. Our carriages traverse a wide green plain. The woman with the dog opens the window to allow in cool Austrian air.

At Villach Station I dash to platform four to find a gleaming black and red train. The connection time is just seven minutes. The final destination for the service is Munich. We are soon passing more snow-capped mountains as the train begins to rise, taking a bridge across a lazy green river and going up, up, up.

This one has a dining carriage. Delicacies such as Viennese-style chicken with parsley potatoes and lingonberry sauce, goulash soup with Kaiser roll, and boiled beef with creamed spinach and pan-fried potatoes are to be had. I order the chicken and drink a bottle of water that comes with some advice: 'MESSAGE FOR YOU: Do not be ashamed of what makes you happy. Whatever it is. And do not give up what fills you with joy. No matter how much time it takes.'

Rehydration and free life-counselling, too.

The chicken is tender, succulent and a decent portion. The lingonberry sauce is both sharp and sweet. The train continues to rise, passing through tunnels. Glimpses of mountains emerge through thick white cloud. A fine castle with turrets and towers commands a peak near Bad Gastein. We run alongside a muddy river before reaching Bischofshofen.

An American woman in a yellow dress and a woman entirely in black, whom I take to be Austrian or German from her accent when she speaks English, sit near me. They begin to talk about relationships.

Woman in yellow: 'The person I was with was too much into drugs and alcohol. I look at my mother and father. You keep on going and you bite your tongue – it's the nature of human relationships. You're in the ocean and it's a very long swim. Or you don't. I had a tonne of respect for him. He could see things seven years before they were going to happen.' By this, I get the impression she means *gaps in the market*. 'But it couldn't last. You've got to be detached about it. Don't get angry.'

Woman in black: 'We met when we were thirty and were together seventeen years. We made a lot of money and had cool jobs. Our whole thing was not based on love, it was based on intellectual decision-making.'

It's like the Museum of Broken Relationships in Zagreb all over again.

They turn to the subject of getting ahead in business.

Woman in black: 'If I come across something, I try to solve it. You've got to think fast and move on.'

Woman in yellow: 'Yeah, you've gotta be observant and solution-orientated.'

They order hotdogs and beer.

We stop at Salzburg, and roll onwards.

Woman in yellow: 'You gotta keep the public finding you online. It's all about integrity. If there's integrity, then that's the starting point. Getting ahead is not just about responding to trends.'

Woman in black: 'Yeah, yeah, totally.'

Their hotdogs and beers are delivered and they begin to devour them.

The woman in black discusses her son: 'He was downloading when he was three. One time I asked him when he was about five how to download something, as I'm not so good, he said: "I told you once and you do not listen! I am going to tell you again one time!"'

The woman in yellow remembers her internet-free childhood and says: 'Even in 1996 people weren't sure websites were going to go anywhere. Look at it now: how cool is that?'

They appear, from what I can gather, to be colleagues enjoying a train holiday together, heading for Munich. They order more beers with Jägermeister shots on the side.

'Bottoms up!' says the woman in black.

'Down the hatch!' says the woman in yellow.

They seem to be having a ball.

My bad
Innsbruck

Although I have travelled slowly on my way to Venice I have taken a circuitous route that has involved quite a bit of moving about (as you may have noticed). I have not spent much time in each place visited as curiosity has dragged me onwards. However, I have found that a day in a destination allows you to sample some of the best bits – to dip your toe in the water, if you like, without becoming marooned or feeling as though you have to see *everything*. You have your ride the next day. The promise of an onwards journey along the tracks and a new place to investigate has kept me going. Stevenson's 'the great affair is to move' has been my motto.

With Innsbruck I'll put my hands up: I messed up a bit.

My idea to drop through the mountains southwards to Verona is OK, but I am not allowing myself enough time in Innsbruck to see the city even vaguely properly because I need to meet Kasia in Venice in two days' time.

I simply got too tempted by the idea of a ride through the mountains. By now I am almost addicted to the clickety-clack of the track. It is the train journey not Innsbruck that has brought me here (sorry, Innsbruck). I really just wanted to experience the ride through the Alps from Austria to Italy.

Arriving so late and leaving in the morning is crazy. I know that.

* * *

The train from Ljubljana arrives into Innsbruck on time. Using my smartphone for directions I reach the River Inn and take a footpath alongside the icy-looking green water (you'd not last long if you fell in there).

The Garni Technikerhaus hotel is close to the river. The Garni Technikerhaus is not in the most distinguished-looking building: grey walls and a grid of windows beyond a car park. It could pass for a low-security prison (reminding me a bit of the Première Classe back in Calais). My smartphone takes me to the back of the hotel via the car park so I do not enter from the front. Inside is a bleak reception and a window for the receptionist that has been closed. No one is about. I read an email I have been sent by Garni Technikerhaus more closely. It says that the reception shuts at 10 p.m. and that guests who arrive later than that will find their key in a 'little box' on the right-hand side of the entrance.

The reception window has a little box on the left-hand side. I look inside. Nothing is there. I am convinced that this little box must be the correct little box even though it is on the left and not the right. I spend a while pondering this. Not a soul stirs in Garni Technikerhaus. I am at a loss what to do.

After some time I exit via the front entrance and find another little box on the right-hand side of the door with the key in it. Always follow the instructions! I walk up a few floors of stairs and enter a room with an orange door. The room is plain and cold-looking with a narrow single bed, a wooden swivel chair and a desk with an angular lamp. It is, however, all very well thought out and could be said to have an *industrial chic* look. It is also exceedingly quiet, not actually cold, and in the morning I have a fine view of the snowy Karwendel Mountains.

I sleep well and feast on a breakfast of hams and cheese in a dining room with orange walls. Other guests are there, too. They exist. I drink a good coffee listening to the 1980s hit 'Gloria'.

Outside it is chillier than at any other time on the trip. Birdsong trills by the scary river as I retrace my steps of last night. Low-hanging clouds cover some of the mountains and even some of the taller buildings; Innsbruck is at 574 metres.

It is a crisp, hopeful morning. I stride onwards to a bizarre sign on a public information board by the footpath. This sign provides advice on how to run and walk properly; just in case any passers-by have forgotten. Detailed diagrams of a man lifting his legs in the correct manner are provided under a heading in English: 'RUN AND WALK BASICS.'

I'm not sure whether this is Austrian humour.

Across the river I enter the Triumphal Arch, a splendid eighteenth-century archway built in an ornate rococo style yet with the grandeur of an entrance to a Roman city. This arch has a story. It was ordered by Empress Maria Theresa to celebrate the forthcoming wedding of her son, the Duke of Tuscany (later Emperor Leopold II), with Princess Maria Ludovica of Spain. However, the empress's husband, Kaiser Franz I, died during the wedding celebrations. The design was altered so that one side of the arch commemorates the wedding and the other the Kaiser. I take a look at both aspects and marvel at their indisputable finery.

This counts as my Innsbruck sightseeing.

I pace onwards to the station.

Well, yes, I had better go back to Innsbruck one day. Then I could see the Goldenes Dachl, with its 2,657 gilded copper tiles on the roof, the biggest attraction in town, built on the orders of Emperor Maximilian I (1459–1519). Train lovers also may wish to note: Innsbruck has a famous cog railway, the Hungerburgbahn, that ascends from near the zoo to a high plateau with great views.

From Innsbruck the line I am taking runs through the Brenner Pass to a height of 1,371 metres before descending to Verona. This is said by the legendary Gardner and Kries (no less) to be a lovely ride and I have always wanted to visit the city of Romeo and Juliet. It is possible, I read, to see the very balcony where 'O Romeo, Romeo! Wherefore art thou, Romeo!' may have been whispered all those centuries ago. There is also a Roman amphitheatre with 44 pink marble tiers accommodating 15,000 people, medieval architecture and a beautiful central square, Piazza Bra.

My good
Innsbruck to Verona

The original Innsbruck Station, commissioned by Emperor Franz Joseph I in 1853, was destroyed in World War Two. This elegant stone station was initially used for regional services in the Tyrol but when the line through the Brenner Pass opened in 1867 it became a key transport hub for the Austrian Empire, both for the movement of goods and soldiers. The Venetia region was then under Austrian control.

It was not the first time the Austrians had built a railway through a mountain range. This honour goes to the line over the Semmering Pass on the way from Vienna, via Ljubljana, to Trieste. This was completed in 1853, with the final section to Trieste polished off in 1857, as previously mentioned.

The leading rail historian Christian Wolmar tells an interesting tale about the completion of the Semmering Pass in his excellent book *Blood, Iron and Gold: How Railways Transformed the World*. Otto von Bismarck had been sent as a German representative to inspect the line and when walking up the mountain to see a tunnel was almost killed when a gangway above a ravine collapsed; he had to cling to a ledge to survive. The accident, as Wolmar points out, could have changed European history. Building Austria's mountain railways was extremely dangerous and of the 20,000 workers on the Semmering Pass 700 died from accidents and diseases such as cholera and typhoid. Every All Saints Day Austrian railway workers commemorate those who died.

Engineering discoveries during the construction of the Semmering Pass made the Brenner Pass much easier to complete; plus it helped that the Brenner Pass did not require tunnels.

* * *

In the latest incarnation of Innsbruck Station, completed after an overhaul in 2004, I drink another coffee and a glass of freshly squeezed orange juice in a canteen by the dingy ticket hall. The station these days has a highly functional design, with a long rectangular space like a giant shoe box. Two abstract frescoes saved from the previous station, the handiwork of the famous Austrian artist Max Weiler (1910–2001), provide a splash of colour above a McDonald's. They really are entertainingly unusual, with bathers in swimming costumes beneath a palm tree surrounded by tropical flowers on the right, a mysterious figure preaching from a pulpit in the centre, and more figures in ordinary clothes slumping on chairs listening to the preacher at the foot of a mountain stretching upwards to a bare-chested ironman of some sort. Perhaps the mural means 'listen to the preacher and paradise awaits', or something like that. Where the ironman fits in, I do not know. Maybe: 'Beware the ironman! Proceed to paradise! But be good along the way!'

It could be that I am reading far more into these frescoes than is necessary. I do know that they caused controversy when they were first unveiled as some took the central figure to be Christ and deemed the depiction to be insulting. Anyway, they date from 1954 and are worth a look.

The canteen has clocks showing the time in Bangkok and Sydney as well as the local time. I watch the minutes tick by and go to platform seven to catch the 09:24 to Verona, due to arrive at 12:56.

There is a ten-euro (£9) ticket reservation charge for this journey. On many trains in Italy extra payments must be made when using an Interrail Pass.

On the platform I read a sign listing the station's house rules. Under a heading that says 'We appreciate order and organisation just as much as you do!' the rules stretch downwards quite a long way. They include securing luggage and prams so they do not roll onto tracks in strong winds or drafts caused by trains, supervising children at all times, neither smoking nor vaping, never crossing the tracks, never daubing graffiti, never playing music, muzzling all dogs, never drinking alcohol, only eating food in designated areas, neither begging nor 'offending public decency', never 'hindering, or disturbing anyone', and never feeding animals, 'especially birds'. There are many other regulations, all of which seem sensible enough. But what a long list! Any passenger who offends will be prosecuted and fined 'at least 40 euros'. All orders of Austrian Federal Railways

(ÖBB) 'must be obeyed'. The house rules sign off with: 'We wish you a pleasant stay and a safe journey.'

I stand very still at a very safe distance from the platform edge keeping myself to myself.

The 09:24 arrives, a cherry-red train with ÖBB written on the side. Its eventual destination is Bologna.

Away we go past a giant ski jump (the 1964 and 1976 Winter Olympics were held in Innsbruck), across a stream and upwards on a mountainside with silver birch trees. Great granite cliffs emerge on each side, as do tiny Alpine villages, each with a church and a cluster of dwellings. The carriage on this modern train is almost empty and I have a compartment of six seats to myself. The train curves round as we rise more steeply than on any train yet; there's something quite satisfying in seeing the carriages bending ahead through the window. I cannot put my finger on precisely why. The conductor stamps my pass and tells me he expects many more passengers to board at Trento.

As the train chugs upwards, I go online and check the latest news. It is interesting and involves Austria.

A BBC report explains that Sebastian Kurz, the country's very young chancellor (he was elected last year aged 31), has given an order to shut down seven mosques and expel any imams found to have links with foreign funding. Images taken at an Austrian mosque have emerged showing children in Turkish soldiers' costumes re-enacting the Battle of Gallipoli in which Allied forces were defeated by the Ottoman Empire in World War Two. Kurz's move is a reaction to this. 'Parallel societies, political Islam and radicalisation tendencies have no place in our country,' he says. Many of the imams being questioned have links to an Islamic organisation that has ties with the Turkish government. Turkey has responded by describing the actions as 'Islamophobic, racist and discriminatory'.

Kurz is the leader of the Austrian People's Party, which is in a coalition with the far-right, anti-immigration Freedom Party of Austria. This party is led by Heinz-Christian Strache, the country's deputy chancellor, who attended a torch-lit protest by a group imitating Hitler Youth when he was younger (he has since said he had merely been 'stupid' doing so). A local councillor who gave a Nazi salute has recently been suspended from the party, which is in the process, it claims, of cracking down on internal antisemitism.

Yet again, immigration and fear of outsiders rearing their ugly heads. Austria has become the only western European country with a government with a far-right presence.

It leaves a bad taste in the mouth.

I try to take my mind off it.

This is lovely scenery. Misty mountains sweep ahead as emerald fields fall further and further below. We enter tunnels that must have been cut to improve on the path of the original 1867 railway. Thick woodland leads to an opening and a greater number of tracks. The Outlet Center Brenner comes into view, promising to be 'THE BEST OUTLET IN THE ALPS'. We have reached Brennero/Brenner Station. The journey to the pass has taken about an hour.

Here a couple of young guys occupy the compartment next to mine and start playing hip-hop music on a mobile phone, not very loudly. I am sure this is in contravention of some ÖBB rule but it does not bother me – and the conductor seems cool about it. We pass a football pitch near the station and begin our descent through a long tunnel into Italy. Beyond the tunnel, slopes are snow covered and stationary cable cars hang above, presumably used only in the winter by skiers. Chestnut horses graze in a field.

The train reaches the town of Vipiteno, where Nazis such as Adolf Eichmann and Josef Mengele are believed to have hidden while waiting for forged passports to escape to South America. On the outskirts is a timber yard and then a hilltop castle made of stone. The sky is milky and people are white-water rafting on a river. Downwards the train goes, coming to the valley floor, where vineyards stretch between granite cliffs on either side of the track;

it's as though we have entered a canyon of wine. The train chunters along through the canyon for quite a while. The cliffs have a violet, metallic tint. The vines are golden green. The sky is a delicious lilac blue. This is, as the newspaper travel supplements so often like to say, *stunning scenery*.

The madcap trip to Innsbruck was worth it.

The guys next door are now listening to R&B. The train clatters across a metal girder bridge over a winding river. We stop at the small town of Chiusa/Klausen. Another hilltop castle looks down on this village, which was where the German Renaissance artist and theorist Albrecht Dürer (1471–1528) stayed on his trip to Italy from Nuremberg in 1494. In this setting he painted watercolours of the Alps before moving on to Venice, where he became acquainted with the ageing master artist Giovanni Bellini. He returned from Italy the following year and his artistic style was greatly influenced by the trip. Chiusa/Klausen looks like an inviting place to leap off. Next time, perhaps.

One of the young guys has begun dancing to the R&B. I can tell because when we go through a tunnel I can see his reflection in one of the windows. He is wearing an orange polo shirt and has short dreadlocks, and is moving smoothly to the beat like some kind of South Tyrolean godfather of soul. We cross more vineyards, still in the canyon of wine, before reaching Bolzano/Bozen, where the two cool music lovers disembark.

An elderly Italian couple joins my compartment; the man assiduously reading the *Corriere Della Sera* newspaper while the woman closes her eyes with her hands folded on her lap. We recross the River Isaco. A field of solar panels shines brightly. A purple-hued cliff soars upwards. I go online and book a room at the Romeo & Juliet Non-Hotel; what a name, but this 'non-hotel' is conveniently near the station and I am intrigued by the whole non-hotel concept. As long as free European Union internet roaming lasts, it is supremely easy to book accommodation on a long train trip in Europe, even at the last minute, even at places as obscure as Slavonski Brod in Croatia.

We recross the river once more. I watch the head of a cyclist – just his head, the rest of his body is obscured by vines – pedalling through the landscape. We amble by Mezzocorona and Zambana and arrive at Trento, where many passengers do indeed board.

At Trento Station an announcement is made that the dining carriage is now open. To the dining carriage I go, soon enjoying goulash soup with Kaiser roll. Everyone else, the four other passengers in the dining carriage, are having the goulash soup with the Kaiser roll so it must be pretty good. It is. The goulash is piping hot and the Kaiser roll is crusty and just right. This is the swankiest dining carriage of the whole trip with white tablecloths, little table lamps and black leather chairs; as close to the *Orient Express* as I've managed yet (admittedly a far cry from the luxury of that train, but a definite step up from some of the beaten-up old carriages I've been in).

As we glide by a grand redbrick castle the waiter comes with the bill for the goulash. I offer him my debit card. He tells me that the machine is not working. I hand him a 50-euro note, all I have on me, and say sorry.

'It is my fault!' he says with a bow. 'You must not apologise!'

He fetches my change. Polite service on this Innsbruck to Verona ride.

I take a look at the online news once again. The father of Meghan Markle, Prince Harry's wife-to-be in two days' time, is pulling out of attending the royal wedding at Windsor Castle for complicated reasons to do with staged photographs. Is he attempting to profit from the wedding, 'royal observers' ask? This controversy is the number one story on the BBC. A man in Florida has sadly, and painfully, died from an 'exploding vape pen'. A student in Alabama has requested that a robot stands in for her at her graduation ceremony as she is too ill to attend. There is a video of the creation, wearing a graduation robe, rolling on wheels across a ceremonial stage with an internet tablet on its head providing a live upload of the ill student in hospital as she reacts to the robot receiving the college certificate. President Donald Trump has declared he paid up to $250,000 (£192,000) to a porn star's lawyer to help hush up her claims of an affair. And finally, with a train-related slant, a Japanese rail company has apologised profusely for a train that left 25 seconds early. A spokesman says the 'great inconvenience we placed upon our customers was truly inexcusable'. This came after another such incident, a month earlier in which a Japanese train departed 20 seconds early. Japanese trains are known for their punctuality and these early departures are being treated as a great scandal in the country.

Just another day in the early twenty-first century.

We pull into Verona Porta Nuova Station.

On the toy train
Verona

It's not exactly a classic. Like the one at Innsbruck, the station was destroyed in World War Two and rebuilt soon after. From the outside it looks like a long flat military barracks made from concrete slabs. A large busy bus station in the foreground does not help matters. Being at the intersection of the Brenner line from Austria and the line between Milan and Venice, a lot of passengers pass through: more than 25 million each year. Inside, the station is chaotic with folk swarming every which way towards the many *binari* (platforms). Some are slumped with backpacks against walls. At the cafes little attempt is made to queue; it's a free-for-all with gesticulations and cries, as though the cafe-goers are attempting to seal multi-million dollar deals on the New York Stock Exchange.

I fight my way through crowds to the ticket office where I take a preliminary ticket with a number from a little machine and wait for my number to flash up on a screen. This system is considered in Italy to be a marked improvement on simple ticket kiosks, which have traditionally resulted in a lot of pushing-in. Italian rail authorities have long pondered how to deal with this problem, initially introducing a single-line queue so people would be funnelled along, in theory making pushing-in impossible. However, as the author Tim Parks explains in his entertaining book *Italian Ways: On and Off the Rails from Milan to Palermo*, this single-line queue system was not entirely pusher-free. There was always the threat of the *furbo* (sly one). Such a character would simply wait by a pillar, looking casual, until a ticket window became free and then step purposefully forwards before anyone could react. Parks experiences such *furbos* at this very station and says he is surprised that other passengers do not intervene. His conclusion is that passengers on Italian trains can always try to bend rules and be pushy so long as they are ready to protest innocence if challenged by the authorities. With this approach, they have a good chance of getting away with whatever it may be. This is just the way things work on trains and at stations in Italy.

Hence the switch to ticket-number machines – as well as more self-service ticket machines – at bigger stations. You can't argue about a ticket number; either you have the ticket or you do not. The rules cannot possibly be broken, no matter how hard a *furbo* tries. The system works well on this occasion. My number flashes up quite soon and a pleasant assistant explains the *biglietti* (ticket) options. If I go on a fast service to Venice, the journey will take 1 hour and 10 minutes, but I will need to pay for a seat reservation. The slower train takes 2 hours and 25 minutes, and I will not need a reservation. I thank her. I'll go for the second option obviously.

Back in the main hall chaos continues to reign. The station was renovated quite recently but marble columns from the post-war remake remain, as does a brilliantly colourful mural of train wheels, viaducts and level-crossing barriers. Train stations and art seem to go together, all the way across Europe.

Outside again, I cross a road and ascend some steps to Case Ferrovieri Porta Nuova (street of the homes of the railwaymen).

This seems like a suitable street for me.

Perhaps unsurprisingly, however, I cannot locate the non-hotel.

I seem to be at the correct street, but all I can find is a nondescript block of apartments at the address given for the Romeo & Juliet Non-Hotel. A metal fence with a couple of gates blocks off intruders to the apartments and I am at a loss what to do.

I look at the booking confirmation on my smartphone. I call Tommy, the owner. Tommy does not answer his phone. I lean against the fence by one of the gates and consider my options. After about five minutes, a group of four people turns up and a tall man with a goatee opens the gate. I ask if I can go through with them as I need to find apartment number eight.

The man with the goatee asks if I am Thomas.

'Yes,' I reply, somewhat taken aback.

'Ah! I am also Thomas,' he says. 'And meet another Thomas.' He points to a skinnier, teenaged version of himself without a goatee. 'My son! Three Thomases!' He chuckles for a while and says: 'We were expecting you. Follow me!'

So this is how a non-hotel works.

The man with the goatee is Tommy. He takes two Chinese tourists to an apartment in one block and his son, who is halfway through eating a slice of pizza, takes me to an apartment in another. My room is reached up steps in a peach-coloured apartment block with another bedroom, a small kitchen and a bathroom. I have been allocated the room with two single beds; the other has a double bed and will be unoccupied tonight, Thomas says. A small wooden sculpture of a man deep in thought occupies the hall. Apart from this there is little further decoration. Thomas finishes his slice of pizza, hands me the key and disappears. I put my bag in my peach-coloured room – the interior of the Romeo & Juliet Non-Hotel seems to match the exterior. I am about to sleep in a peach.

I set off to investigate Verona.

From the station to the centre is about a 15-minute walk past the bus station, busy roads and a roundabout upon which the Porta Nuova after which the station was named is to be found. An Italian flag flutters above a solid stone structure constructed in the early half of the sixteenth century – just before Shakespeare, father of the city's tourism boom, was born in 1564. A ramp leads to three grand archways; the two on either side of the central archway were added by the Austrians in the nineteenth century. Until 1912 this southerly gate to the city served its purpose, but in that year breaches were made in the walls to create traffic lanes.

It certainly stands out – and it's intriguing to see the course of the ancient city walls on the tourist map I picked up at the station. A wall once twisted and turned, protecting a loop of land surrounded by the River Adige to the north; the centre of the old town with the Roman amphitheatre by Piazza Bra. An extra loop of land to the north of the River Adige also had fortifications and gates. What a magnificent city it must once have been.

And still is. The street from Porta Nuova is long and straight and heads directly to the Roman amphitheatre so getting lost is just about impossible. Halfway along I stop for a slice of oily, peppery tuna-and-onion pizza accompanied by an Aperol Spritz at a cafe that also offers Aperol Spritz *da asporto* (to go), as though you've ordered a cappuccino or an orange juice.

Ah, *la dolce vita*!

* * *

The *Romeo and Juliet* balcony is on Via Cappello, where Juliet's house is located 'according to legend' at number 23. I head in this direction down the long street coming to Piazza Bra and the amphitheatre. For a moment or two I just stop and stare. Of all the sights I have visited on these train journeys this is the most captivating (and I have seen a lot). The amphitheatre is the third largest in Italy: 140 metres long and 110 metres wide, with two storeys of arches dating from the first century and used until AD 404 when Emperor Honorius banned gladiatorial games.

I buy a ticket, go inside and sit on a marble tier admiring the sheer majesty of the structure, restored during the Renaissance after being plundered for masonry in the centuries following AD 404. A stage is at one end, seats are in the middle and spotlights rise above; the summer concert season is about to begin. Operas are regularly held – the acoustics are said to be excellent – and pop concerts have been staged from time to time: Pink Floyd, Paul McCartney, Whitney Houston and Radiohead have performed. Bloody fights have taken place here. Glorious music has floated across the arena, too.

Via Cappello is around the corner, down narrow lanes with sixteenth-century houses and bars with more Aperol Spritz drinkers. And there it is: Juliet's balcony, in a cobbled courtyard packed with tourists. A statue of Juliet stands at one end. People crowd around taking pictures of the statue and the stone balcony. Up there, Juliet discussed the trouble with being a Capulet, and down here Romeo did the same about being a Montague. They told each other how much they loved one another. Somebody once decided this was the spot. A million pictures and more later, this little courtyard is a Veronese cash cow.

It has long been a tourist attraction. Charles Dickens visited Italy in 1844 and 1845 making his base in Genoa while taking a break from novel writing; between *Martin Chuzzlewit* and *Dombey and Son*. During this time, he travelled around the country extensively and collected his thoughts for a travel book, *Pictures from Italy*.

Dickens visits both Verona and Venice and is greatly taken by both. Romeo and Juliet become the focus of his visit to Verona, which he finds 'so fanciful, quaint, and picturesque a place, formed by such a rich variety of fantastic buildings, that there could be nothing better at the core of even this romantic town: scene of one of the most romantic and beautiful stories'.

Yet when Dickens visits Via Cappello he is not impressed. He writes that the House of the Capulets is 'now degenerated into a most miserable little inn' with muddy market carts passing by its yard in 'ankle-deep dirt'. He goes on to describe a 'grim-visaged dog, viciously panting in a doorway, who would certainly have had Romeo by the leg, the moment he put it over the wall'.

Dickens visits the amphitheatre – 'so well preserved, and carefully maintained, that every row of seats is there, unbroken' – before pounding the streets for hours: 'I walked through and through the town all the rest of the day, and could have walked there until now, I think.' Afterwards, he reads *Romeo and Juliet* in his 'own room at the inn that night – of course no Englishman had ever read it there, before' (even back then people were moving about Europe on tours quite a bit). His overall take on Verona? 'With its fast-rushing river,' he writes, 'picturesque old bridge, great castle, waving cypresses, and prospect so delightful, and so cheerful! Pleasant Verona!' He likes the city *quite a lot.*

Amid all the modern-day tourists around the House of the Capulets today, if not ankle-deep dirt and grim-visaged dogs, I'm getting flashbacks to Bruges. Yet a short distance from Via Cappello in Piazza delle Erbe all is quiet, with a handful of market stalls and a column topped by a lion, the symbol of Venice. Magnificent palaces and medieval merchants' houses surround the square, just as they would have during Dickens's visit.

Piazza Erbe is a hidden heart of the city with many an artery-like lane disappearing in mysterious directions. I turn into one to find a long run of glitzy fashion shops: blazers, furs, summer dresses with golden belts, high-heel shoes, T-shirts with shouty slogans (LOVE LIFE, EAT THE RICH and BE A BITCH), silk shawls, loafers and miniskirts. Verona is perfect for rail enthusiasts, male or female, thinking of hanging up their anoraks and trying something slicker, or at least a little different.

Back on Piazza Bra I hand over a few euros and take my seat on the city's tourist 'train'. I suppose I had to really. It is gold and cream coloured, shaped like an old-fashioned steam train at the front and has two 'carriages' holding 40 people. We are parked next to an armoured vehicle beside which soldiers in black berets, bulletproof vests and shades are posing and keeping an eye on things. They do not seem too bothered by us.

This is another very slow train; faintly ridiculous, I'll admit, but a handy way to get orientated. On board are a handful of French tourists. Classical music plays as we wait around for a while, although no further tourists are forthcoming. With two blows of a whistle we move off on our half-hour ride, learning that the city has 260,000 inhabitants and is a UNESCO World Heritage Site. A recorded commentary is repeated in four languages with the legend of Romeo and Juliet getting a mention in more or less the first breath. Our train cannot take us to the famous courtyard on Via Cappello, we are told, but we are advised to visit as this is the 'setting of the most famous love story in history'. I wonder if a visitor to Verona has ever just not bothered.

Tourists take pictures of us – we have become an attraction in our own right – as we drive past a redbrick castle, Castlevecchio, from the fourteenth century and probably on the site of a former Roman castle, we learn. The castle was built by the Scaliger family. We observe a beautiful Roman arch. The 'train' crosses a bridge over the swiftly flowing River Adige with a view in the distance of a sunny hill covered in cypress trees. Classical music plays again and the commentary ceases.

More tourists take pictures of us. We recross the river on another bridge (all bridges in Verona were destroyed by the fleeing Nazis and had to be rebuilt). We turn into a lane that leads to the elegant medieval cathedral. The Gothic facade of the Church of St Anastasia is followed by Piazza Erbe. We return to the river, with more classical music playing. 'Maria Callas, the famous opera singer, lived for many years in this quarter,' says the commentator, before we spin round, passing the eleventh-century Church of San Fermo Maggiore, and return to Piazza Bra, coming to a halt next to the armoured vehicle with the posing soldiers.

I am not sure that the hardest of hardcore rail enthusiast would care for all of this.

It is, however, quite fun.

* * *

Back at the Romeo & Juliet Non-Hotel I have a snooze and wake to hear thunderclaps and heavy rain. It's a deluge and the heavens have opened. There's no way I'm going out in that.

But hanging about alone in a room with two single beds in the Romeo & Juliet Non-Hotel for an evening does not really bear thinking about.

For a while I do so. To pass the time, I read the Respect Verona rules on the city's tourist map. Just as at Innsbruck Station, there are many. One must not 'bathe in the fountains' (a diagram shows a figure leaping into a fountain with arms in the air), nor may one, rather mysteriously, 'defeat and dehumidify' (a picture of a figure spray-painting a wall accompanies this rule). Eating near monuments is forbidden, as is 'circulating naked' (a diagram shows a shirtless man and a woman in a bikini). Anyone considering stopping off at Verona Porta Nuova Station should bear all of this in mind. There are 'possible fines', although the minimum amount is not stated.

I think I really need to take a walk. I am reading city rules on tourist maps. I need to get some air.

The downpour ends abruptly. I venture, via many puddles, to Piazza Bra and eat a probably-overpriced-but-good pasta with ragu sauce at a cafe with red tablecloths facing the square. I order a glass of red wine and begin to read a book, rather than a tourist map. Fewer people are dying in terrible ways in *The Bridge on the River Drina* by Ivo Andrić – my train-inspired discovery in Serbia – but a fair few still are. During a particularly troubled period an Austrian guard on the bridge, who is huge in stature but simple-minded, has just committed suicide after a pretty young Turkish woman with whom he has become infatuated fools him into believing that she is taking her ageing grandmother across the bridge. In fact, the huddled, shuffling figure is a fugitive wanted by the authorities. His superiors discover his lapse and he admits to the sequence of events. He is court marshalled (he has both failed in his duties and broken an order banning Christian-Muslim relations), but he is not properly overseen while left with his rifle. The description of the taking of his life is vivid.

Not the happiest of holiday reads. Perhaps I should simply stop reading for a while altogether.

I do so, and gaze across Piazza Bra sipping another glass of red.

This may sound awful yet it's true: one of the great joys of a train trip is that, should you wish to, *you can have a drink*. No need to worry about breathalysers (or finding a parking space, for that matter). Just roll along, order a bottle of whatever, watch the scenery go by from the window, or life unfold at your destination. Taking a long train journey can be relaxing in more ways than one.

The streets in which Shakespeare's Capulets and Montagues clashed, where the ancient grudge is played out, feel ghostly as the light fades. The families exchange insults and brawl here in Act One of *Romeo and Juliet*, forcing the Prince of Verona to intervene:

> Rebellious subjects, enemies to peace,
> Profaners of this neighbour-stained steel –
> Will they not hear? – What ho! You men, you beasts,
> That quench the fire of your pernicious rage
> With purple fountains issuing from your veins.
> On pain of torture, from these bloody hands
> Throw your mistempered weapons to the ground.

It all happened here somewhere near the amphitheatre in Verona.

Shakespeare did not invent the plot of *Romeo and Juliet* so he cannot take all the credit for the tourism euros. The story was popular in Italy long before he penned his version. Shakespeare's direct source for his play was *The Tragicall Historye of Romeus and Juliet* by Arthur Brooke, a narrative poem published in 1562, two years before the Bard was born. Shakespeare's version, which brought life, inventiveness and brilliance to the tale, was published around 1597. Soon after hitting the stage his play was described in a quarto note as 'hath been often (with great applause) plaid publiquely'. Brooke sadly died in a shipwreck crossing the English Channel a year after he completed his work.

I order another glass of red.

I decide I very much like Verona, despite all the crowds by Juliet's balcony. It is a mellow city once the day's tourist hordes have gone. Locals take evening strolls and the amphitheatre broods beneath an ebony sky. Star-crossed lovers, perhaps, walk hand in hand. This is the time to see Verona, when Romeo and Juliet were exchanging sweet nothings.

Romeo:

> O speak again, bright angel, for thou art
> As glorious to this night, being o'er my head,
> As is a winged messenger of heaven
> Unto the white upturned, wond'ring eyes
> Of mortals that fall back to gaze on him,
> When he bestrides the lazy-passing clouds,
> And sails upon the bosom of the air.

Juliet:

> 'Tis but thy name that is my enemy.
> Thou art thyself, though not a Montague.
> Nor arm nor face, nor any other part
> Belonging to a man. O be some other name.

What's in a name? That which we call a rose
By any other word would smell as sweet.

I drink another glass for good luck.
Tomorrow I am catching a final slow train – to Venice.

CHAPTER TEN

VERONA TO VENICE IN ITALY

CHE BELLA CORSA! (WHAT A RIDE!)

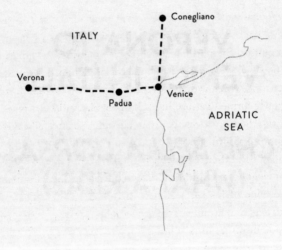

It is said Mussolini 'made the trains run on time'. But this expression can be read in different ways. One take: despite Mussolini's fascist policies, the dictator at least got one thing working well. Another is: who in their right mind would accept the slaughter and torture of fascism just to have the 12:30 from Verona to Venice depart punctually?

I prefer the second interpretation.

But is it true: did the trains run better?

The answer is equivocal.

In *Italian Ways: On and off the Rails from Milan to Palermo*, Tim Parks says that the long decline of Italian railways began during fascism in the country. Before the 1922 March on Rome, when Mussolini gained power, a great deal of cash had been ploughed into the Italian train network, which was regarded as important to maintain the unity of the newly formed nation. Indeed, many blackshirts involved in the 'march' travelled on specially arranged trains (some railway workers were supporters of the fascists).

So Mussolini inherited a well-run railway and cannot take credit for what went before him. But once in power, Il Duce did make train efficiency one of his key policies, introducing *treni popolari*, with cheap tickets and simple carriages to take working-class people to the seaside or on mountain holidays. He oversaw the electrification of tracks to reduce reliance on expensively imported coal; in 1937 one such train broke the world speed record by touching 106 miles an hour. Yet at the same time, many rail workers were laid off (unions were a power threat), the economy struggled, driving on newly built roads became popular and the railways were ultimately, of course, destroyed in World War Two. No trains were running on time after that.

These days train efficiency is generally considered pretty good and the Italian need for speed that harks back to the 1937 record-breaker has come to the fore. The journey time from Rome to Venice can be as little as 3 hours and 45 minutes, while from Rome to Florence is a mere 1 hour and 32 minutes, and Rome to Naples is 1 hour and 10 minutes. Reasonably priced Frecciarossa (red arrow) trains operated by Trenitalia whizz along at 186 miles an hour, with dining carriages with waiters and comfortable seats. There are also pointy-nosed Frecciargento (silver arrow) services with a top speed of 155 miles an hour. These have a cafe/bar rather than a fancy restaurant. The country has 10,000 miles of state-owned tracks and it is quite easy to get about on them.

Italians have always loved their railways.

The first railway, or *ferrovia* (ironway), opened in 1839, just nine years after the original Manchester–Liverpool line, with English-made locomotives taking passengers on the 11-minute journey over five miles between Naples and Portici in what was then the Kingdom of the Two Sicilies. This track was soon extended to 22 miles around the Bay of Naples and was a big hit, not least with King Ferdinand II, who often enjoyed rides to the seaside. A total of 58,000 passengers were notched up in the first month; so much money was flowing in that the owners began to reduce fares for 'ladies without hats, servants in livery and non-commissioned officers'. Which was nice of them.

Railway mania swept the nation, with rapid growth in lines including north–south tracks on either side of the Apennine mountains. The line between Milan and Venice, along which I am about to travel, was completed in 1857, requiring a remarkable two-mile viaduct with 222 arches across a lagoon. Historians believe that more than half of public spending on infrastructure between Italian unification, also known as the Risorgimento (the resurgence), and World War One was on railways.

This was, as mentioned earlier, a crucial period. Just as in Belgium and Germany in the late nineteenth century the country was becoming one – and trains were at the heart of matters.

Prossima fermata
Verona to Venice

After a lie-in at the Romeo & Juliet Non-Hotel and a wander round Verona, I walk up the hill past Porta Nuova to the station. The frenetic scrum of the ticket hall is, as ever, going strong. At the main cafe I fight my way forward waving euros, eventually taking possession of a slice of pizza oozing with mozzarella, parmesan and pesto. Well worth the elbow-barging: absolutely fantastic; best station-food yet.

Someone has left a *La Gazzetta dello Sport* on my table and I gather from the front page that the famous goalkeeper Gianluigi Buffon is leaving Juventus Football Club. I hang around for a bit reading about Italian football gossip, the best I can. With little else to do as I've got here too early, I explore the station, ascending some steps to discover, somewhat surprisingly, a *ristorante birreria bavarese* (Bavarian restaurant and beer hall) on the platform above. A cardboard cutout of a buxom waitress clasping a massive glass of beer marks the entrance. Inside people are drinking similar massive glasses of beer. It's all very jolly.

I stop to consider this Bavarian beer hall. There is something about it that is not quite right. Verona Porto Nuova Station may not be the best choice of venue for a German-themed restaurant and beer hall.

This station was, after all, in the hands of the Nazis after Italy's 1943 surrender in World War Two. Before the Germans destroyed all the bridges and left Verona, the station was used for freight train deportations to death camps.

The Auschwitz survivor Primo Levi, captured in December 1943, was some weeks later loaded onto such a train with a dozen wagons along with 649 other 'pieces', as the Nazi guards described their prisoners, in the town of Carpi in the province of Modena, about 60 miles south of Verona. The train went north past Verona, through the Adige Valley and over the Brenner Pass. On board Levi and his fellow occupants were thirsty, cold and suffering from blows from the guards. At the

Brenner Pass, the 45 people in Levi's wagon all stood in silence, not knowing whether they would ever return. Through slits in the wagon, Levi saw the names of Austrian, Czech and, finally, Polish towns and cities at stations. In February 1944 after a journey of about four days the train arrived at Auschwitz. Guards selected those deemed fit to work for the Reich. Of the 650 people on board, 525 separated from those considered healthy died soon after. Of the 45 people in Levi's wagon only four returned home. His was by far the most fortunate wagon, as Levi explains in his harrowing memoir *If This Is a Man*.

As I said, a Bavarian beer hall at Verona Porto Nuova Station does feel distinctly out of place; if not simply completely wrong.

* * *

The 12:30 to Venezia Santa Lucia Station draws up at platform four.

I enter a carriage with two levels and plush blue seats. A bald conductor with a red tie and a bushy moustache checks my almost completely ruined Interrail Pass as the train creaks away, soon arriving at the *prossima fermata* (next stop), Verona Porta Vescovo Station, where more passengers board. A television monitor in a corner advertises an exhibition in Treviso featuring the works of the French sculptor Auguste Rodin. We pause at Caldiero Station to collect yet more passengers. We pull away. An advert for an exhibition about the nineteenth-century English writer, painter and art critic John Ruskin flashes up. It is being held at the Doge's Palace in Venice. Ruskin was 'a strenuous opponent of expanding mechanisation and materialism' and loved Venice's medieval buildings, the advert says. Not much of a lover of trains, then. I read a little pamphlet that was given out at Verona Porta Nuova Station. The pamphlet is all about great restaurants at stops between Verona and Venice and comes with a quote from the German poet and writer Johann Wolfgang von Goethe: 'On market days, the eyes can rejoice at the sight of mountains of garlic, vegetables and fruit.' Quite a cultural train, this one.

Poppies line the track near Lonigo. The train enters countryside with vineyards mixed with orchards of fruit trees and the occasional factory. Every inch of land seems to have been put to productive use. Hills with villas with terracotta roofs undulate on the horizon near Montebello Vicentino. The landscape is sunlit and warm. We slide by a yard with slabs of marble and apartments with washing hanging from balconies near Altavilla.

I read an online article about Italy's current politics. It appears likely that the anti-establishment Five Star Movement will soon form a government with the far-right League party. These parties together won more than half of the vote in a recent national election. They plan to get tough on immigration. Italy has, of course, been the destination of so many migrant boats from north Africa. The *Financial Times* has recently described the leaders of Five Star and the League as 'modern barbarians' on account of their right-wing extremism and derisive attitude to asylum seekers. Matteo Salvini, leader of the League party, responded to this attack by saying: 'It's better to be a barbarian than a slave that sells Italy's dignity, future, businesses and borders.'

Another country – more troubled times.

I find myself talking to a man sitting in the seats across the aisle from mine. He is in his forties, tanned and smartly dressed in a casual style with a jumper, jeans and black trainers. Italians just seem to have the knack of dressing well. He also seems to exude *education*. I ask if he speaks English as I want to quiz him on what he thinks about Five Star and the League.

'Yes, of course!' he says, as though quite surprised anyone might imagine he did not.

Giacomo is a professor at Bologna University, which is, as he quickly says: 'The oldest university in Europe!'

The university was founded in 1088 and has been taking students ever since. This really is a cultural train.

He asks me to guess what he teaches, and I have a go with *politics*.

'No, no! Economics and law!' he replies, as though in complete disbelief that anyone might imagine otherwise.

I wasn't so far off. He is happy to talk politics anyway.

'They really don't know what is required to deal with a complex Italian society. They are populist: they speak to the belly not to the mind,' he says as an opening salvo. As he does so he joins me on my side of the aisle. When he speaks, he waves his hands close to his face, like a true Italian, and leans forwards as though letting me in on a closely guarded secret. When referring to 'they' he means Five Star and the League.

'For example, they support a flat tax not a progressive tax. They talk about fifteen per cent. But that is not *realistic* at all. In Italy we have huge public spending debt.' He leans forward even more, gesticulating as though conducting an orchestra tackling an intense passage of music. 'It is our way, to be organised by the state. If we do not raise taxes, there will be fiscal pressure. Not *realistic!*'

Giacomo loves the word realistic.

We discuss migrants crossing from Africa.

'Their immigration proposals! Not *realistic!*' he says. 'The League would like to send back home lots of these persons. But it is a historical phenomenon. So, not *realistic!*' He pauses to catch his breath. 'The only *realistic* way is to manage it. You can't stop the river flowing. Managing it has not just got to be an Italian policy. It has to be Europe-wide. It is not just Africa we are dealing with, it is Romania and the Middle East.'

Giacomo believes that Italy presents a one-country version of the troubles that currently beset Europe as a whole.

'We have a problem in Italy, a very big problem between the south and the north,' he says, gesticulating with broader sweeps of his hands. 'Southern Italy is not wealthy. This is like Europe. The north of Italy is comparable to Germany, Austria and France. The south is like Greece and the south of Spain. We are a microcosm of Europe! We have it all in the same country – and that's the problem. There are much better railways, roads and schools in the north.'

He returns to the recent election. 'It is totally, totally *unrealistic*!' he says, waving as wildly as ever. 'The Five Star Movement and the League. They will have to change. Economic forces are stronger than they are!'

He returns to immigration.

'Like your man Farage,' says Giacomo, referring to the former leader of the UK Independence Party. 'They want to leave Europe to stop people coming. But that cannot happen in Italy!'

He mentions the 1957 Treaty of Rome, which – along with the Maastricht Treaty – sets out the constitutional basis for the European Union. Italy was among six countries to sign up to the treaty along with West Germany, France, Belgium, the Netherlands and Luxembourg. 'Italy was one of the founder countries of the EU,' he says. 'But Italy was the only country interested in the political as well as the economic side of it. Germany and France cared most about their core markets: steel and coal. The Netherlands, Belgium and Luxembourg were interested in the arrangement for financial reasons.'

Italy, so soon after World War Two, understood the political importance of togetherness, Giacomo explains. 'Yes, we see that Great Britain has made the choice to leave,' he says, arms truly flailing. 'And now it seems that we may try to do the same. In the end it's all just a political movement.' He is talking about the Five Star Movement and the League. 'In the real economy nothing will change. *Unrealistic*! It's all *unrealistic*!'

With that Giacomo shakes my hand and gets off at Vicenza Station; notable for its palm trees and poppies planted in beds by the platform. Railways do seem to loosen tongues.

The train continues to Grisignano di Zocco Station, where a man is crudely pickaxing the edge of a water fountain by the station house. It is difficult to determine exactly why he would want to do this. Mestrino and Padova come and go before we cross a small green river and recently ploughed fields on the way to Busa di Vigonza Station. The television screen begins to show CCTV footage of different parts of the train. We reach Pianiga, which has walls of tinted panels near the station to keep the sound of trains from houses. The panels are painted with pictures of birds here and there; presumably to stop real birds flying into them.

Two thirty-something men with huge suitcases sit in the booth formerly occupied by Giacomo.

They are from Toronto in Canada and have spent a fortnight travelling around Italy on trains. Bohdan – blue shirt and curly hair – works in human resources at a bank. Tyler – flowery shirt, cool shades – is a vet. It is their first time in Italy and the pair particularly like Tuscany, but do not like Rome.

Bohdan: 'Too many tourists and it was dirty: garbage everywhere.'

They are returning to Venice after taking a fast train from there to Rome.

Tyler: 'The best thing about Italian trains is the speed.'

Although we are on a slow train.

Tyler thinks that the 'general consensus' is that Britain leaving the EU is a mistake.

Bohdan does not have an opinion and says that he has a British friend who does not have an opinion either.

This is as far as our conversation goes. Canadians on the slow train to Venice do not seem to be quite as opinionated and chatty as the Italians.

They disembark at Venezia Mestre Station along with a lot of other passengers. The train has reached Venice! But we are on the mainland side, which does not seem to count properly. We crawl past a telecommunications office and a mysterious tumbledown house with broken windows and weeds in gutters. We cross the lagoon on the two-mile causeway.

Speedboats zip along channels. We are overtaken by a nasty, fast bullet train. The water opens out. Rowers in dragon boats race by (a competition of some sort seems to be on). Magnificent palaces with terracotta roofs rise on the horizon as does, on the left, the bell tower of St Mark's Square. Pale blue water glimmers. More bell towers shoot upwards. More majestic palaces emerge, seeming to float on the water.

The serene one, La Serenissima, awaits.

A sign for Venezia Santa Lucia appears on the left. We have reached the station. The train squeals to a stop at platform 16, two minutes late. Everyone gets off. A hipster kindly takes my picture at the front of the red, grey and blue train. I have, after many, many miles, made it to Venice.

Magnifico!

Che bella corsa! (What a ride!)

A glass of bubbly or two
Venice and Conegliano

It is not, after all, to be my final train journey on this adventure. Two more trains are to come.

* * *

If I thought Verona Porta Nuova Station had been busy, it has absolutely nothing on Venezia Santa Lucia Station. Just getting out is a task. Tourists scramble in a chaotic clamour that makes Verona seem a tranquil oasis. I follow signs for the Grand Canal. Hordes with backpacks and roll-along bags block the way. They jostle. They barge. They read smartphones. This must be a pickpocket's paradise. Nobody seems quite sure where they are going nor what they are doing. Yet the anticipation is immense. I want to see the Grand Canal. I want to see it badly. Venice, despite all the much-reported *overtourism*, is one of my favourite cities.

I have never visited Venice by train, though I once left the city on the railway here. This was on the first *Orient Express* train to pass through into eastern Europe via Dresden and Kraków, with scores of eastern European rail enthusiasts snapping pictures along the line as the Pullman carriages ventured to pastures new: a bizarre experience watching out from the dining carriage.

In the ticket hall of Venezia Santa Lucia Station *biglietti* machines take centre stage and a mosaic featuring stars and planets decorates the walls. Amid all the madness a floppy-haired teenaged tourist is playing a not-very-well-tuned public piano in a corner (not very well). This is the busiest station yet. I reach one of the doorways and there it is: to me, the best sight to be had at the end of any train journey: Venice! Glorious Venice!

Apologies if I am gushing.

Across the way is the fine copper dome and pillars of the Church of San Simeone Piccolo. *Vaporettos* (water buses) gurgle past. Shiny black gondolas glide by with gondoliers in straw hats and couples clutching one another... are proposals in the air? Sunlight illuminates a long terrace of peach, ochre and pale-yellow buildings occupying the opposite bank. The canal has a magical translucent quality, as though glowing from deep below. It is lovely and gorgeous and exciting.

Apologies if I am gushing (part two).

Varnished speedboats churn by sedately. I sit on the top of the steps of Venezia Santa Lucia Station and watch. This terminus – there's no way a train could go any further without the construction of a bridge, the destruction of many ancient palaces and upsetting UNESCO quite a lot – feels a suitable target for a long train ride in Europe. I turn around. The station building has a low roof and is built in concrete in a modernist style with the letters 'FS' above the centre, which stands for Ferrovie dello Stato (Italian State Railways). Santa Lucia Church and a convent were demolished to make way for the structure, which was based on a 1934 design but eventually completed in 1952.

Amid all the Renaissance splendour the station really should not fit in. The facade is faintly sinister with its dozen concrete steps to the dark rectangular opening to the ticket hall. Yet it does. This is an awe-inspiring place to arrive.

Vessels of various shapes and sizes bob past, some bearing tourists, others laden with supplies for hotels and restaurants, some piled with teetering stacks of cannisters, yet more fixed with cranes or with long deep holds waiting to be filled with who knows what. It is a hive of activity and seemingly impossible that the gondolas should keep going with such cool amid the swirl and chop of competing wakes. Yet in the thick of this magnificent madness, a gondolier breaks nonchalantly into a mournful yet uplifting song.

I gaze ahead transfixed. I think I like Venezia Santa Lucia Station a little more than the one back in Katowice in Poland.

Apologies if I am gushing (part three).

A man tries without success to sell me a selfie stick. A series of porters attempt similarly unsuccessfully to take and transport my backpack. A lot of people are eating ice cream. Wheelie bags clatter across the wide cobbled courtyard in front of the station. I turn left and walk through the northern Cannaregio *sestieri* (neighbourhood) of Venice with the Grand Canal to the right. My target? The Quintessential Venetian Apartment offered by Pietro that I have booked for three days. Kasia is flying in this afternoon.

I have changed the owner's name, and the exact wording of his advert, as I have received a long text from Pietro that says: 'In Venice we do not do short term rent. If anyone asks u something, we are friends and I am hosting u and I sleep on the armchair.' Authorities in Venice have recently imposed a ban on new holiday accommodation in the city centre due to a shortage of living options for locals, and I believe this message has something to do with that. Pietro has also warned: 'Washing machine centrifuge: max 500 laps. If higher then all the palace [sic] kind of an earthquake. And please attention, when it opens, it is a bit broken.' On top of this: 'Please don't use at same time washing machine and dishwasher.' Also: 'My wardrobe is on right of bed, locked, u can use the one on left.' And: 'Avoid noise in condo.' Advice is given on where to dispose of rubbish – in the 'communal basin in the front of the house is most practical'. By 'communal basin', I am guessing Pietro means the public bin.

Travelling by train and winging it with budget rooms (with a few quirks) is so much more fun than staying at regular hotels, even if the experience can be a tad frustrating at times.

Key fetched from the reception of a nearby hotel where Pietro is friends with the owner, I find the Quintessential Apartment down a tiny alley and up a dingy staircase to the top floor. The first object I see after negotiating an old-fashioned sliding lock is a shisha pipe. This is in a dimly lit bedroom with a glass chandelier hanging from a beamed ceiling. A black cape and a spooky white mask hang from a coat stand. There is no toilet paper, kitchen roll (although an empty roll is on a dispenser), washing up liquid or dishwasher tablets. There is, on the plus side, one wine glass. The small kitchen also has a little table, a humidor with a few cigars, whisky and vodka bottles and a set of crystal glasses on a high shelf, a decanter and one large yellow armchair. A picture of a swarthy man riding a quad bike in a desert is framed by the front door. This I take to be Pietro, cape-wearing owner of the shisha pipe and the Quintessential Apartment.

The best thing is the little balcony overlooking a canal and a domed church. It is superb to be in a quiet residential part of Venice amid the terracotta roofs with your own private suntrap. I go to buy various missing items and some food, on the way being berated in Italian by an elderly man yelling out of a window in the alley. Perhaps he is asking if Pietro is on the armchair. I give him an Italian shrug and open the palms of my hands to face upwards. Then I drop provisions back at the apartment and go to find Kasia at Venezia Santa Lucia Station.

* * *

Kasia is already there, waiting beneath the 'FS'. After all the miles on the tracks and the many encounters with strangers along the way it's great to see her here in Venice. What better place to meet at a station after an absence, with the gondolas gliding past in the sunshine? The last time we saw each other was by a dusty bus stop next to a roundabout in Kraków. We return to the Quintessential Apartment, cook a spaghetti bolognaise with plenty of parmesan cheese and drink a bottle of Pinot Grigio (we are, after all, in Italy). On the balcony of Pietro's Quintessential Venetian Apartment, we put our feet up and listen to the peal of early evening bells, looking across the rooftops and spires.

'So you made it!' says Kasia, gazing out across the lagoon city and sipping her Pinot Grigio. She had been in some doubt when I was in the depths of Transnistria and, later, in Vrbas and Slavonski Brod. 'I wasn't sure you would.'

Timing the journey back to Italy had been tricky.

We raise our glasses and watch the sun set in a tangerine swirl that turns first lilac then purple and then coal-black, with stars twinkling and the moon casting milky light on the canal below. The warmth of the day remains in the stone balcony. A woman on a terrace opposite us hums quietly as she waters her potted plants. Somewhere in the distance a gondolier sings a song, which echoes up between the narrow, ancient buildings. Oh, Venice, oh, Venice!

Apologies for gushing (part four).

The next day we visit the sights like good, dutiful overtourists.

We soon learn to go with the crazy overflow of visitors in the alleys on the way to Rialto Bridge and St Mark's Square. It is a terrible crush... more a case of 'Oh no, Venice!' this morning.

We stop by posters that seem to be announcing an event. Next month yet another protest is planned against what we are in the midst of experiencing. A picture of the canals shows a theme park rising in the background beside a giant cruise ship. Messages read: *'COME TO DISNEYLAND!' 'SVENDIAMO TUTTO!'* [SELL OFF

EVERYTHING!] *'PIÙ HOTELS PER TUTTI!'* [MORE HOTELS FOR EVERYONE!] *'MEGA OSTELLO!'* [MEGA HOSTEL!] *'LASCIATE OGNI PERANZA VOI CHE ABITATE!'* [ABANDON ALL HOPE OF LIVING!].

I don't think the poster writers really want all of this to happen. At the foot of the invitation to join the protest is a final message: *'TUTTI INSIEME PER UNA CITTA PIÙ DEGNA!'* [ALL TOGETHER FOR A MORE DIGNIFIED CITY!] There are further calls for *turismo sostenibile* (sustainable tourism). The overall aim of the march? *'CIAO POVERTY!'* And who could argue with that?

Bruges, 'Venice of the North', may have a bad dose of *overtourism*; Venice itself seems at the point of keeling over from the condition.

We consider the Ruskin exhibition but the queue is too long, take a *vaporetto*, and then lose ourselves off the beaten track in alleyways. This is the way to do it. Away from the main sights are tranquil squares, empty passages and tiny restaurants that seem to be mainly for locals. We stop at one, Trattoria Bandierette in the *sestieri* of Castello, to the east of St Mark's. Inside are simple wooden tables, faded yellow walls, exposed brick columns and a handful of well-dressed elderly customers (men in jackets and ties) eating linguine with clams and drinking wine. Dusty bottles on shelves line the window at the front, blocking the sunlight and adding to the atmosphere of secrecy. Faded black-and-white pictures of Venice depict the days before the masses arrived on giant cruise ships and easyJet. Specials are written neatly on a little chalkboard. This is the opposite of overtourism. If anything, it's *undertourism*. A waiter with a moustache takes our order of black ink squid with polenta in Venetian style and grilled sea bream. Both are delicious (although my teeth turn black). We while away an hour or so in this delightful hideaway from the hordes. *Bellissimo!* Oh, Venice, oh, Venice! *Bellissimo, bellissimo!*

Am I gushing yet again (part five)?

It's hard not to. Dickens, who loved Verona so much, felt even more strongly about Venice, which he describes in a chapter entitled 'Italian

Dream' in *Pictures from Italy*. He is so enamoured by the lagoon city that he imagines he has visited Venice in his sleep as the reality is too unbelievable to him. After floating by boat in darkness and silence (few tourists or cafes and bars for tourists then) from the mainland and along 'phantom streets', the canals, to St Mark's Square, he awakes the following morning:

> The glory of the day that broke upon me in this Dream, its freshness, motion, buoyancy; its sparkles of the sun on the water; its clear blue sky and rustling air; no waking words can tell. But, from my window, I looked down on boats and barks; on masts, sails, cordage, flags; on groups of busy sailors, working at the cargoes of these vessels; on wide quays, strewn with bales, casks, merchandise of many kinds; on great ships, lying near at hand in stately indolence; on islands, crowned with gorgeous domes and turrets: and where golden crosses glittered in the light, atop wondrous churches, springing from the sea!

Dickens fell for Venice hook, line and sinker. He goes on to imagine the ghosts of 'old Shylock passing to and fro upon a bridge' with Shakespeare's spirit haunting the lagoon and stealing along the canals. He revels in the 'crimson flush' of sunsets, 'the whole city resolving into streaks of red and purple, on the water'. And when he leaves to continue his grand tour of Italy, he remains awestruck by the 'luxurious wonder of a dream so rare', still disbelieving what he's seen.

The ghosts along the 'phantom streets' do not seem to have gone away. After our excellent lunch at Trattoria Bandierette, Kasia and I wander along the empty backstreets of Castello, crossing little humpback bridges over deserted canals by eerie passageways that cannot have changed much since Dickens's time. Yes, the tourist hordes have well and truly invaded St Mark's and the Rialto Bridge, but Venice in its quiet corners remains dream-like. That will never change, no matter how many incurious cruise ship passengers pour down the gangplanks and follow each other like lemmings to the main sights (so long as the city remains above the rising waves of our climate-change world, that is).

Kasia seems to have got the train bug – and she has a plan. She has read that the town of Conegliano, about 35 miles north of Venice, is in the heart of Prosecco country. Why not go for a day trip there tomorrow by train for a glass of bubbly before flying home? 'It'll be fun,' she says, 'and we won't have to hide away from the cruise ship people.' Kasia hates crowds.

I could think of worse ideas.

We'll escape La Serenissima for a day – and swarms of passengers with day-pass plastic wristbands that even Dickens could not have dreamed of – and go on a final train adventure.

* * *

Which is how we find ourselves back at Venezia Santa Lucia Station. We are about to catch the 10:05 to Conegliano, due in at 11:00. But first a taste of *overtourism* up close and personal.

A queue has formed at what appears to be the main cafe in the ticket hall. This is an improvement on Verona Porta Nuova Station's free-for-all but the cafe is in a cramped space with the general carnage of people that never seems to go away at Venezia Santa Lucia Station swirling all around. In the queue, a seriously large American woman with a seriously large roll-along suitcase has just bought two tall takeaway coffees. She balances the two takeaway coffees on top of one another, somehow manages to swivel, takes the seriously massive suitcase in her other hand and attempts to leave the cafe. She goes one step. The coffee balancing on top of the other coffee flies off and splatters all over the floor, miraculously not soaking anyone. At this very moment, a man who I take to be Italian, who I have already noticed has been trying to push ahead, seizes the moment to make his move and gain a place.

He is, you might say, a first-rate *furbo* (sly one) – like a Formula One driver snatching an audacious opportunity to pass on a tight bend, he slides by. I step ahead slightly to prevent his manoeuvre and at the very same time, another American woman ahead of me steps back so that she steps on me. 'Step back, will you please!' she shrieks at me, with astonishing anger. In contrast to the American with the suitcase, she is tiny and extremely mean-looking, positively fuming with rage. I apologise begrudgingly as she did, after all, step back on *me*. After I do so she regards me with even greater fury, as though I am the source of all the world's evil and ought to be lined up against a wall and summarily given my due Mussolini-style. At this moment, of course, the *furbo* pushes past all three of us and orders an espresso. It really is quite impossible to defeat a *furbo*.

Kasia, sensing my annoyance, says: 'Bad infrastructure. The cafe is too small. People want food, water and coffee, not some make-up products.' We had noticed a couple of cosmetic shops in the station. 'Anyway, you can't take a suitcase in here – it's just crazy,' she says. The seriously large American woman had started it all off, though the *furbo* and the tiny furious American woman had not exactly helped matters. Why had the seriously large American woman not left her case with the person to whom she was delivering the extra coffee? Or perhaps, as a seriously large American, she required two coffees?

Sometimes life throws up unsolvable mysteries.

This is Venice and it is busy-busy. Too many tourists in one place: overtourism in action.

We decide to get away from the main cafe at Venezia Santa Lucia Station. Coffee-less, we board the 10:05 to Conegliano.

The train is jam-packed with more holidaymakers. We find two seats by a woman with a wailing baby. Her husband, clearly finding the toddler an irritation, leaves his wife and child and goes to the gap between the carriages to make a phone call. Yet another *furbo* of sorts. They're all over the place.

Across the beautiful lagoon we go, arriving at Treviso not long afterwards, where the father returns and all three disembark along with the majority of our carriage. They must be going to the airport.

In blissful silence we spin through farmland and vineyards towards distant misty mountains. A classic Italian bell tower arises near Spresiano and we cross the swirling River Piave. Just before we arrive at Conegliano, Kasia realises that she has not validated her ticket at a machine on the platform back in Venice. The tiny furious American woman who had been set off by the actions of the seriously large American woman had distracted our attention. We spend a while watching *furbo*-like for a conductor, but none is to be seen. The train pulls in to a stately looking mid-nineteenth-century station with a distinguished facade and arched doorways. We have arrived in Conegliano without being fined for an invalidated ticket.

This is a quiet town with a population of about 35,000. From the station we go along a street that leads straight to the picturesque main square. What a heavenly place!

Apologies for gushing (part six).

The square is dominated by a neoclassical theatre guarded by sphinxes with heads in the shape of maidens and, it is impossible not to notice, enormous naked breasts with prominent nipples. On the right-hand side of the square is another neoclassical building with statues of Giuseppe Garibaldi, the key military leader during Italian unification, and Vittorio Emanuele II, the first king of the united Italy. Above the square is a hill with the walls and tower of a tenth-century castle rising above cypress trees. The town was once home to the Renaissance artist Cima da Conegliano (1459–1517), whose works hang in the National Gallery in London and who painted the altarpiece featuring a Madonna and child at the town's Duomo.

A food and drink festival is about to begin, although hardly anyone is about. As far as we can tell we are the only foreign tourists. Trenitalia has transported us in less than an hour from the crazy Venetian alleyways to a provincial backwater about to launch into some kind of annual celebration. A ticket system is in operation. Festival goers buy tickets and take these to a stall with a bar to select Prosecco wines. Pasta with various sauces is available at another stall. Ice cream and pastries are to be had at another. Songs by James Brown are playing on a sound system manned by two teenagers who are dancing to the beat as though they are DJs at a mega-club on Ibiza, though the music is not too loud and the audience has yet to arrive.

We climb the hill to the castle without passing a soul and find the tower is home to a museum that is closed. The tower and the walls are more or less all that remain of the castle, which now has a well-tended garden with a lawn, beds of flowers, cypress trees, statues of classical figures and a solitary palm tree. In one corner is a cafe/restaurant, with a view across terracotta rooftops. We sit in the cool shade of a cypress tree and toast travelling Europe by slow trains. I do not wish to gush any further but there is plenty to gush about this castle and this very splendid setting with a glass of Prosecco in hand.

Down the hill once again, James Brown is a little louder and children are dancing to the music along with the DJs. Locals eat gnocchi with ragu sauce on long picnic tables. We do the same before buying tickets to try the various different types of Prosecco (I had no idea non-fizzy Prosecco existed). Sitting at a table on the terrace of the town hall by the bust of Garibaldi drinking non-fizzy Prosecco is a fine way to spend an afternoon in Italy.

A woman pushes a pram with a very pampered hound on board. Kids chase one another. An opera singer takes to the steps of the theatre with a microphone from the DJs and sings 'O Sole Mio' ('My Sunshine'), her voice wobbling and the sound system failing to cope with her screechy high notes.

'Oh my God, my ears are bleeding,' says Kasia.

Mine are not feeling so good either.

But then the sound system is fixed and ears cease to bleed as a troop of dancers in traditional red costumes with unusual pointy hats takes to the steps playing string instruments and drums. They dance frenetically for a while. The Conegliano Vespa Club arrives by the square after a rally of some sort. They park their shiny classic scooters in a side street, looking like a comedy version of Hell's Angels, and go to the gnocchi and ragu stalls.

We read a pamphlet that explains Prosecco comes from the glera grape and that there are various different types – DOCG (Denomination of Origin Controlled and Guaranteed), DOC (Denomination of Origin Controlled, but not apparently guaranteed) – and methods of production, including the Martinotti process, which involves large pressurised vats and the *talento* process, where fermentation takes place in bottles. Those who drink of Superior DOCG should do so in the year after the harvest to enjoy best the wine's 'fruity, floral, organoleptic characteristics'. We look up 'organoleptic' to find the meaning is 'related to the sense of human organs'. Not only must drinkers of Superior DOCG be aware of organoleptic characteristics, they must also ensure that they drink from 'Prosecco calyx glasses, rather than wide glasses, and avoid flutes or cups at 9°C of temperature'. Calyx are wider than champagne flutes and we appear to be drinking from them. What a great deal one needs to know when sampling Italian bubbly.

Kasia and I return to the station and catch the 14:50 back to Venice, crossing the lagoon to see four enormous cruise ships moored to the right. Each must hold a thousand passengers. From a distance they look like floating car parks above the pastel-coloured palazzos. No wonder more local protests are soon to be held. So many people. So little space.

The train, my very last one, glides along. The madness of Venezia Santa Lucia Station awaits.

On a balcony in Cannaregio
Venice

These slow trains to Venice, including the day trip to Conegliano, have covered almost 4,000 miles (3,990 miles, to be as precise as I can).

On the sunny balcony of Pietro's Quintessential Venetian Apartment, I try to put this in perspective. The mileage is almost equidistant as the crow flies from London to Chicago to the west, Afghanistan to the east, Uganda to the south, and somewhere around the top of Greenland to the north. It has been a very long journey indeed and I have enjoyed (almost) every moment.

High points from a train perspective have come in different forms: the simple thrill of moving off on the rambling line through Kent; the escape from France (without getting stuck); the welcoming and amusing Belgian Trains conductors; the amazing efficiency of Deutsche Bahn; the Z-land of Poland as seen from Polskie Koleje Państwowe, followed by the wonderful rattling sleepers in Ukraine and the sensation of dropping off the map on the *Ivo Andrić* into northern Serbia. The crawl through the Balkans into Croatia was a delight. The trip on the funny steam train with Mr Dusan at the Railway Museum of Slovenian Railways in Ljubljana was a lark. The sight of the mountains on the ride from Austria over the Brenner Pass to Verona was exhilarating. The first glimpse of the lagoon in Venice took my breath away.

These are just the rides.

Another train-related enjoyment, as I have mentioned, has been the stations. What a variety, from the simple suburban platform in Mortlake to the grandeur of Gare de Lille Flandres, to the sheer scale of Leipzig Station and the moving Holocaust memorial at Dresden Station. In Poland I was met by both Kasia and a maharaja's palace at Wrocław and enjoyed the tucked-away elegance of Opole Główne Station with its fine old steam engine. The HALL OF ENHANCED COMFORT added a curiosity factor in Lviv. Odessa was memorable for its military videos in the ticket hall, followed soon after by the statues of George Stephenson and James Watt on the splendid facade of Budapest-Keleti, sleepy Vrbas, Tito-era Slavonski Brod, the chapel in Zagreb, the James Joyce plaque in Ljubljana, the striking mural at Innsbruck, the madness of Verona Porta Nuova, and the even madder Venezia Santa Lucia.

Then there were the people, both on and off the rails, from the guards at Dover, to the refugee coordinators in Calais, the government officials in Maastricht, the communists in Bonn, backpackers in Poland, lovelorn air-mile aficionados in Ukraine, sleeper companions in Hungary, cafe owners in Serbia, museum directors in Croatia, professors of economics and law from Bologna University.

It is not just the clatter of the tracks that seems to rattle out stories, although trains certainly do have this effect, it is also the interest others have in hearing about a lengthy rail ride. A long-distance train traveller has a tale to tell. You roll into town after a journey that can, as I found time and again, open doors, as people simply seem interested in how on earth you arrived at wherever you've ended up. This is something that air passengers just don't have: a story. When it comes down to it, the traveller by plane does *not want* a story: delays, turbulence scares, vomiting neighbours, screeching children, diversions, sleepless nights, dreadful service and worse, if things really do go wrong. In answer to the question 'How was your flight?' most people would prefer simply to say 'Fine, thanks'. And that's it.

But that's not likely to break the ice with strangers. Meanwhile, on board there is no dining carriage in which to meet fellow travellers. You find your seat, sit there and generally do what you are told. Paul Theroux describes time on planes as being 'truncated' and designed so your mind empties as you wait for the wheels to touch down. It is the *getting there* that is important for the airline passenger, Theroux says, not the *how you did it*.

T. S. Eliot is credited with the saying: 'The journey, not the arrival, matters.' This is accurate up to a point so far as train travel is concerned. The journey certainly matters a lot, but arrivals do, too.

Discovering histories, meeting interesting people and the very act of staying overnight in a new place all add to the journey. As I have said, I could not begin to be comprehensive about the places visited. Snapshots: that's all I have offered and I knew that as I embarked from London, so long ago now it seems. That is all part of the pleasure of travelling by train: you arrive somewhere and move on. Snapshot taken from whichever angle you prefer.

From the refugee centre and the World War Two museum in Calais to the medieval squares and morning mass in Lille, the overtourism of Bruges, the table where the Maastricht Treaty was signed, and onwards, this has been my approach. The train traveller has no obligation to see all the sights, he or she may merely take in what is of particular interest before catching the next ride. The train is the thing. It's all about the train (well, mostly).

Another enjoyment offered by travelling by rail is the opportunity to read. Tim Parks describes train travel as being oddly conducive to reading and he is right. There is no way you could spend 3,990 miles merely staring out of your carriage window, unless the scenery induces many a long snooze (but then you might miss your station). There is plenty of time to dip into the dramas of Agatha Christie's *Murder on the Orient Express*, the eerie but enticing *Bruges-La-Morte* by Georges Rodenbach, John le Carré's thrilling *A Legacy of Spies*, Ivo Andrić's captivating *The Bridge on the Drina*. Books and trains go together like rail tracks and sleepers.

Railways also provide the time to think. You can down tools for a while, just go wherever the lines take you, as the German rail enthusiast said back at Budapest-Keleti Station: once on board, that's it, you're going where the train goes, no more decisions to make. Drift along, enjoy the unexpected and reflect on things. I did just this, and as I have said, the sense of getting away from it all, the escapism – very quickly – infected me. In Dover, I made a move that I had been meaning to make for some time. The freedom of the tracks with Europe waiting to be explored seemed to tip the balance in my mind.

We live in an era of mass-market airline travel and the ticking off of 'bucket-list' destinations. Travel for many seems to have become a concerted effort to see places that most of those in the early twentieth century would only have been able to read about in books or watch on films. Take camel rides by the pyramids, marvel at the Taj Mahal, drink fine wines overlooking Uluru and generally see as many sights as possible before you kick the bucket. Yes, this may sound appealing – enjoy the world while you're still in it! – although some believe the saying derives from a person committing suicide by kicking away a bucket and hanging from a beam. Not so appealing.

Whatever you do, don't forget to post something on social media so your friends are jealous.

A recent study by the International Air Transport Association found that people took to the skies almost twice as often as they did 18 years ago at the turn of the twenty-first century. More than four billion people caught flights last year and the reason given is the great affordability of airfares in the era of budget airlines. Ryanair is now the busiest airline in Europe, taking 130 million passengers a year, and the next biggest is easyJet, with 83 million. One-way transatlantic flights are to be had for £140. Flying is so cheap – and likely to become even cheaper – that many simply do not even for a moment consider trains as a way of discovering the world. Trains are associated with long, cramped, boring commutes. Who in their right mind would use up their holiday messing about with connections on branch lines when you can get where you want more quickly for less cash and less bother?

But this totally misses Eliot's point – it also ignores that planes pump out carbon dioxide directly into the atmosphere and are not at all good for the planet. The environmental impact of trains is well established as being much less than that of planes; a matter I've left alone till here, as the case has been made by many others.

The Interrail Pass, invented in 1972, had its heyday during the twentieth century. For a long time, until 1998, a mid-twenties age limit was set, but after then passes became available to all. Prices are reasonable. For the cost of three of those budget transatlantic flights you can spend 22 days on a European adventure. But the lure of a long weekend break in Barcelona, Athens, Rome and – yes – Venice is always there. Fly away and tick off the Parthenon or the Colosseum on Friday-to-Monday getaways and only take a single day off work if it's a Bank Holiday.

This is obviously a totally different type of travel; a far cry from the train travel that I hope to have captured on this series of 38 rides.

* * *

Sunshine bakes the terracotta rooftops of Cannaregio. Locals are meeting on a makeshift terrace across the canal by the domed church as bells toll in the direction of Venezia Santa Lucia Station. Not a tourist is in sight at sunset (other than us). Tucked away in the eaves, this is the perfect spot to look back over the past few weeks.

* * *

Another reason I took to the rails for this journey was a curiosity to see Europe from the tracks during a period of great change.

The Continent is obviously in a state of flux. At such times railways tend to come to the fore. Budapest-Keleti Station, with its faded grandeur and tasty omelettes, has seen a major refugee crisis unfold. This crisis shed light on the priorities of a far-right government in charge of the central European nation. While rejecting immigration from a war-torn country in the Middle East, Hungarian leaders have also distanced themselves from the country's complicity with the Germans in World War Two; some would say rewriting history by doing so.

Similar attempts have been made in Poland, which is witnessing a major backlash against immigration. As is Germany, where I met anti-fascist activists shortly after arriving in Bonn, and in Austria, where I travelled in the opposite direction along the line that took Primo Levi and so many others to Nazi death camps.

In Calais I met Eritreans who had risked their lives crossing the Mediterranean Sea after fleeing troubles and taking trains to reach as far as the Channel. In Italy, where Mussolini was once so train obsessed, the far right is on the verge of power once more. In the Balkans I visited countries that have only fairly recently concluded a conflict that involved genocide. Feelings remain bitter and resentful, as the tall man wearing black in Vrbas in Serbia and the guest house owner in Slavonski Brod in Croatia quickly revealed. In Ukraine, I went to a sandy beach resort 100 miles across the Black Sea from invading troops. A low-key war has been raging quietly in the east of the country since 2014.

Europe is deeply troubled. On a long train ride, it is possible to take its pulse from the tracks.

Where does the UK fit in to all of this? Well, it seems hell-bent, one way or another, on opting 'out'. Whether this will actually happen and, if so, whether it will work, only time will tell. I began this book mentioning Winston Churchill's hope for a 'kind of United States of Europe'. Yet the dreams of the man who led Britain in the defeat of Hitler have been cast aside. The 51.9 per cent of Britons who voted Leave in the EU referendum of 2016 – 26 per cent of the country's population – had their say and they 'won'. For now. Who really knows what lies ahead? Uncertainty seems the only certainty – no matter how things play out.

Travelling by train from the station close to my home I was able to move freely across almost 4,000 miles of the Continent. I truly hope such rail adventures will be possible for generations to come. For now, though, buy a ticket! Find a seat on a slow train! Venezia Santa Lucia Station is a good target and a glass or two of Prosecco is a suitable reward. Kasia and I take a bottle we bought in Conegliano out of the freezer. It is perfectly chilled and tastes suitably fruity, floral and organoleptic.

Saluti!

Arrivederci! Ciao!

AFTERWORD

So Brexit did happen, despite the lingering doubts. When I first sat down to write this afterword it was 'Brexit Day', 31 January 2020 – or 'Liberation Day' as some were dubbing it. The *Daily Express* was jubilant: 'YES, WE DID IT!' The *Daily Mail* was less triumphant, yet optimistic: 'A NEW DAWN FOR BRITAIN'. The *i* newspaper opted for: 'UK'S LEAP INTO THE UNKNOWN'. Meanwhile, *The Guardian*'s front page depicted a crumbling sandcastle topped by a plastic Union Jack on a beach in front of Dover's white cliffs: 'SMALL ISLAND: AFTER 47 YEARS, BRITAIN LEAVES THE EU AT 11PM TONIGHT – THE BIGGEST GAMBLE IN A GENERATION'.

Of all the papers, only the *Daily Star* (quite entertainingly) ignored the big news: 'TONIGHT IS A TRULY HISTORIC MOMENT FOR OUR GREAT NATION… THAT'S RIGHT, IT'S THE END OF DRY JANUARY!'

Britain leaving Europe was indeed the Big Story – at least, for a while.

Trouble was on its way in the form of a disease first recorded in December 2019 in the Chinese industrial city of Wuhan (a place I visited while writing my book *Ticket to Ride: Around the World on 49 Unusual Train Journeys* and didn't much like back then). The rest is history as the coronavirus (or COVID-19) pandemic spread like wildfire with death tolls rising, lockdowns, travel restrictions and economic turmoil that will probably take years from which to recover.

For a period, Britain's departure from the European Union was forgotten as concerns necessarily shifted to supplying hospitals and fighting the disease. The word 'Brexit', seldom far from news readers' lips, disappeared as the lockdown took over, only tentatively returning as the worst of the outbreak passed.

* * *

Everything now has changed as emergency measures are taken worldwide to protect health and restore wealth. Yet in many ways, matters on the Continent are likely to remain much as before. If anything, the coronavirus has simply sharpened the focus.

Brexit may have represented post-Second World War Europe beginning to unravel, with growing populist movements on the Continent reflecting this instinct to get away and 'go it alone', but the coronavirus has not cared what your politics happen to be.

Every nation has been forced to respond – and what is interesting is precisely *how*.

Britain's bumbling efforts have yet again raised questions about the competency of its leaders (as well as eyebrows overseas). Somehow, despite repeated reassurances that the situation is under control, the United Kingdom has the second highest number of recorded deaths by the coronavirus on the planet at the time of writing. Compare this to Germany, which – thanks to its well-resourced health system – has had a quarter of the fatalities, and you get an idea of Britain's abject failure to handle the crisis.

On the Continent, however, there has been another reaction. Authoritarian leaders have assessed how to deal with the pandemic and have unashamedly co-opted the disease to grab or attempt to grab greater powers. In Hungary, an indefinite 'state of danger' has been declared. In Poland, rulers have indulged in electoral skullduggery. Censorship of social media has tightened in Turkey. Increased surveillance and heavy fines for spreading 'false information' have been introduced in Russia.

On one level, the motivation behind *Slow Trains to Venice* was simply to head off and enjoy the freedom of the tracks, see some sleepy out-of-the-way places and indulge in a bit of gentle 'train geekery'. The smell of oil. The clatter of the wheels. The judder along little branch lines leading wherever next.

But on another, I wanted to get close to Europe at a time my country was doing the opposite. Setting forth from Britain's shores for 4,000 miles was a chance to watch the Continent go by from the carriage window and to consider what 'Europe' means.

I wanted to see for myself from the rail side. I also wanted to make a straightforward historical point, which is why this book begins with Churchill's quote about Europe and putting an end to the 'frightful nationalistic quarrels' that led to the Second World War.

During troubled times, Churchill recognised that togetherness is key. Some people are now comparing Europe today with the 1930s when Hitler was on the rise. Discontent with immigrants and frustration about living standards have fuelled knee-jerk politics in many countries. The effect of the coronavirus, which looks set to trigger widespread economic misery, will not be likely to help much.

* * *

For the time being, with so many lockdowns in place, getting about in Europe is tricky. It is impossible to set forth as I did so freely. But things will no doubt return to 'normal' soon enough and it may just be that our appetite for air travel will not be quite as strong as before. Perhaps this is the moment to hit the tracks.

Oh yes, and just in case you were wondering, the Belgian Rail conductors did indeed send me a Belgian Rail tie and belt.

A few months after my return the postman knocked and handed me a cardboard box. Inside was an orange tie with a 'B' pattern and a belt with a 'B' buckle.

Thank you very much, Louis and Luca.

25 May 2020, Mortlake, London

ACKNOWLEDGEMENTS

Setting off into Europe without too much of a plan – just a destination – meant I knew at the outset that the story of the journey would be as much about the people encountered as the places visited. It would be no good to say: 'And then the train arrived at XX, and then I went to XX, following which XX was interesting and XX looked nice from the carriage window.' Fortunately I met a string of interesting folk who brought life to the adventure and I would like to thank all who spared their time; most are mentioned in the text. Special thanks go to my parents Robert Chesshyre and Christine Doyle for listening to me rabbit on about the train rides so much. I would also like to thank Jamie Fox, Ben Clatworthy, Danny Kelly, Kate Chesshyre, Edward Chesshyre, Alasdair MacTavish, Kate Quill, Laura Ivill, Kate McWilliams, Mike Atkins, Damian Whitworth, Nicola Jeal, Stephen McClarence, Alex Frater, Alice Tomic, Julia Brookes and Zsuzsa Simko for their encouragement. Kasia was both brilliant company and full of great ideas for the chapters on Poland and Venice. Special thanks, once again, to Denise Kelly for her assistance with the cover. Frank Barrett, the former travel editor of *The Mail on Sunday,* offered sage advice. Helena Caletta of the Open Book in Richmond has been incredibly supportive, as has Stanfords maps and travel bookshop in Covent Garden. Thanks also to Amanda Monroe of Voyages-sncf.com for her help and advice, as well as to the Costa Coffee employees at Warsaw University library, who allowed me to nurse Americanos for hours on end during the edit.

The terrific enthusiasm of Claire Plimmer, editorial director at Summersdale, pushed me along and made this book possible. I would also like to thank Sophie Martin for overseeing the book's production, Dean Chant for publicity, Debbie Chapman for her first-rate edit, Lucy York for her thorough copy-edit, and Hamish Braid for the maps.

Since publication of the hardback of this book, the coronavirus pandemic has of course altered the way we travel for some time to come. Getting about in Europe is more difficult than ever and this is nothing whatsoever to do with countries putting up border controls to keep out immigrants. Many thanks to all involved at Summersdale for continuing with the publication of this paperback in such a troubled year – and let's hope we all keep healthy and get travelling again soon (preferably by train, naturally).

TRAINS TAKEN

1. Mortlake to Clapham Junction – South Western Railway, 11 minutes, 5 miles
2. Clapham Junction to Victoria – Southern Railway, 6 minutes, 3 miles
3. Victoria to Dover Priory – Southeastern, 2 hours and 3 minutes, 90 miles
4. Calais to Lille – SNCF, 1 hour and 20 minutes, 63 miles
5. Lille to Kortrijk – Belgian Rail, 37 minutes, 17 miles
6. Kortrijk to Bruges – Belgian Rail, 57 minutes, 29 miles
7. Bruges to Liège-Guillemins – Belgian Rail, 2 hours and 4 minutes, 120 miles
8. Liège-Guillemins to Maastricht – Belgian Rail, 33 minutes, 19 miles
9. Maastricht to Liège-Guillemins – Belgian Rail, 33 minutes, 19 miles
10. Liège-Guillemins to Cologne – Deutsche Bahn, 1 hour and 1 minute, 71 miles
11. Cologne to Bonn – Deutsche Bahn, 23 minutes, 18 miles
12. Bonn to Cologne – Deutsche Bahn, 23 minutes, 18 miles
13. Cologne to Hanover – Deutsche Bahn, 2 hours and 40 minutes, 178 miles
14. Hanover to Leipzig – Deutsche Bahn, 2 hours and 42 minutes, 149 miles
15. Leipzig to Dresden – Deutsche Bahn, 1 hour and 24 minutes, 69 miles
16. Dresden to Wrocław – Trilex express, 3 hours and 47 minutes, 160 miles

17. Wrocław to Opole – Polskie Koleje Państwowe (Polish State Railways), 1 hour and 2 minutes, 53 miles

18. Opole to Gliwice – Polskie Koleje Państwowe, 1 hour and 5 minutes, 46 miles

19. Gliwice to Katowice – Koleje Śląskie (Silesian Railways), 29 minutes, 15 miles

20. Katowice to Kraków – Polskie Koleje Państwowe, 2 hours and 3 minutes, 50 miles

21. Bochnia to Przemyśl – Polskie Koleje Państwowe, 2 hours and 29 minutes, 125 miles

22. Przemyśl to Lviv – Ukrainian Railways, 1 hour and 52 minutes, 61 miles

23. Lviv to Odessa – Ukrainian Railways, 10 hours and 31 minutes, 515 miles

24. Odessa to Lviv – Ukrainian Railways, 10 hours and 31 minutes, 515 miles

25. Lviv to Budapest – Ukrainian Railways and Hungarian State Railways, 12 hours and 20 minutes, 360 miles

26. Budapest to Vrbas – Hungarian State Railways and Serbian Railways, 6 hours and 11 minutes, 165 miles

27. Vrbas to Novi Sad – Serbian Railways, 48 minutes, 27 miles

28. Novi Sad to Belgrade – Serbian Railways, 1 hour and 30 minutes, 58 miles

29. Belgrade to Slavonski Brod – Serbian Railways and Croatian Railways, 4 hours and 56 minutes, 137 miles

30. Slavonski Brod to Zagreb – Croatian Railways, 2 hours and 45 minutes, 126 miles

31. Zagreb to Zidani Most – Croatian Railways, 1 hour and 25 minutes, 50 miles

32. Zidani Most to Ljubljana – Slovenian Railways, 1 hour and 2 minutes, 39 miles

33. Ljubljana to Villach – Slovenian Railways, 1 hour and 42 minutes, 77 miles

34. Villach to Innsbruck – Austrian Federal Railways, 2 hours and 32 minutes, 228 miles
35. Innsbruck to Verona – Austrian Federal Railways, 3 hours and 32 minutes, 171 miles
36. Verona to Venice – Trenitalia, 2 hours and 25 minutes, 74 miles
37. Venice to Conegliano – Trenitalia, 55 minutes, 35 miles
38. Conegliano to Venice – Trenitalia, 55 minutes, 35 miles

Number of countries visited by train: 13 (plus side trips to Transnistria in Moldova and Bosnia and Herzegovina that were not by train)

Total distance: 3,990 miles

Please note: distances and times are approximate

OVERNIGHT STAYS

- Hôtel Première Classe Calais Centre-Gare, Calais, France
  www.premiereclasse.com

- Hôtel Première Classe Lille Centre, Lille, France
  www.premiereclasse.com

- Charlie Rockets Jeugdherberg, Bruges, Belgium
  www.charlierockets.com

- Botel, Maastricht, the Netherlands
  www.botelmaastricht.nl

- Max Hostel, Bonn, Germany
  https://max-hostel.de

- Hentschels Apartments, Leipzig, Germany
  www.hentschels-leipzig.de

- Apartamenty Kościuszki, Wrocław, Poland
  www.booking.com

- Apartamenty Młyńska 15, Katowice, Poland
  http://mlynska15.pl

- Lubomirskiego Apartments, Kraków, Poland
  www.booking.com

- Plazma Hotel, Lviv, Ukraine
  http://plazma-hotel.lviv.ua

- Black Sea Hotel, Odessa, Ukraine (day stay only)
  https://blacksea-hotels.com

- Sleeper train from Lviv to Odessa in Ukraine and back
  www.uz.gov.ua

- Sleeper train from Lviv in Ukraine to Budapest in Hungary
  www.uz.gov.ua

- Locomotive Hostel, Budapest, Hungary
  www.locomotive-hostel-budapest.com

- Hotel Bačka, Vrbas, Serbia
  www.hotelbacka.rs

- Hostel Play, Belgrade, Serbia
  www.play-hostel.hotels-in-belgrade.com/en/

- For accommodation in Slavonski Brod, Croatia, see
  www.booking.com (as I do not wish to reveal the exact
  guest house so as not to identify the owner)

- Hostel Kaptol, Zagreb, Croatia
  www.hostelkaptol.com.hr

- A Writer's Place, Ljubljana, Slovenia
  www.booking.com

- Garni Technikerhaus, Innsbruck, Austria
  www.garni-technikerhaus-bed-breakfast.allinnsbruckhotels.com

- Romeo & Juliet Non-Hotel, Verona, Italy
  http://romeo-juliet-non.hotelsverona24.com

- For accommodation in Venice try www.airbnb.com (as I do not
  wish to reveal the exact apartment we stayed in so as to protect the
  identity of the owner)

No hospitality was taken.

USEFUL WEBSITES

- The Man in Seat 61 – for excellent advice on most routes in Europe
  www.seat61.com

- Interrail – to buy an Interrail Pass (a month-long pass with
  continuous travel costs from about £580, while seven days' travel
  within a month is from about £290)
  www.interrail.eu

- OUI SNCF – for information on French services
  https://en.oui.sncf/en

- Deutsche Bahn – for German services and other journeys in Europe
  www.bahn.com

- Trainline – for information on trains in Europe
  www.trainline.com

- Eurostar – if you really want to catch a fast train (and then go slow)
  www.eurostar.com

- Rail Europe – sells tickets and passes
  www.raileurope.com

- Rail.cc – a group of friends offers advice on rail travel in Europe
  www.rail.cc

- OpenRailwayMap – handy website that shows rail lines across
  the globe
  www.openrailwaymap.com

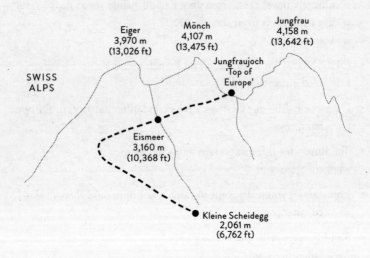

SWISS
ALPS

Eiger
3,970 m
(13,026 ft)

Mönch
4,107 m
(13,475 ft)

Jungfrau
4,158 m
(13,642 ft)

Jungfraujoch
'Top of
Europe'

Eismeer
3,160 m
(10,368 ft)

Kleine Scheidegg
2,061 m
(6,762 ft)

NOTES ON SWISS TRAINS: THE TOP OF EUROPE

Writing about trains in Europe without mentioning Swiss trains just feels wrong. Trains in Switzerland are a key part of the way of life, dating back to the 1880s when the tunnel through the St Gotthard Pass created a link between Germany and Italy, a remarkable engineering feat that had an economic imperative important to both nations: the export of coal to the south. Italy wanted coal. Germany had it to sell. The Swiss swiftly succumbed to railway mania. A country that had previously effectively shut down during snowy winter months began to create lines in a web across the mountainous terrain. Switzerland in winter was open for business.

Not going on any Swiss trains on the way to Venice, due partially to the French rail strikes blocking the way, was disappointing. Travelling through the mountains in Switzerland is exhilarating, as I have described in my previous train book *Ticket to Ride: Around the World on 49 Unusual Train Journeys*. The journey between the snow-clad peaks in Pontresina in Switzerland and Tirano in Italy on the Bernina Express is especially wonderful, reaching a height of 2,253 metres, the highest train crossing between mountains in Europe.

But this is not the highest train ride in Europe. Far from it.

The Jungfrau Railway reaches a giddy 3,454 metres.

* * *

Just a month after returning from Venice, Kasia and I book a ride.

We are on a walk from the Eiger to the Matterhorn and have stopped at the picturesque town of Wengen. Wengen is near Kleine

Scheidegg Station (sitting at a height of 2,061 metres) from where the Jungfrau Railway rises 1,393 metres in about five and a half miles, weaving for half an hour through tunnels in the Eiger and the Mönch mountains before reaching Jungfrau mountain. This cog railway provides access to the Aletsch Glacier and an astronomical observatory – plus quite a few shops, restaurants and bars. The railway opened in 1912 after 16 years of construction and was the brainchild of an eccentric Swiss industrial magnate named Adolf Guyer-Zeller.

Thank goodness for eccentrics. It may sound dull to go through a long tunnel in a mountain, but this is far from the case. Having walked from Männlichen, reached by cable car above Wengen, enjoying sweeping views of the famous north face of the Eiger (finally conquered in 1938), we arrive at the station and board the 11 a.m. tomato-red train to the top.

The train begins to go very steeply upwards passing the old Hotel Bellevue des Alpes (dating from 1840 and where *The Eiger Sanction* starring Clint Eastwood was filmed) and a small lake before stopping at Eigergletscher Station. Here more passengers board. Soon afterwards we enter a tunnel and a strange sensation takes hold: that we are climbing a mountain from the inside.

The carriage is full of Japanese tourists, one of whom, directly in front of us, does not stop using her smartphone for a single moment from Kleine Scheidegg to Jungfrau, described as 'The Top of Europe' in a little 'passport' we have been given with our tickets. Halfway up we stop for five minutes inside the mountain at a station called Eismeer. Many of the passengers – not the Japanese woman with the phone – get out here to check out the view from a platform that opens onto the mountain, although we are in thick cloud and cannot see a thing.

We rush back to the train and proceed upwards once more before arriving in a kind of Alpine Disneyland. As instructed, we follow signs from the station that say 'TOUR'. This takes us past various shops offering noodles, Tissot and Omega watches, pocket knives, Lindt chocolate and oxygen canisters (for anyone who is feeling the thin air too much). In one room we pause to watch a 360-degree film of the mountains. A bar sells brandy and Scotch whisky. We follow a corridor and go to a viewing platform by the observatory and can see: *almost nothing*. The peaks are wrapped in thick cloud. We can make out a little of the Aletsch Glacier, but not all that much. The temperature, according to a display by a tattered Swiss flag, is 1.5°C. We look around for a while with the Japanese tourists. One section of the platform has been closed due to a 'falling icicle'. Nobody is using oxygen canisters.

We all follow another corridor on the TOUR that takes us past grainy black and white pictures of the people who constructed the tunnel. In 1899 six men tragically died in a dynamite accident. Soon afterwards there were strikes as the daily wage of workers was incredibly low; the 'management reacted with dismissals', says a panel. Beyond is a freezing room with skilfully crafted ice sculptures depicting Charlie Chaplin, eagles and a football (the FIFA World Cup is on). After the ice sculptures comes Restaurant Bollywood, serving Indian buffet meals as well as spaghetti bolognaise. A sign by this self-service restaurant says 'NO PICNICS'. Meanwhile, our 'passport' tells us: 'Mountain air makes you hungry and thirsty. Refresh yourself in our restaurants.'

We queue for quite a long time for the train back – and we are soon going downwards as though on a very slow rollercoaster. The conductor checks all tickets, giving each passenger a Lindt chocolate as she does so.

Back at Kleine Scheidegg we disembark and Kasia and I head for the trail back to Wengen, passing a field of cows with clanking bells. As we do so, we look back and see the observatory at the top of Jungfrau. The clouds have completely lifted. The views up there on the Top of Europe must be amazing.

Half an hour later and we would have seen the Alps from above in all their glory.

A pity... but it was an interesting ride.

BIBLIOGRAPHY

Andrić, Ivo *The Bridge on the Drina* (translated by Edwards, Lovett F.; Sezam Book, first published 1945)

Bradley, Simon *The Railways: Nation, Network and People* (2015, Profile Books)

Christie, Agatha *Murder on the Orient Express* (2017, HarperCollins, first published 1934)

Christie, Agatha *The Mystery of the Blue Train* (1974, Fontana Books, first published 1928)

Dunton-Downer, Leslie and Riding, Alan *Essential Shakespeare Handbook* (2014, Dorling Kindersley)

Engel, Matthew 'Croatia: the fragile heart of the Balkans' (2018, *The New Statesman*), quote from Hrvoje Andrić, page 207

Fleming, Ian *From Russia With Love* (2012, Vintage, first published in 1957)

Gardner, Nicky and Kries, Susanne *Europe by Rail: The Definitive Guide* (2017, Hidden Europe Publications)

Greene, Graham *Stamboul Train* (1963, Penguin, first published 1932)

le Carré, John *A Legacy of Spies* (2018, Penguin, first published 2017)

Levi, Primo *If This Is a Man* (2011, Abacus, first published 1958)

Masters, Tom et al *Eastern Europe* (2005, Lonely Planet)

Morris, Jan *Venice* (1993, Faber & Faber, first published 1960)

O'Brien, Sean and Paterson, Don, editors *Train Songs: Poetry of the Railway* (2013, Faber & Faber)

Orwell, George *Decline of the English Murder and Other Essays* (1965, Penguin, first published 1946)

Parks, Tim *Italian Ways: On and Off the Rails from Milan to Palermo* (2013, Harvill Secker)

Rodenbach, Georges *Bruges-La-Morte* (2012, translated by Mitchell, Mike; Dedalus, first published 1892)

Salter, Mark and Bousfield, Jonathan *The Rough Guide to Poland* (2002, Rough Guides)

Shakespeare, William *Romeo and Juliet* (1984, Heinemann Educational Books, earliest recorded performance 1594)

Theroux, Paul *The Great Railway Bazaar* (2008, Penguin, first published 1975)

Theroux, Paul *To the Ends of the Earth: The Selected Travels of Paul Theroux* (1991, Ballantine Books)

White, Ethel Lina *The Lady Vanishes* (2017, Pan Books, first published 1936)

Wolmar, Christian *Blood, Iron & Gold: How the Railways Transformed the World* (2009, Atlantic Books)

Woodcock, Chris, editor *European Rail Timetable April 2018* (2018, European Rail Timetable)

INDEX

INDEX

INDEX

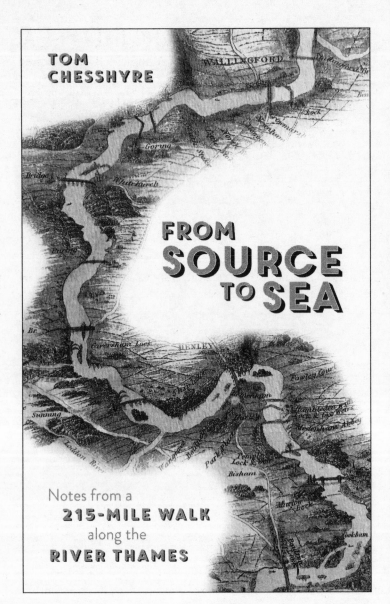

TOM
CHESSHYRE

FROM
SOURCE
TO SEA

Notes from a
215-MILE WALK
along the
RIVER THAMES

FROM SOURCE TO SEA
Notes from a 215-Mile Walk Along the River Thames

Tom Chesshyre

£16.99
Hardback
ISBN: 978-1-84953-921-0

Over the years, authors, artists and amblers aplenty have felt the pull of the Thames, and now travel writer Tom Chesshyre is following in their footsteps.

He's walking the length of the river from the Cotswolds to the North Sea – a winding journey of over two hundred miles. Join him for an illuminating stroll past meadows, churches and palaces, country estates and council estates, factories and dockyards. Setting forth in the summer of Brexit, and meeting a host of interesting characters along the way, Chesshyre explores the living present and remarkable past of England's longest and most iconic river.

TICKET
TO RIDE

AROUND THE WORLD ON
49 UNUSUAL TRAIN JOURNEYS

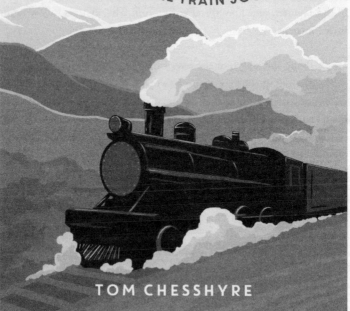

TOM CHESSHYRE

TICKET TO RIDE
Around the World on 49 Unusual Train Journeys

Tom Chesshyre

£9.99
Paperback
ISBN: 978-1-84953-826-8

Experience the world by train

Why do people love trains so much?

Tom Chesshyre is on a mission to find the answer by experiencing the world through train travel – on both epic and everyday rail routes, aboard every type of ride, from steam locomotives to bullet trains, meeting a cast of memorable characters who share a passion for train travel. Join him on the rails and off the beaten track as he embarks on an exhilarating whistle-stop tour around the globe, from Sri Lanka to Iran via Crewe, Inverness, the Australian outback and beyond.

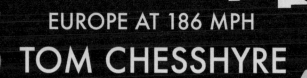

TALES FROM THE FAST TRAINS

EUROPE AT 186 MPH

TOM CHESSHYRE

TALES FROM
THE FAST TRAINS
Europe at 186 mph

Tom Chesshyre

£9.99
Paperback
ISBN: 978-1-84953-151-1

Tired of airport security queues, delays and all those extra taxes and charges, Tom Chesshyre embarks on a series of high-speed adventures across the Continent on its fast trains instead. From shiny London St Pancras, Tom travels to places that wouldn't feature on a standard holiday wish-list, and discovers the hidden delights of mysterious Luxembourg, super-trendy Rotterdam, much-maligned Frankfurt and lovely lakeside Lausanne, via a pop concert in Lille.

It's 186 mph all the way – well, apart from a power cut in the Channel Tunnel on the way to Antwerp. Is our idea of 'Europe' changing as its destinations become easier to reach? And what fun can you have at the ends of the lines? Jump on board and find out!

Have you enjoyed this book?

If so, why not write a review on your favourite website?

If you're interested in finding out more about our books,
find us on Facebook at **Summersdale Publishers** and
follow us on Twitter at **@Summersdale**.

Thanks very much for buying this Summersdale book.

www.summersdale.com